D1507539

The Budget and
National Politics

The Budget and National Politics

Dennis S. Ippolito

Emory University

W. H. Freeman and Company
San Francisco

Library of Congress Cataloging in Publication Data

Ippolito, Dennis S
  The budget and national politics.

  Includes bibliographies and index.
  1. Budget—United States.   I. Title.
HJ2052.I76   353.007'22   78-5102
ISBN 0-7167-0298-3
ISBN 0-7167-0297-5 pbk.

Copyright © 1978 by W. H. Freeman and Company

No part of this book may be reproduced by any
mechanical, photographic, or electronic process, or
in the form of a phonographic recording, nor may it
be stored in a retrieval system, transmitted, or
otherwise copied for public or private use, without
written permission from the publisher.

Printed in the United States of America

1 2   3   4   5   6   7   8   9

For Nancy and Christopher,
and for my mother.

Contents

Preface

The relationship between the federal budget and national politics is direct and substantial, although perhaps not widely appreciated or understood. Despite the complexities involved, a close look at the budget can result in a great deal of understanding about the costs and purposes of government. For example, the budget determines the level and scope of federal activity through its allocations of financial support to agencies and programs. It records the policy preferences of executive and legislative participants in the budgetary process and the constituencies and interests these participants represent. The federal budget has also become a major instrument for pursuing social and economic objectives, such as the redistribution of financial resources in society and the management of economic growth, prices, and employment. In each of these contexts, the budget introduces a necessary measure of political realism by requiring that policy goals finally be evaluated in terms of actual costs and available resources. Budget decision making is, in sum, a crucial and continuing part of the political process.

The purpose of this book is to introduce the student to the political relevance of the budget by examining the institutional responsibilities and conflicts, decision-making factors, and policy implications that characterize the budgetary process. Its scope is modest, extending primarily to presidential and congressional influences on budgetary policy. Chapter One, a general introduction to the budget system and budget process, discusses cognitive elements of budget decision making and important budget concepts and trends. Chapters Two, Three, and Four cover presidential and congressional involvement in budget policy determination and implementation. Chapter Two examines budget formulation in the executive branch and the various presidential purposes associated with budget decision making. Chapter Three, dealing with the power of the purse, presents an historical overview of the problems that Congress has encountered in exercising this power effectively and analyzes the objectives, operation, and impact of the 1974 Congressional Budget and Impoundment Control Act. Chapter Four focuses on budget implementation, particularly congressional attempts to restrict executive spending discretion. The policy implications of budget decision making are examined in Chapter Five, which deals with current controversies involving defense spending, income programs, and health programs. Finally, Chapter Six appraises two recently introduced techniques for budget decision making—zero-base executive budgeting and congressional sunset legislation—and also presents some speculations concerning future budget conflicts between the President and Congress.

In preparing this book, I have had the benefit of several thorough and thoughtful critiques. David A. Caputo of Purdue University, George C. Edwards of Tulane University, James P. Pfiffner of the University of California, Riverside, James A. Thurber of American University, and the late Jeffrey Pressman of the Massachusetts Institute of Technology all reviewed an earlier version of the manuscript and suggested many of the subsequent improvements. I am most grateful to them for their help and, of course, absolve them of any responsibility for what is written here. Also, while this study draws from many sources, I would like to acknowledge specifically Professor Aaron Wildavsky's contributions to our understanding of the politics of the budgetary process.

February 1978   *Dennis S. Ippolito*

The Budget and
National Politics

One

An Overview of the Federal Budget

The purpose of this book is to examine the role of the budget in national politics. This requires particular attention to the responsibilities and relative influence of the major executive and congressional participants in the budgetary process. It also requires an understanding of those characteristics of the budget upon which political decision makers focus their attention and the extent to which executive and congressional participants share a common focus. The uses of budgets are various and diverse, but for this examination the budget is interpreted as a political document.[1]

The budget that the President submits to Congress each year and the actions that Congress takes in response are a crucial set of political decisions. These decisions are, in effect, official answers in the debate about what the federal government should do, how much it should spend, and how it should finance its activities. In addition to their direct effects on government programs, federal taxing and spending policies also have substantial economic consequences. The level of spending, the composition of revenues and expenditures, and the budget surpluses or deficits that result affect economic activity, employment, prices, and productivity.

The "power of the purse" has long been recognized as a major bulwark of national authority. Writing in defense of the proposed Constitution in Federalist No. 30, Alexander Hamilton stated boldly that "money is, with propriety, considered as the vital principle of the body politic; as that which sustains its life and motion and enables it to perform its most essential functions." It was not long until Hamilton, as the first Secretary of the Treasury, engaged Congress in the first of many executive-congressional struggles over the exercise of the power of the purse.

Throughout our history, taxing and spending controversies have often focused attention on urgent matters of public policy or on the effectiveness of the Constitution's checks and balances between the President and Congress. Recent years have been no exception; the combined effects of inflation and recession have provided new challenges in the use of the budget as an element of economic policy.[2] The "energy crisis" has had a severe impact on economic and budgetary goals and assumptions.[3] There has been growing concern over the military balance between the United States and the Soviet Union, which has been reflected in budget debates over the size and composition of defense spending.[4] In 1972, an especially bitter confrontation between the Nixon administration and Congress over budget and impoundment policies provided the stimulus for a critical review of the congressional budget process. A recent and major revamping of the budgetary process, the 1974 Congressional Budget and Impoundment Control Act, has affected the relative influence of Congress and the executive on budget matters and has also altered the power of major committees in Congress.[5]

Viewed in this context, the political implications of the budget are clear. What is politically important—whether it be what government does, who decides it, or who benefits from it—is usually translated into the financial language of budget decisions. As Aaron Wildavsky, a leading budgetary scholar, has explained:

> The size and shape of the budget is a matter of serious contention in our political life. Presidents, political parties, administrators, Congressmen, interest groups, and interested citizens vie with one another to have their preferences recorded in the budget. The victories and defeats, the compromises and the bargains, the realms of agreement and the spheres of conflict in regard to the role of national government in our society all appear in the bud-

get. In the most integral sense the budget lies at the heart of the political process.[6]

These preferences and the manner in which they are recorded are often the subject of complex and detailed policy controversies—for example, the necessity, feasibility, or estimated costs over a multiyear period of a proposed major weapons system. These specific types of controversies, moreover, are usually accompanied by conflicts over budget *aggregates*—spending totals, revenue totals, and the economic impact of resulting deficits or surpluses. During early 1977, for example, three sets of budget "preferences" were recorded. The outgoing Ford administration submitted its recommendations for fiscal year (FY) 1978. Several weeks later, the new Carter administration sent to Congress its proposed revisions of the Ford budget. In May, Congress adopted its initial guidelines for consideration of the fiscal 1978 budget. In Table 1.1, the overall, or aggregate, figures are presented along with the recommended outlays for various governmental functions. Some interesting comparisons emerge, with both Congress and the Carter administration supporting higher outlays and larger deficits than did the Ford administration. The differences are especially pronounced on the outlay side, with approximately $20 billion separating the Republican President from his Democratic successor and the Democratic-controlled Congress. Receipts also differ, largely as a result of permanent tax cuts recommended in the Ford budget, many of which were rejected by President Carter and by Congress. The planned deficit, moreover, shows the Democrats supporting a larger "stimulus" than did the Republican administration, although on this point there is also a significant difference between the Carter recommendations and the congressional target. The fiscal 1978 disagreements on budget aggregates between the Ford recommendations and congressional targets paralleled those in previous years, reflecting the same kinds of partisan and ideological predispositions about spending and revenues. One interesting aspect of the fiscal 1978 budget, however, is that the new Democratic administration, mindful perhaps of its characterization as ideologically moderate, recommended higher spending than Ford, higher taxes than Congress, and a deficit that fell almost in the middle.

There are also some important policy differences in these three budgets. In Table 1.1, the highest outlay recommendation for each budget function has been designated. The Ford outlay recommendation is highest in only one functional area, national defense, although

Table 1.1

Executive and Congressional Budget Estimates and
Recommendations for Fiscal Year 1978 (in billions of dollars)

	Aggregates		
	Ford administration January 1977	Carter administration February 1977	Congress May 1977
Total outlays	440.0	459.4	460.9
Total receipts	393.0	401.6	396.3
Deficit (–)	–47.0	–57.8	–64.6
	By selected functions[a]		
National defense	*112.3*	111.9	111.0
International affairs	7.3	*7.8*	7.3
General science, space, and technology	4.7	4.7	4.7
Natural resources, environment, and energy	19.7	*20.5*	20.0
Agriculture	2.3	2.3	*4.4*
Commerce and transportation	19.3	*20.1*	19.4
Community and regional development	7.9	10.0	*10.8*
Education, training, employment, and social services	19.4	26.5	*27.2*
Health	43.2	*44.5*	44.3
Income security	143.9	146.5	*147.7*
Veterans benefits and services	18.3	19.1	*20.2*
Law enforcement and justice	3.8	*3.9*	*3.9*
Revenue sharing and general purpose fiscal assistance	8.1	*9.7*	*9.7*

Note: Italicized figures represent the highest outlay recommendation for each function.

[a]Figures for general government, interest, allowances, and undistributed offsetting receipts have not been included here.

Source: Adapted from *Congressional Quarterly Weekly Report, 35*, No. 9 (February 26, 1977), 351–353; *The Budget of the United States Government, Fiscal Year 1978* (Washington, D.C.: Government Printing Office, 1977), pp. 69–201; *Congressional Record, 123*, No. 80 (May 11, 1977), H-4331.

the lowest outlay recommendation (by Congress) is only $1.3 billion
less. Carter administration recommendations are highest in four functional categories—international affairs; natural resources, environment,
and energy; commerce and transportation; and health—with combined
outlays for these functions $3.4 billion above the Ford proposals and

$1.9 billion above congressional targets. Congress has adopted the highest outlay levels in five categories—agriculture; community and regional development; education, training, employment, and social services; income security; and veterans benefits and services—and the differences are substantial. Combined outlays for these functions are $18.5 billion higher than the Ford recommendations and $5.9 billion higher than the Carter recommendations. There is only one function— general science, space, and technology—where all sides agree on an outlay level, although the law enforcement and justice outlay levels are also quite similar. For the last functional category, revenue sharing and general purpose fiscal assistance, the Democrats agree on a funding level $1.6 billion above the Republican position.

During 1977, then, a Republican President, a Democratic President, and a Democratic-controlled Congress were seeking to achieve economic objectives and specific policy goals through decisions on the fiscal 1978 budget. The broad outlines of their agreements and disagreements reflected a mix of economic, philosophical, and political judgments and beliefs. As always, the actions and commitments finally taken on the fiscal 1978 budget would significantly affect future budgets.

The Budget System and Budget Process

The federal budget serves as the formal system for financial administration within the federal government. By scheduling receipts (what the government will receive through various taxes, tariffs, and other revenue-raising methods) and outlays (what the government will spend for various functions), it provides the means for managing programs and controlling finances. The budget covers a fiscal year that now runs from October 1 through September 30. Fiscal year 1978, for example, covers the period from October 1, 1977, through September 30, 1978.

Executive Preparation

While the budget process will be covered in detail in Chapters Two through Four, it is helpful at this point to understand the general responsibilities of the "participants." The President is responsible for formulating and transmitting budgetary requests and information to Congress.[7] This includes: (1) an accounting of how funds have been spent in the past; (2) a plan of estimated receipts and outlays; (3) a discussion of the importance or priority that the President assigns to various programs and governmental activities—that is, his recommendations about program needs; and (4) requests to Congress to provide authority—through legislation—to spend public money. The President's budget therefore reflects the administration's judgments about the needs of individual programs. It also incorporates recommendations about fiscal policy—the total outlays and receipts that the administration believes are appropriate given current and prospective economic conditions. The executive side of the budgetary process involves the President, presidential staff and advisers [particularly the Office of Management and Budget (OMB), the Council of Economic Advisers, and the Treasury Department], and the government agencies that administer various federal programs.

Congressional Action

Congressional action on the budget involves the actual legislation that determines receipts and outlays. Taxes and other methods of raising revenue are specified by legislation, and Congress may consider presidential requests for changes in revenue laws or may initiate such actions on its own. Tax legislation follows the normal legislative process, with the major committee responsibilities lying with the Ways and Means Committee in the House and the Finance Committee in the Senate.

The expenditure side is somewhat more complex, and two separate actions are required. Legislation is first needed to authorize—to set up or continue—a federal program or federal agency. In some instances, authorizing legislation also sets a limit on the amount that can be subsequently appropriated for a particular program. The periods covered by authorizations vary—some are indefinite, some are for a specified number of years, and an increasing number are for one year (thus requiring annual authorization). Authorizing legislation is handled by the legislative committee in each chamber having jurisdiction over the program or agency involved. For programs or agencies that have not been authorized or whose authorization has lapsed, authorizing legislation must be passed by Congress and signed by the President.

The appropriations actions that Congress takes allow agencies to incur obligations—that is, to take actions that require immediate or future payments of money—by granting them *budget authority*. As with authorizations, budget authority can be granted for varying periods of time. For many agencies, budget authority must be voted annually by Congress. In certain cases, such as appropriations to pay interest on the federal debt or to pay beneficiaries under most federal trust funds, Congress has provided permanent budget authority, so that annual congressional action is not required. Appropriations legislation must, of course, be passed by Congress and signed by the President.

The House and Senate Appropriations Committees have jurisdiction over budget authority, which is provided through the congressional appropriations process.[8] Appropriations bills, like revenue bills, are first considered by the House of Representatives. The House Appropriations Committee, through its subcommittees, considers the appropriations requests for specific agencies. Once appropriations bills have been approved by the House, they are sent to the Senate, where a second review process is conducted. If the House and Senate versions of a bill differ, a conference committee meets to resolve the differences. This committee includes members from both the House and Senate Appropriations Committees; once it reaches an agreement on an appropriations bill, the measure goes to the House and then to the Senate for approval. If both houses pass the bill, it is then transmitted to the President for his approval or veto.

Under the new procedures adopted in 1974, Congress now sets budget targets to guide its consideration of revenue and spending legislation. Subsequent to receipt of the President's budget, but no later than May 15, Congress must adopt a budget resolution setting totals for receipts, outlays, and budget authority. It then considers specific revenue and appropriations measures. By September 15, action is to be completed on these measures and on a second budget resolution, which sets binding ceilings on outlays and budget authority and a floor on receipts for the ensuing fiscal year. Any changes in revenue or spending bills already enacted or in the statutory limit on the debt necessitated by this second resolution must then be accomplished by September 25, so that the congressional budgetary process will be completed by October 1, when the new fiscal year begins.

Execution and Control

Once the necessary legislation has been passed to provide an agency with budget authority for the fiscal year, the director of the OMB—acting for the President—is responsible for insuring that the budget authority is used in an effective and orderly manner. This is usually accomplished by apportioning funds to the agency, usually on a quarterly basis or in relationship to certain activities or programs. If despite the apportionment additional budget authority does become necessary, requests for supplemental appropriations must be sent to Congress.

It is also possible for the President to recommend to Congress that budget authority provided for an agency or program not be used. If this is to be temporary—a *deferral*—the President transmits a special message to Congress with his request and supporting information. If either the Senate or the House disapproves the request, the funds must be made available for obligation. (In no case can a deferral go beyond the end of a fiscal year.) If the President determines for reasons of fiscal policy or otherwise that authority is not needed at all, he sends to Congress a special message requesting a *rescission* of budget authority. If not approved by both houses of Congress within 45 days, the rescission request fails and funds must be made available for obligation. This procedure, adopted in 1974, substantially restricted the executive's discretionary spending authority and was aimed specifically at the practice of impoundment. Several Presidents had asserted, though none so forcefully as Richard M. Nixon, various bases for their authority to delay or cancel the spending of appropriated funds. Congress finally reacted to this by imposing new statutory procedures circumscribing the President's authority to withhold funds.

Review and Audit

While the individual agencies and departments are responsible for insuring that authorizing and appropriations legislation is followed—that funds are spent for the purposes specified by law—additional monitoring is conducted within the executive branch by the OMB. Within Congress, in addition to the regular oversight or supervision conducted by the committees that authorize and appropriate funds, regular audits, examinations, reviews, and evaluations are conducted by the General Accounting Office. This is headed by the Comptroller General, who is responsible to Congress. The review and audit process is designed to insure not only that financial transactions are conducted properly but also that funds are spent efficiently and effectively.

Elements of Budget Decisions

While budgeting may appear to be in large part a technical process, budget decisions are not always correspondingly exact or precise. There is, as most Presidents admit, a degree of uncertainty about the information and recommendations that they transmit to Congress. A similar uncertainty also infuses Congress' handling of the budget. As Louis Fisher, a leading budget specialist, has remarked, "No one is 'right on top of things' " when it comes to budget matters. "No one will ever be."[9] As a guide to dealing with this unavoidable complexity, it is helpful to classify the various elements of budget decisions as assumptions, estimates, facts, or choices.

The Economy (Assumptions)

Budget decisions must take into account assumptions about economic conditions. Just as the budget's size and composition may affect economic activity, economic conditions may also affect the budget. Budget receipts and outlays, for example, are linked to certain economic conditions. Receipts from taxes vary with individual and corporate incomes. As the unemployment rate increases, outlays for unemployment benefits rise. What the government must pay in interest on the federal debt is affected by general market rates. Most federal retirement and social insurance benefits now have automatic cost-of-living increases. And, of course, inflation affects what the government must pay for goods and services.

Both the executive branch and Congress, therefore, must make assumptions about current and future economic conditions. What will occur with respect to economic growth, prices, and the unemployment rate? The economic projections issued by the President or by Congress reflect assumptions about precisely these matters. As both sides recognize, these assumptions are always risky, especially for longer-range forecasts. In its report on budget options for FY 1977, for example, the Congressional Budget Office (CBO) stated:

> As always, there are dangers that the economy will not actually follow the projected path. Crop failures here or abroad, a major strike, a rapid rise in short-term interest rates—all contrary to the assumptions made here—would change the outlook for inflation

and unemployment. In addition, the forecast rests on judgments about a number of critical aspects of economic behavior, among them the rate of household saving, the vigor of investment, the relation of monetary growth to interest rates, and the persistence of inflation.[10]

The President's budget for FY 1977 was equally cautious:

> The assumptions for calendar years 1975 . . . , 1976, and 1977 are forecasts of probable economic conditions during these years. *The longer range assumptions for the period 1978 to 1981 are not forecasts of probable economic conditions,* but rather assumptions consistent with moving gradually toward a relatively stable price level and higher level of employment. Any economic forecast is subject to substantial error.[11]

Of course, the presidential and congressional assumptions are not always the same. There can be, and frequently are, differences in their evaluations of where the economy is and their assumptions about where it is headed given certain conditions. Thus a major element of contention is how to use the budget to affect those conditions and thus to move the economy in the desired direction. Naturally, the assumptions about future conditions substantially affect estimates of future receipts and outlays.

Receipts and Outlays (Estimates)

Estimates of receipts and outlays are affected by the economic assumptions discussed above. These estimates also depend, however, on taxing and spending policies. The 1974 Congressional Budget and Impoundment Control Act sought to provide some perspective in evaluating budget proposals by requiring estimates of what would happen to the budget—that is, to receipts and outlays—if current tax provisions were to remain in force and if current government programs were to be maintained at existing commitment levels.[12] This *current services budget* could then be used as a basis for evaluating the budgetary impact of changes in existing tax or spending policies.

The estimates contained in the President's budget, then, are contingent on Congress acting favorably on the taxing and spending recommendations that the administration is sponsoring. These estimates are therefore subject to serious reservations initially, since Congress often does not subscribe to the President's proposals or program priorities. The fiscal 1978 budget submitted by the outgoing Ford administration in January 1977, for example, contained receipt and outlay estimates that were clearly unrealistic, since Congress was unlikely to accept the recommendations for changes in the tax laws and in domestic social welfare programs.

In addition, estimates of receipts and outlays have often been inaccurate even when there has been congressional and executive agreement about tax provisions and spending programs. There is considerable difficulty in estimating in advance what the government will actually spend or take in during a fiscal year, and this difficulty even extends to estimates made once the fiscal year is under way. Unanticipated changes in economic conditions, for example, can significantly alter outlays and receipts.

The problems inherent in making short-range projections are obviously multiplied when long-term estimates of receipts and outlays are developed. The five-year projections of receipts and outlays used by the President and Congress are at best very general guides to future taxing and spending levels. Indeed, past projections have tended to overestimate receipts and underestimate outlays, providing an erroneous impression about future deficits or surpluses.

Prior Spending (Facts)

The President's budget includes information on the past expenditure of funds. This typically includes actual outlays for specific functions and agencies during previous fiscal years, as well as actual long-term outlays in broad spending categories such as defense or agriculture. While this might appear to be necessarily factual, figures for the year in which the budget is being submitted (the fiscal 1978 budget, for example, is submitted during FY 1977) are estimates, so that actual outlays for programs and agencies may increase or decrease if unforeseen developments occur. Beyond current outlays, however, past outlays are settled, and to that extent there are facts on which the President and Congress can agree and that can be used in making decisions about future spending.

Policy and Program Support (Choices)

Budget decisions determine how much will be spent for governmental activities. This involves two broad types of choices: what activities the government will perform, which also answers the question of which activities it will not perform; and how funds should be distributed given the competing claims of various programs and the limits on available resources. Policy and program support choices, then, characteristically reflect a mix of practical and philosophical considerations.

The range of available choices in any given year, however, is usually quite limited. Radical changes in the size or composition of the budget are highly unlikely from year to year. In large part, this simply reflects the fact that much of one year's budget has been determined by actions taken previously. Some spending, for example, is mandatory since the government has legal commitments that must be met. Interest on the federal debt, social security payments, veterans pensions, and other contractual obligations into which the government has entered are examples of spending commitments that cannot be eliminated and that account for a substantial share of total spending. Other spending may not be mandatory but may still be resistant to change, since it is supported by powerful political interests. Executive attempts to close domestic defense installations typically encounter intense and often successful opposition from members of Congress who represent the affected areas. During his first months in office, President Carter ran afoul of members of both parties in Congress when he proposed the curtailment or abolition of a large number of major water projects. Congressional opponents of his proposal argued that the justification for these projects had been adequately established in the past, that massive amounts of money had already been spent, and that commitments had been made to their states and districts. Whatever the merits of such arguments in this specific instance, the fact remains that a portion of the budget reflects similar long-term commitments that are difficult to change.

It is also important to recognize that many programs and agencies are continued from year to year, because they have operated satisfactorily in the past and therefore occasion no challenge. In effect, legal commitments and political realities operate to limit the short-term flexibility in the budget. Moreover, using last year's budget as the primary guide for this year's budget serves as a practical aid to calculation.[13]

Rather than engaging in a yearly, comprehensive evaluation of all programs and agencies and then deciding on the comparative worth of existing programs as compared to possible alternatives, budget decision makers have usually followed an *incremental* approach. They do not reconsider all or even most programs, but rather focus much of their attention on marginal increases or decreases in existing programs. Some programs are reconsidered in a given year, but these are generally programs about which specific questions or challenges have arisen.[14] According to Wildavsky, this incremental approach has been the most important aid to calculation in dealing with the budget's complexity and magnitude:

> Budgets are almost never actively reviewed as a whole, in the sense of considering at one time the value of all existing programs compared to all possible alternatives. Instead, this year's budget is based on last year's budget, with special attention given to a narrow range of increases or decreases.[15]

The incremental approach, however, does limit short-term flexibility in the budget, and alternative approaches have been proposed that would allow comprehensive consideration of existing programs and thus increase short-term flexibility. The Carter administration, for example, has announced its intention of employing *zero-base* budgeting in developing the executive budget. This budgeting approach requires that costs for all programs be calculated annually in terms of demonstrable needs rather than past commitments or existing legislative mandates. Each agency must therefore provide justifications for all of its programs and all of its expenditures, as if these programs and costs were being considered for the first time.

The zero-base approach thus differs drastically from the incremental approach. Theoretically, it requires the comprehensive reconsideration that the incremental approach cannot provide and therefore enlarges the potential range of program and policy choices. Whether it will have any significant effect in practice is difficult to predict, although its past use at the state level has not had an appreciable effect on outcomes.[16]

The fact that most changes in the budget are marginal, however, does not mean that these changes are unimportant. As the CBO has noted, even marginal changes in the budget may have a substantial impact on future budgets:

These marginal changes, in their turn, often continue to have a significant impact well into the future. A decision to begin procurement of a major weapons system, to redefine eligibility for pensions or other benefits, or to eliminate a specific tax may have profound implications for future budgets.[17]

From year to year, the areas where important policy decisions are made can change. In its fiscal 1977 report, for example, the CBO identified five major policy areas in which significant budget decisions had to be made: (1) national security (whether there should be a build-up and modernization of general purpose forces and more spending on strategic weapons); (2) jobs (what federal spending might be needed for public service employment, public works, and other job programs); (3) health (whether the federal government should enact comprehensive national health insurance or more limited plans, or focus on improving health services for the poor and elderly); (4) aid to state and local governments (how much aid should be granted and what types of specifications should be made about the use of this aid); and (5) federal pay (what level of increase federal workers should receive).[18]

In previous years, Democratic-controlled Congresses and Republican administrations viewed these and related types of issues in different ways. A particularly important difference was the relative priority assigned to spending for defense versus spending for human resources, such as education, health, and housing. By 1976 there was somewhat greater agreement between the President and Congress about the necessity of increased defense spending, but there was continued division over spending levels in other areas. Despite the Democratic victory in the 1976 presidential election, program and policy choices and priorities have continued to divide the President and Congress.

Fiscal Policy Intentions (Choices)

A second important element of budget choice is fiscal strategy—how the government should use its taxing and spending powers to affect economic activity. The major question here typically involves the balance between receipts and outlays: Should the budget be balanced, is a deficit necessary to stimulate the economy, or is a surplus required to provide restraint?[19] A simplified depiction of the options available and of the potential effects is shown in the table below.

Anticipated Economic Effects of Taxing and Spending Decisions[a]

		SPENDING		
		Increase	Maintain	Decrease
TAXES	Increase	Neutral	Moderate restraint	Major restraint
	Maintain	Moderate stimulus	Neutral	Moderate restraint
	Decrease	Major stimulus	Moderate stimulus	Neutral

[a]Assuming an initial balance between revenues and expenditures and matching increases or decreases of roughly equal amounts.

When the United States moved out of a severe recession in 1975, the questions arose over whether a mild stimulus was still needed to maintain recovery, how long such a stimulus might be required, and what the effects of a continued deficit would be on inflation. These questions remain especially difficult, since the unemployment rate has been quite high during the recovery. The general assumption has been that when unemployment increases, the government can increase spending, decrease taxes, or do both in order to increase private spending and thus increase production and jobs. But continued deficits resulting from such a strategy can produce inflation and also have a negative effect on business and consumer confidence. Whether there was a trade-off between unemployment and inflation and precisely how this trade-off worked was especially troublesome in 1975 and 1976, since the available estimates were usually based on periods when both unemployment and inflation were considerably lower.[20]

Certain fiscal policy measures work automatically. When unemployment increases, for example, government spending increases as unemployment benefits are paid and government revenues decrease as personal and corporate incomes fall. This operates as an "automatic stabilizer" or cushion during economic fluctuations. As a way of estimating the effects of discretionary fiscal policy, a full-employment budget concept has been developed. This assumes an economy operating at full capacity (usually defined as 4.0 percent unemployment in the civilian labor force) with the resulting governmental receipts and outlays. The difference between actual receipts and outlays and what receipts and outlays would be under full employment provides a rough measure of the direction and magnitude of discretionary fiscal policy.

There is, then, limited information and knowledge about key elements of budget decisions. Executive and congressional participants must necessarily take positions with a certain degree of risk, and this risk is of course compounded by the political implications of the choices made. But even if we ignore the political considerations affecting budget decisions, it is clear that these decisions are rarely if ever made on the basis of facts and information on which all of the participants agree. Indeed, even in the case of prior program spending, there may be considerable disagreement about a program's utility or desirability. The budget is large and complex, its range of realistic choices is limited in the short run, and its susceptibility to changes in economic conditions and other unanticipated developments is considerable. Each year budget decision makers must grapple as best they can with the limits on what they know. They must make choices about programs and policies despite the difficulties involved in comparing the relative worth of defense spending, education programs, and health services. Inevitably, these judgments must take into account what is available in terms of resources, possible in terms of planning, and feasible in terms of politics.

Interpreting the Budget: Concepts and Trends

During recent years, there has been particularly intense debate over the flexibility, size, and composition of the federal budget. One of the common problems in following this debate is the confusing assortment of figures and terminology being used. While it is impossible to eliminate all of the confusion, an understanding of some basic budget concepts and of recent budget trends should help to clarify the annual budget debates.

Budget Concepts

A useful starting point in examining executive and congressional actions relating to spending is to distinguish between budget authority and outlays being considered for a given fiscal year. As noted previously, budget authority allows an agency to incur obligations and to make payments. However, since budget authority can be provided for varying periods of time, each year's budget typically includes *outlays,* or actual spending, based on budget authority enacted in previous years as well as budget authority to be enacted specifically for that budget. Figure 1.1 shows the relationship between budget authority and outlays for the fiscal 1978 budget submitted by the Ford administration. Of total recommended outlays of $440.0 billion for FY 1978, slightly less than 30 percent ($129.2 billion) was based on unspent budget authority enacted during prior years. Remaining outlays were to come from new budget authority recommended for FY 1978. However, of this new recommended budget authority, more than one-third ($169.7 billion) was to be spent in future years.

Not all of the budget authority that is enacted into law for a fiscal year, then, is likely to be spent or obligated during that year. A portion of it will be carry-over authority earmarked for specific purposes in

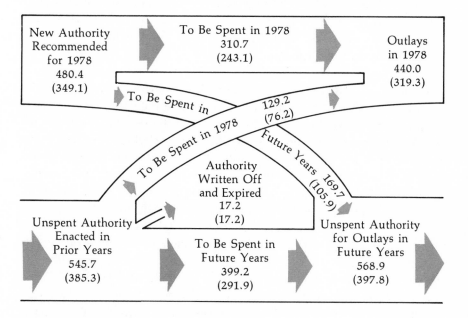

Figure 1.1

Relation of budget authority to outlays in the fiscal 1978 budget. (Figures are in billions of dollars. Figures in parentheses represent federal funds only. The difference between the total budget figures and federal funds shown in parentheses consists of trust funds and interfund transactions between fund groups.) [Source: *The Budget of the United States Government, Fiscal Year 1978* (Washington, D.C.: Government Printing Office, 1977), p. 205.]

future years. The federal budget for a fiscal year, therefore, will contain two figures for each program or function. One figure represents the outlays or actual spending for that program or function during the fiscal year; the second figure represents budget authority enacted, some of which will be obligated or spent during the fiscal year and some of which will be spent in future years. In the fiscal 1978 Ford administration budget, for example, $122.9 billion in budget authority was recommended for national defense, but recommended outlays or actual spending for the fiscal year were $112.3 billion.

Figure 1.1 also shows the amounts of budget authority and outlays for federal funds as opposed to trust funds. Federal funds are derived largely from general taxes and borrowing and are used to support general government functions. Trust funds, which include the social security and unemployment compensation programs, are earmarked for specific purposes and programs and are not available for general government purposes. For FY 1978, approximately three-fourths of recommended outlays were federal funds, with the remainder accounted for primarily by trust fund outlays.

Controllability.   As used by budget officials, controllability reflects the extent to which outlays in a given year can be increased or decreased under existing law. Thus, "relatively uncontrollable" outlays are those which "are mandated under an existing law" or which "represent the liquidation of a contractual obligation . . . that was made prior to the start of the fiscal year in question."[21] Over the past decade, the amount of uncontrollable spending has grown dramatically, and now accounts for approximately three-fourths of all federal spending.

Table 1.2 shows the types of outlays that fall within the "relatively uncontrollable" classification and also the changes in these outlays in recent years. From 1967 to 1976, relatively uncontrollable spending increased from $93.5 billion (or 59 percent of total outlays) to $267.7 billion (or 73 percent of total outlays). The specific programs that contributed most heavily to this growth are found in the "payments for individuals" category. Here spending grew more than fourfold, from $41.6 billion to $174.4 billion.

It should be noted that there are degrees of uncontrollability within this classification. Legal commitments made by government in previous years, such as interest on federal securities or payments on bonds for public housing construction, must be met when due and are, in this

Table 1.2

"Relatively Uncontrollable" Spending (in billions of dollars)

	Fiscal year			
	1967	1971	1975	1976
Payments for individuals				
Social security and railroad retirement	22.5	37.2	68.4	76.2
Federal employees' retirement and insurance	3.8	6.6	13.3	15.6
Unemployment assistance	2.6	6.6	14.0	19.8
Veterans benefits	5.0	7.6	12.4	13.9
Medicare and Medicaid	4.6	11.2	21.6	26.3
Housing payments	.3	.7	2.1	2.5
Public assistance	2.8	7.4	16.9	20.2
Subtotal, payments for individuals	*41.6*	*77.3*	*148.7*	*174.4*
Net interest	10.3	14.8	23.3	26.8
General revenue sharing	——	——	6.1	6.2
Farm price supports	1.7	2.8	.6	.6
Other programs	3.0	5.2	8.0	8.8
Spending from prior-year contracts				
National defense	21.2	21.6	23.6	19.1
Civilian programs	15.8	18.6	27.1	31.8
Subtotal, spending from prior-year contracts	*37.0*	*40.2*	*50.7*	*50.9*
Total	93.5	140.4	237.5	267.7
Percentage of total outlays	59%	66%	73%	73%

Source: Adapted from *The Budget of the United States Government, Fiscal Year 1977* (Washington, D.C.: Government Printing Office, 1976), pp. 354–355; *The Budget of the United States Government, Fiscal Year 1978* (Washington, D.C.: Government Printing Office, 1977), p. 212.

context, absolutely uncontrollable. Payments to meet contract obligations, such as those arising from construction projects and weapons systems, can sometimes be deferred, but they must be made eventually. Even if it were desirable to cancel such projects, substantial penalty payments would still be required. Spending under entitlement programs, such as public assistance or social security, can be controlled to a limited degree by changes in authorizing legislation. For example, automatic cost-of-living increases established for certain retirement programs could be limited or eliminated in the future. Or eligibility standards for participation in public assistance or food stamp programs could be made more stringent, thus limiting the number of people receiving benefits and lowering the program costs. In the past, cuts in entitlement programs have been rather rare, but the possibility does exist for imposing controls on future increases if not necessarily on current costs.

It should also be noted that even theoretically controllable types of spending may be difficult to change in the short run. Of the 25 to 30 percent of the budget now classified as relatively controllable, a considerable portion cannot be readily changed without significant and unlikely changes in public policy. For example, 68 percent of the fiscal 1976 budget for defense and international affairs was classified as controllable. However, a detailed study of this controllable spending found that, at most, less than 10 percent of the entire budget could be reasonably adjusted without significant policy shifts and that certain cuts could actually lead to higher long-term costs.[22] Thus, in the absence of radically different policies regarding military preparedness, theoretically controllable defense-related outlays are, in reality, not subject to substantial short-term decreases.

A considerable portion of federal spending, then, is affected by legal obligations and policy commitments that are not amenable to short-term modifications. As the controllability problem has become more acute, however, both Congress and the President have sought to impose tighter controls on existing uncontrollable spending so as to limit future growth and to increase, at least to a limited extent, budget flexibility.

Tax Expenditures. A relatively new budget concept that has received considerable attention is that of tax expenditures. *Tax expenditures* are revenues lost because of provisions in the tax laws that reduce an individual's or a corporation's tax liability. Included are special exclusions, exemptions, and deductions that reduce taxable income (such as the deductibility of mortgage interest on owner-occupied homes), preferential tax rates, special tax credits, and tax deferrals. The resulting revenue losses are called tax expenditures because they are, in effect, payments by the federal government, except that they are accomplished through a reduction in taxes paid rather than by a direct grant.

Tax expenditures are designed *"to encourage people to do certain things,* for example, to give to charity or to buy business machinery, *and to help people in special cases,* such as the blind or those with unusually high medical expenses."[23] It is extremely difficult to estimate tax expenditures precisely, since changes in the tax treatment of one item can alter the method of calculating taxes or the rate bracket applied. Thus, the amount of revenue lost because a particular tax expenditure provision exists is not necessarily the same as the net revenue gain that would result if the provision was eliminated.[24]

Despite measurement problems, estimates of tax expenditures are required under the 1974 Congressional Budget and Impoundment Control Act. In FY 1976, total tax expenditures were estimated at $91.8 billion. Of this total, $21.0 billion went to the corporate sector and $70.8 billion to individual households.[25] The largest component of the latter was the deductibility of mortgage interest and property taxes on homes ($11.8 billion). It is estimated that under current laws tax expenditures will total $124.7 billion in FY 1978 and increase by approximately $10 billion per year through 1982.[26]

The issues relating to tax expenditures involve whether it is better for the government to "subsidize" an activity through the tax system or to do so by regular expenditure, since the former may have differing effects on high- and low-income groups; and whether the review of tax expenditures is careful enough to eliminate or modify those provisions that now provide unnecessary or undesirable subsidies.[27] Presumably, the requirement for yearly estimates will allow the executive branch and Congress to assess more adequately their past decisions concerning tax expenditures and to evaluate new proposals for such subsidies in terms of budgetary impact and program priorities.

Budget Functions. There are several different methods used to present budget information. For example, the annual budget includes outlays and receipts for each agency and branch of government. However, budget outlays and related information are also presented in terms of the major function or purpose being served regardless of organizational or agency lines. Under this classification, federal activities and programs are designated according to their predominant purpose, and each activity or program can be classified under only one function. The presentation of the federal budget on this functional basis has been done since 1948, but it has assumed increased importance and utility recently. Under the 1974 revision of the budgetary process, Congress now uses the functional classifications in developing its spending targets and guidelines. Therefore, an available and informative means of examining executive and congressional budget preferences and priorities is to compare the President's budget recommendations for each broad function with the congressional targets and subsequent ceilings. (These comparisons are presented in Table 1.1.)

Under the current classification scheme, there are fifteen functional classifications, as well as categories for allowances and undistributed offsetting receipts. A brief description of each functional classification is presented below. Included for each function are fiscal 1976 outlays.

The Budget by Function

National Defense (military programs of the Department of Defense; military assistance; military-related nuclear programs; defense-related activities of civilian agencies)—fiscal 1976 actual outlays, $89.9 billion.

International Affairs (diplomatic and consular activities; foreign economic and financial assistance; foreign information and exchange activities; international financial programs)—fiscal 1976 actual outlays, $5.1 billion.

General Science, Space, and Technology (space research and technology programs of the National Aeronautics and Space Administration; physical science programs of Energy Research and Development Administration)—fiscal 1976 actual outlays, $4.4 billion.

Natural Resources, Environment, and Energy (general energy programs; pollution control and abatement programs; water resources and power; land management and conservation)—fiscal 1976 actual outlays, $11.3 billion.

Agriculture (farm income stabilization programs; agricultural research and services)—fiscal 1976 actual outlays, $2.5 billion.

Commerce and Transportation (development and support of ground, air, water, and other transportation; home mortgage programs; Postal Service subsidies; aids to business; regulatory activities)—fiscal 1976 actual outlays, $17.2 billion.

Community and Regional Development (assistance to state and local governments for construction of public facilities, provision of public services, and economic development; disaster relief and insurance programs)—fiscal 1976 actual outlays, $5.3 billion.

Education, Training, Employment, and Social Services (assistance to state and local governments for elementary, secondary, and vocational education; student aid and institutional support for higher education; educational research; training and employment programs and labor services; assistance to states and localities for delivery of social services to individuals and families)—fiscal 1976 actual outlays, $18.2 billion.

Health (health care services; research and education; prevention and control of health problems; planning and construction)—fiscal 1976 actual outlays, $33.4 billion.

Income Security (general retirement and disability insurance programs; federal employee retirement and disability; unemployment insurance; public assistance and income supplement programs)—fiscal 1976 actual outlays, $127.4 billion.

Veterans Benefits and Services (income security; education, training, and rehabilitation programs; hospital and medical care; housing assistance programs)—fiscal 1976 actual outlays, $18.4 billion.

Law Enforcement and Justice (federal law enforcement and prosecution; judicial activities; correctional and rehabilitative activities; law enforcement assistance to state and local governments)—fiscal 1976 actual outlays, $3.3 billion.

General Government (federal activities including operation of the legislative branch, Executive Office of the President, tax and revenue collection; government-wide operations affecting property, supplies, and personnel)—fiscal 1976 actual outlays, $2.9 billion.

Revenue Sharing and General Purpose Fiscal Assistance (aid to state, local, territorial governments for general fiscal assistance)—fiscal 1976 actual outlays, $7.1 billion.

Interest (cost of borrowing or income from lending money, primarily consisting of interest on the public debt)—fiscal 1976 actual outlays, $34.6 billion.

Allowances (statutory pay increases for federal civilian agency employees; contingencies for relatively uncontrollable programs)—estimated for budget's fiscal year.

Undistributed Offsetting Receipts (employer share of employee retirement funds; interest received by trust funds; rents and royalties on the outer continental shelf)—fiscal 1976 actual receipts, $14.7 billion.

Budget Trends

In the period from 1956 through 1976, federal spending increased more than fivefold, from $70.5 billion to $366.5 billion, with the increases in 1975 and 1976 being especially steep. This has increased concern about the level and composition of federal spending and, not incidentally, of the taxing and borrowing policies needed to support that spending. In this section, budget trends and their implications will be examined by focusing on spending, taxing, and borrowing.

Spending Increases.   As Table 1.3 indicates, federal spending has grown dramatically in recent years. The fiscal 1975 budget, for example, was $56.5 billion greater than the preceding year's budget, and spending

Table 1.3

Budget Outlays and Estimated Outlays, 1956–1979 (in billions of dollars)

Fiscal year	Total outlays
1956	70.5
1957	76.7
1958	82.6
1959	92.1
1960	92.2
1961	97.8
1962	106.8
1963	111.3
1964	118.6
1965	118.4
1966	134.7
1967	158.3
1968	178.8
1969	184.5
1970	196.6
1971	211.4
1972	232.0
1973	247.1
1974	269.6
1975	326.1
1976	366.5
TQ[a]	94.7
1977	401.9
1978 estimate	462.2
1979 estimate	500.2

[a]This was the three-month transition period from July 1, 1976, through September 30, 1976, which resulted from changing the beginning of the fiscal year from July 1 to October 1.

Source: *The Budget of the United States Government, Fiscal Year 1978* (Washington, D.C.: Government Printing Office, 1977), p. 436; *The Budget of the United States Government, Fiscal Year 1979* (Washington, D.C.: Government Printing Office, 1978).

for FY 1976 increased by an additional $40.4 billion. Thus, in only two years the budget grew by almost $100 billion. While estimates for FY 1978 and FY 1979 show a reduced rate of growth, the projected increases are still substantial.[28]

It is necessary, however, to take into account factors such as inflation and economic growth in evaluating increases in government spending or activity. For example, inflation directly affects government spending. If prices for goods and services purchased by the government increase over time, the government is forced to spend more money to support the same level of activity. One method for taking the effect of inflation into account is to use *constant dollars,* in which spending is measured according to the prices of a base period. This eliminates the effects of fluctuations in the price level, so that increases or decreases in constant dollar spending over a period represent real changes in the volume of goods and services purchased. In Figure 1.2, current and constant dollar outlays (spending) are shown for the period 1956 through 1976. As indicated, a considerable portion of the increase in government spending has been a result of inflation. Indeed, over this period constant dollar spending approximately doubled, while spending in current dollars increased by more than five times.[29] It should also be noted that the effects of inflation on spending were particularly severe from 1974 through 1976.

In addition to assessing the impact of inflation on government spending, it is also necessary to examine the relationship between government spending and economic growth. This relationship shows the relative importance of the federal government in the economy and, when measured over time, indicates whether government spending is growing at a faster rate than the economy as a whole.[30] Table 1.4 illustrates this by presenting federal spending or outlays as a percentage of the gross national product (GNP), since GNP is a comprehensive measure of the size of the economy. As indicated, there has been—with the exception of World War II outlays as reflected in the 1946 figure—a long-term increase in the percentage of GNP represented by federal outlays. A portion of the recent growth, however, is the result of the economic recession, which greatly increased government expenditures for unemployment compensation and at the same time limited the growth in GNP. If the recessionary effects are discounted, the increase in outlays as a percentage of GNP has been smaller—from approximately 17 percent in 1956 to slightly less than 20 percent in 1976.[31]

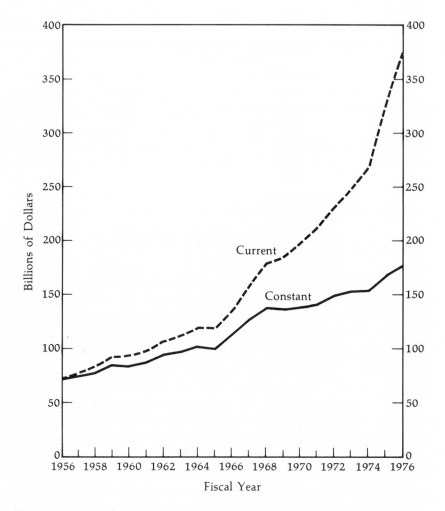

Figure 1.2
Federal outlays in current and constant dollars, in fiscal years 1956 through 1976.
(Constant 1956 dollars are used. 1976 outlay total reflects the Second Concurrent
Resolution on the Budget for 1976.) [Source: Congressional Budget Office,
*Budget Options for Fiscal Year 1977: A Report to the Senate and House Committees on the
Budget* (Washington, D.C.: Government Printing Office, March 15, 1976), p. 4.]

Nevertheless, the relative importance of the federal government in
the economy has increased, since federal outlays have grown faster
than the economy as a whole. Of course, state and local government

Table 1.4

Budget Outlays as Percentages of Gross
National Product, 1941–1976

Fiscal year	Percentage
1941	12.5
1946	27.4
1951	14.7
1956	17.1
1961	19.2
1966	18.7
1971	20.7
1976	22.8
1977 estimate	22.5
1978 estimate	21.6

Source: Figures for 1941 through 1951 from *The Budget of
the United States Government, Fiscal Year 1976* (Washington, D.C.: Government Printing Office, 1975), p. 67;
figures for 1956 through 1978 from *The Budget of the
United States Government, Fiscal Year 1978* (Washington,
D.C.: Government Printing Office, 1977), p. 435.

spending has also risen, so that the combined government, or public
sector, proportion of GNP had risen to more than one-third by the
mid-1970s, up significantly from the levels of one or two decades previously. As a result of this past growth in the relative size of public sector spending, both the Ford and Carter administrations have
stressed the importance of keying increases in federal outlays to increases in GNP, so as to arrest or eventually to reverse this trend.

In addition to the overall increases in spending, significant changes
have also occurred in the composition of federal outlays—that is, in the
relative importance of spending for various functions. The major shift
has taken place in defense-related expenditures. As Figure 1.3 shows,
national defense outlays now account for slightly more than one-fourth
of total outlays, as compared with more than one-half of all outlays
during the mid-1950s. Ths decline became particularly sharp in the
post-Vietnam period and was not reversed until the fiscal 1976 budget.
Estimates of current and future spending now project national defense
expenditures to account for between 25 and 28 percent of total outlays.

At the same time, domestic transfer payments (to individuals) and
grants-in-aid (to state and local governments) have increased substantially as components of federal spending. *Domestic transfer payments,*
which consist primarily of income security and other domestic assis-

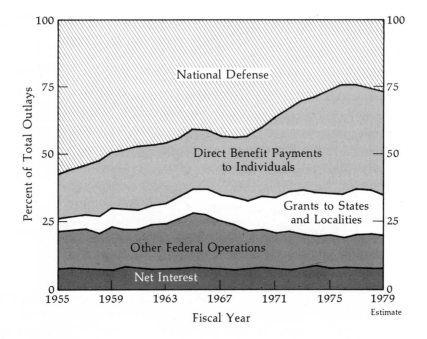

Figure 1.3
Expenditure category proportions of total outlays, in fiscal years 1955 through 1979. [Source: *The United States Budget in Brief, Fiscal Year 1978* (Washington, D.C.: Government Printing Office, 1977), p. 16.]

tance programs, are now the largest single category of federal spending, representing more than 40 percent of total outlays. While grants to states and localities account for a considerably smaller share, this share is over three times as large as in 1955.

The major increases in constant dollar spending have likewise been concentrated in payments to individuals and in grants. As Figure 1.4 indicates, defense spending in constant dollars actually declined slightly from 1955 through 1975 (with the exception, of course, of the Vietnam war period), and only since FY 1976 has there been an increase in real defense spending. By way of contrast, constant dollar spending for domestic transfer payments and grants increased by some $200 billion during this period.

It is apparent, then, that while inflation has accounted for part of the growth in federal spending over the past two decades, there has also been a substantial increase in real spending. The increase in real spending, however, has not been uniform throughout the budget. On

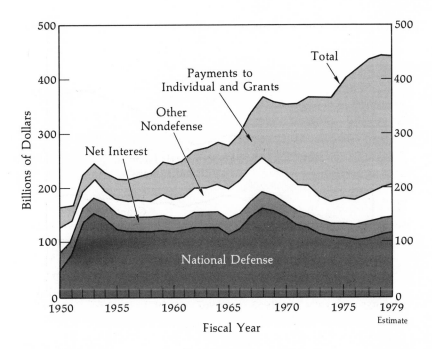

Figure 1.4
Federal outlays in constant 1978 dollars, in fiscal years 1950 through 1979.
[Source: *The Budget of the United States Government, Fiscal Year 1978* (Washington,
D.C.: Government Printing Office, 1977), p. 72.]

the contrary, most of this increase has occurred in domestic assistance
benefit programs and grants-in-aid. Spending in these categories now
accounts for well over óne-half of all federal outlays, and future estimates show only a small decrease in this share. At the same time, the
long-term decline in real defense spending has been arrested only recently, and the proportion of federal spending devoted to defense has
declined to less than one-half of its 1955 level.

Taxes.   The largest proportion of federal revenues is drawn from individual income taxes, with a slightly smaller share drawn from payroll
taxes levied on wages and salaries (social insurance taxes such as social
security). As Figure 1.5 indicates, an estimated 68 percent of the federal
budget dollar for FY 1978 stems from these sources, with most of the
remainder coming from corporation income taxes and borrowing.
  If we examine that portion of federal revenue derived from tax re-

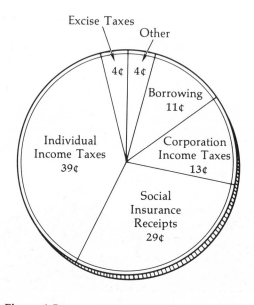

Figure 1.5

Estimated sources of the budget dollar for FY 1978. [Source: *The Budget of the United States Government, Fiscal Year 1978* (Washington, D.C.: Government Printing Office, 1977), p. M2.]

ceipts (thus excluding borrowing), we find a major shift in the government's reliance on the various forms of taxes. Since the mid-1950s, the proportion of federal receipts derived from individual income taxes has changed very little—43 percent in FY 1956 as compared with 44 percent in FY 1976 (see Figure 1.6). Social insurance taxes, however, accounted for approximately 12 percent of federal receipts in FY 1956 but had risen to 31 percent in FY 1976. This rapid increase is a result of many factors—growth of the labor force and wage rates, liberalized benefits and expanded coverage of programs, and higher taxable wage bases and contribution rates. Because of this increase, insurance taxes are now significantly higher than income taxes for many low- and moderate-income households.[32] During this same period, the proportion of total receipts derived from corporation income taxes and excise taxes has declined markedly. Projections through the early 1980s show a leveling off of the corporation income tax share (at around 15 percent) but a further decline in the share derived from excise and other taxes.

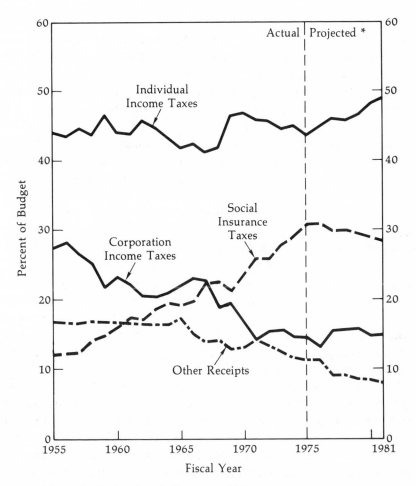

* Assumption of real GNP growth of 5 percent annually.

Figure 1.6
Receipts by source as a percentage of total receipts. [Source: Congressional Budget Office, *Budget Options for Fiscal Year 1977: A Report to the Senate and House Committees on the Budget* (Washington, D.C.: Government Printing Office, March 15, 1976), p. 9.]

Individual income taxes and social insurance taxes, therefore, will continue to provide 70 to 75 percent of total federal receipts. To the extent that future budgets are reasonably balanced between outlays and revenues, available budget receipts will be the primary determinant of spending. As a consequence, any permanent income tax reductions that are enacted now will reduce the growth in federal receipts in future years and thereby limit the possibility for major new spending programs. At the same time, it is widely recognized that without such reductions or corresponding changes in tax rates, many taxpayers will be penalized as inflation pushes them into higher tax brackets. When this occurs, their tax liability increases while their real income does not. An obvious problem confronting the Carter administration and Congress, then, is how to achieve significant tax relief, especially for middle-income households, without foreclosing major program initiatives.

Deficits.   While federal receipts have more than quadrupled over the past 20 years, federal spending has risen even faster. One of the most important aspects of the federal budget debate has been the focus on the size and frequency of the resulting deficits. As shown in Table 1.5, deficits occurred in all but four years from 1956 through 1976, raising the total federal debt from $272.8 billion to $631.9 billion. The deficits in FY 1975 and FY 1976, moreover, were unusually large, and the estimated deficit for FY 1977 is also substantial. Indeed, the total deficits incurred during these three years exceed by a considerable margin the combined deficits of the preceding 20 years.

While these figures are enormous and, to many, unsettling, some additional factors should be noted. First, the long-term trend for the total federal debt in relation to GNP is down, which means that the economy has been growing at a faster rate than the debt. Even with the very large recent increases, the federal debt is less than 40 percent of GNP, down more than one-third from the level in 1956. Second, the same pattern holds for the federal debt held by the public—that is, individuals and private institutions—as opposed to government agencies, primarily trust funds, that invest accumulated surpluses in government securities. The federal debt held by the public increased from $222.2 billion in FY 1956 to $480.3 billion in FY 1976, but as a percentage of GNP, this represented a decline from 54.1 percent to 29.8 percent. Third, there has been a relatively steady decline in the federal debt held by the public in terms of total debt in the economy. As Figure 1.7 indicates, private debt (which includes corporate, farm, consumer, commercial, and financial debt) has accounted for more than one-half of total indebtedness since about 1950, and this share has gradually

Table 1.5

Federal Surplus or Deficit and the Federal Debt, 1956–1976

Fiscal Year	Surplus or deficit in current dollars (billions)	Total federal debt		Federal debt held by public	
		In current dollars (billions)	As percentage of GNP	In current dollars (billions)	As percentage of GNP
1956	+4.1	272.8	66.4	222.2	54.1
1957	+3.2	272.4	62.9	219.4	50.6
1958	−2.9	279.7	63.3	226.4	51.2
1959	−12.9	287.8	61.1	235.0	49.9
1960	+0.3	290.9	58.4	237.2	47.6
1961	−3.4	292.9	57.5	238.6	46.9
1962	−7.1	303.3	55.6	248.4	45.5
1963	−4.8	310.8	53.9	254.5	44.1
1964	−5.9	316.8	51.4	257.6	41.8
1965	−1.6	323.2	49.1	261.6	39.8
1966	−3.8	329.5	45.6	264.7	36.6
1967	−8.7	341.3	44.1	267.5	34.6
1968	−25.2	369.8	44.5	290.6	35.0
1969[a]	+3.2	367.1	40.6	279.5	30.9
1970[b]	−2.8	382.6	39.8	284.9	29.7
1971	−23.0	409.5	40.2	304.3	29.8
1972	−23.2	437.3	39.3	323.8	29.1
1973[c]	−14.3	468.4	37.8	343.0	27.7
1974	−3.5	486.2	35.8	346.1	25.5
1975	−43.6	544.1	37.8	396.9	27.6
1976	−74.1	631.9	39.3	480.3	29.8
1977 est.	−57.2	716.7	39.2	560.3	30.7

[a]During 1969, three government-sponsored enterprises became completely privately owned, and their debt was removed from the totals for the federal government. At the dates of their conversion, gross federal debt was reduced $10.7 billion, debt held by government accounts was reduced $0.6 billion, and debt held by the public was reduced $10.1 billion.

[b]Gross federal debt and debt held by the public were increased $1.6 billion due to a reclassification of the Commodity Credit Corporation certificates of interest from asset sales to debt.

[c]A procedural change in the recording of trust fund holdings of Treasury debt at the end of the month increased gross federal debt and debt held in government accounts by about $4.5 billion.

Sources: Congressional Budget Office, *Budget Options for Fiscal Year 1977: A Report to the Senate and House Committees on the Budget* (Washington, D.C.: Government Printing Office, March 15, 1976), p. 11; *Special Analyses, Budget of the United States Government, Fiscal Year 1977* (Washington, D.C.: Government Printing Office, 1976), p. 50; *Budget of the United States Government, Fiscal Year 1978* (Washington, D.C.: Government Printing Office, 1977), pp. 435, 437.

increased to almost 80 percent. State and local government debt has also increased its share of net indebtedness. But the federal debt held by the public has dropped to less than one-fifth of net indebtedness.

Of course, the interest paid on the federal debt has necessarily increased as the debt has grown. Total interest, for example, was $15.8

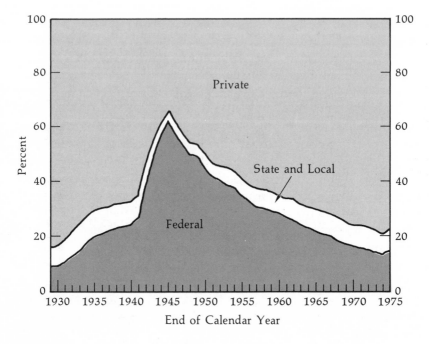

Figure 1.7

Distribution of net indebtedness among private sources, the federal government, and state and local governments. (Federal net indebtedness is the
federal debt held by the public, including the Federal Reserve System. Private net indebtedness includes the debt of the government-sponsored enterprises, which are federally established and chartered but privately
owned.) [Source: *Special Analyses, Budget of the United States Government,
Fiscal Year 1978* (Washington, D.C.: Government Printing Office, 1977),
p. 47.]

billion in 1969 but climbed to almost $35 billion in FY 1976. Net in-
terest—that is, interest paid on the publicly held debt as opposed to
interest paid to government trust funds—is between 75 and 80 percent
of this total. In terms of all federal outlays, the proportion accounted
for by net interest outlays has been fairly stable, generally between 7
and 8 percent. The federal debt, then, is costly and does affect financial
markets, but despite recent large deficits, the relative impact of the
debt as measured against economic growth or government spending
has not increased. If very large deficits continue to be incurred, however, these relationships could change.

Summary

Federal spending and tax policies have important social and economic effects, which guarantee that budget decisions will be politically important. In recent years, there has been increasing concern about the size and composition of federal spending, and this has been reflected in the annual budget conflicts between the executive and legislative branches. As head of the executive branch, the President has administrative responsibilities and policy preferences that underlie his involvement in the budgetary process. Correspondingly, the traditional base of congressional influence is the power of the purse—a power that it guards jealously if not always successfully.

Thus the budget is one focus for executive-congressional conflict. As subsequent chapters will discuss, executive participation and congressional participation have changed substantially in recent decades. The recently enacted budgetary reforms have the potential to effect equally profound long-term alterations in the budgetary process, particularly with respect to Congress' independence and influence in determining budget policy.

It should be kept in mind, however, that regardless of the rhetorical claims and flourishes that the competing sides may employ, budget decisions and their impact are complex, elusive, and imperfectly understood. Whether it be economic assumptions, outlay and revenue estimates, or fiscal policy choices, budget decision makers must frequently utilize data or other information about which there is considerable disagreement. Thus, on one level, the impact of budget aggregates on the economy must be considered, but there are generally questions about what shape the economy is in, where it is heading, and what effects a planned deficit (or surplus) will have. Even when there is consensus about the need for an economic stimulus in the form of a planned deficit (or restraint through a planned surplus), details such as amount, form, timing, and duration are likely to provoke debate.

In addition to budget aggregates and fiscal policy, budget decision making also affects the level of support for specific agencies and programs. The range of short-term policy choices available in the budget is characteristically quite narrow. The budget for a given fiscal year is based in large part on the previous year's budget. This relationship reflects binding financial commitments that are carried over from year to year, the political support that numerous programs have developed over the years, and the practical difficulties encountered in phasing out old programs or phasing in new ones. Legal commitments, political realism, and considerations of feasibility restrict the range of budget choices. As a result, budgets have usually been handled through an incremental approach, with attention focused primarily on a limited number of increases or decreases from the previous year.[33] But while choices are generally limited and changes generally marginal, some of these choices and changes can have a substantial impact on future budgets. An incremental approach, in other words, does not rule out significant long-term change.

As the discussion of budget trends indicates, the size and composition of the budget can change markedly over the long term. Federal spending over the past two decades has increased substantially, even when inflation is taken into account, and the growth in spending has exceeded the growth in the overall economy. Moreover, the composition of federal spending has changed drastically, with a reversal in the share of spending devoted to defense as opposed to social insurance and domestic assistance programs. Finally, since spending has also increased faster than receipts, deficits have occurred frequently, with recent deficits being especially large.

The budget developments during the mid-1970s have resulted in widespread concern about spending growth and deficits, but there is still likely to be substantial controversy over the relative merits of balanced budgets, new social programs, and lower taxes in the future. This controversy will no doubt be reflected in conflicts between the executive branch and Congress, as both sides struggle not simply against each other but also to achieve some degree of rational control over the extraordinary complexity of the budget decision process.

Notes

1. For a discussion of the various purposes of budgets, see Aaron Wildavsky, *The Politics of the Budgetary Process*, 2nd ed. (Boston: Little, Brown, 1974), chap. 1.
2. See Senate Committee on the Budget, *Seminars, Macroeconomic Issues and the Fiscal Year 1976 Budget*, 2 vols., 94th Congress, 1st Session (Washington, D.C.: Government Printing Office, May 1975).
3. See Senate Committee on the Budget, *Seminars, Energy Policy, the Impact on Budgetary and Economic Goals*, 94th Congress, 1st Session (Washington, D.C.: Government Printing Office, September 1975).

4. See Senate Committee on the Budget, Task Force on Defense, *Seminars, Service Chiefs on Defense Mission and Priorities*, 3 vols., 94th Congress, 2nd Session (Washington, D.C.: Government Printing Office, 1976).

5. The effects of this legislation will be covered in detail in subsequent chapters, particularly Chapter Three. The new process received a "trial run" for the fiscal 1976 budget and was fully operative for the fiscal 1977 budget.

6. Wildavsky, *Politics of the Budgetary Process*, pp. 4–5.

7. The President now submits two budgets to Congress. In November, a "current services estimate" is prepared. This projects the budget authority and outlays necessary to continue federal programs in the next fiscal year without policy changes. The President's budget, submitted in January or February, is formally titled *The Budget of the United States Government, Fiscal Year 19—. The Budget of the United States Government, Fiscal Year 19—: Appendix* contains detailed budget information, including the proposed text of appropriations legislation, budget schedules, budget estimates, lists of permanent positions in each agency, and related information. In addition, there are *The United States Budget in Brief, Fiscal Year 19—* and *Special Analyses, Budget of the United States Government, Fiscal Year 19—.*

8. Other forms of budget authority may be provided outside the regular appropriations process. "Borrowing authority" allows agencies to finance activities by borrowing funds directly from the Treasury or from the public. "Contract authority" allows agencies to incur contractual obligations in advance of appropriations. These are sometimes referred to as "backdoor spending." In an attempt to centralize control over spending, Congress has provided in certain instances for the Appropriations Committees to share jurisdiction over these types of budget authority with the legislative committees.

9. Louis Fisher, *Presidential Spending Power* (Princeton, N.J.: Princeton University Press, 1975), p. 6.

10. Congressional Budget Office, *Budget Options for Fiscal Year 1977: A Report to the Senate and House Committees on the Budget* (Washington, D.C.: Government Printing Office, March 15, 1976), p. 21.

11. *The Budget of the United States Government, Fiscal Year 1977* (Washington, D.C.: Government Printing Office, 1976), p. 25 (emphasis in original).

12. There has been continued disagreement about the "current services" estimates. This sometimes reflects apparent uncertainty about just what spending would indeed occur of its own "momentum," but a more general problem is that estimates for some programs do not take into account anticipated changes in economic conditions, such as inflation.

13. See Wildavsky, *Politics of the Budgetary Process*, chap. 2.

14. Ibid., pp. 13–16.

15. Aaron Wildavsky, *Budgeting: A Comparative Theory of Budgeting Processes* (Boston: Little, Brown, 1975), p. 6.

16. Ibid., pp. 294–296.

17. *Budget Options for Fiscal Year 1977*, pp. 2–3.

18. Ibid., pp. vii–xvii.

19. There have been recent analyses suggesting that the government's ability to affect the economy is much more limited than is sometimes assumed. One important reason for this is the political constraint affecting fiscal policy choices. See *National Journal, 8,* no. 3 (January 17, 1976), 86.

20. See Barry M. Blechman, Edward M. Gramlich, and Robert W. Hartman, *Setting National Priorities, The 1976 Budget* (Washington, D.C.: Brookings Institution, 1975), chap. 2.

21. Ibid., p. 192.

22. Ibid., pp. 203–204.

23. *Budget Options for Fiscal Year 1977*, p. 381.

24. See Congressional Budget Office, *Five-Year Budget Projections: Fiscal Years 1978–1982, Supplement on Tax Expenditures* (Washington, D.C.: Government Printing Office, April 1977), pp. 2–3. See also *Special Analyses, Budget of the United States Government, Fiscal Year 1978* (Washington, D.C.: Government Printing Office, 1977), pp. 119–142.

25. Blechman et al., *Setting National Priorities*, pp. 186–187.

26. *Five-Year Budget Projections*, p. 16.

27. Blechman et al., *Setting National Priorities*, pp. 188–189.

28. The 1978 budget also contains figures for "off-budget federal entities." These are partially or totally federally owned, but their transactions are excluded from budget totals under statutory provisions. This designation includes such organizations as the Federal Financing Bank, Rural Telephone Bank, and U.S. Railway Association. Total outlays for off-budget federal entities were $7.2 billion in FY 1976, and fiscal 1977 estimated outlays were $10.8 billion.

29. Even this may overstate the case for real spending increases. It has been argued that the prices paid by government increase more rapidly than prices generally because of the proportion of outlays paid to federal employees, whose wages in the past have typically risen faster than prices generally. Blechman et al., *Setting National Priorities*, pp. 5–7. It should be noted, however, that whatever its other merits or failings, the federal bureaucracy has not increased in size in recent years. Federal civilian employment in FY 1977 is estimated at 2.83 million. This is approximately the same as five years previously and slightly lower than in FY 1967 (2.88 million). Civilian personnel costs are considerable, however, estimated at $45.7 billion for FY 1977, more than double the total costs in FY 1967.

30. Blechman et al., *Setting National Priorities*, p. 4.

31. *Budget Options for Fiscal Year 1977*, p. 3.

32. *Special Analyses*, p. 10.

33. See Wildavsky, *Politics of the Budgetary Process*, pp. 13–16.

Two

Executive Planning and Formulation

Although the President's formal responsibility for executive budget planning and formulation was not established until 1921, presidential budget leadership has quickly developed a variety of purposes and objectives. The budget is often an effective tool for achieving administrative, policy, or political goals, and its utilization has become an important component of presidential leadership. Moreover, the final spending and taxing decisions made in the budget are sometimes interpreted as a measure of the relative influence of the President and Congress over national policy making. Indeed, in recent years there has been criticism that Congress has allowed the President to gain dominance in budget matters, and Congress has responded by changing drastically its internal budget procedures and limiting the President's ability to evade congressional budget decisions.[1] At the same time, it is apparent that the federal budget is not amenable to sharp or sudden short-term changes, so that Presidents face significant practical as well as political constraints in budget planning and formulation.[2] The budget represents, then, an opportunity for Presidents to achieve certain purposes. The relative emphasis placed on each of these purposes and the degree of success in achieving them, however, is only partially a matter of presidential determination. Much also depends on the actions of other political leaders and on objective circumstances.

First, the budget can serve the President as a means of administrative management and control. By affecting the resources available for agencies and programs, the President can seek to promote better planning of what is done, more effective supervision of how it is done, and more systematic evaluation of how well various objectives are accomplished. In August 1965, for example, President Lyndon Johnson announced that a "planning-programming-budgeting system," which had been introduced earlier in the Department of Defense, would be applied to the domestic operations of the federal bureaucracy. This major management "innovation" was not successful, but the belief persists, as reflected in the Budget Bureau reorganization during the Nixon administration and the zero-base budget system advocated by President Carter, that budgets can be and should be effective management tools. This is an important purpose, but it is one to which recent Presidents have given sporadic attention at best.

Second, and considerably more compelling to most inhabitants of the White House, the fiscal policy effects of the budget are an important part of the President's economic program and relate directly to his general responsibility for economic management and stabilization. Assessments of an administration's performance are affected by the state of the economy, which means that Presidents must pay attention to prosperity as well as to peace. In this context, budget totals and the balance between spending and revenues are matters that command serious presidential attention.

Third, budget decisions can affect a President's political support and image. By emphasizing particular programs or criticizing others, by challenging Congress' spending preferences, by trumpeting the need for fiscal responsibility, or by reiterating commitments to greater economy and efficiency, a President can attempt to dramatize his leadership role and to generate public support for his economic policies and program preferences. When done effectively, this tactic can provide a major advantage in dealing with Congress or other political opposition; recent Presidents have repeatedly exercised this option.[3] Whether this advantage will continue as Congress develops its new budgetary process is uncertain, although it might be anticipated that the President's superior ability to publicize actions and initiatives will still provide an edge in budget debates. In any case, the budget does present an opportunity for the kind of symbolic leadership that Presidents find useful.

Fourth, the budget allows the President to argue his policy preferences and innovations within the context of a comprehensive budgetary program, which means that the President can initiate attempts to reorder budget priorities. For example, in attempting to change the relative emphasis between defense spending and domestic program support, an administration is able to focus attention on the relationships between spending choices. Presidents can therefore use their annual budget submission to initiate debate about cutting, continuing, or expanding existing programs or about establishing new programs, and they can do so as part of a coherent plan for the total budget.

There are, then, several avenues for presidential influence through the budgetary process, despite the constraints on budget planning and formulation. The focus on one or another of these objectives has, of course, varied from administration to administration, just as actual presidential involvement in budget decision making has varied.[4] But by the mid-1970s, the growth of federal spending had become such a serious political and economic problem that presidential politics and presidential-congressional relations focused to an unusual extent on the President's budgetary leadership.

During the twentieth century, the President's budgetary responsibilities have become institutionalized. A formal statutory responsibility has been established along with a growing staff capability to assist the Chief Executive. Most important, Presidents cannot easily evade the political accountability relating to the economic and programmatic implications of the budget. In this chapter, the development of presidential budget leadership will be examined, along with the executive budgetary process and the major participants in that process. Finally, some recent budget controversies will be discussed in order to illustrate the attempts to exercise presidential budget leadership.

Development of Presidential Responsibility

While the 1921 Budget and Accounting Act signaled the beginning of formal presidential budget leadership, there is evidence of significant, if sporadic, presidential involvement in budget matters during the period from 1789 to 1921. What the 1921 act did reflect, however, was agreement that direct presidential involvement was necessary to promote economy and efficiency in government, to develop a true "national budget" in order to achieve economic stability, and to counter—

along with internal reforms in Congress—the splintering of congressional control over money matters that had developed during the latter part of the nineteenth century. This suggests, of course, that Presidents could and would perform functions that Congress was either unwilling or unable to perform.

The Pre-1921 Period

The traditional practice established after the adoption of the Constitution was to have annual estimates prepared by the various executive agencies. These were then submitted in the "Book of Estimates" by the Secretary of the Treasury. Since Congress has always emphasized the importance of its control of the purse, it is not surprising that it attempted to use this power to establish control over the executive departments. The role of the Secretary of the Treasury was to be perfunctory, restricted to transmitting the estimates of spending and sometimes supplying estimates of revenue. The President was not to have direct budgetary responsibilities, and the executive departments were to deal only with congressional committees in determining their budgets. This meant that "centralized Executive authority in budgetary matters was to remain in abeyance for over a century."[5]

Despite congressional intentions, several Presidents, along with their Treasury secretaries, did attempt to exercise some degree of budget leadership.[6] This took a variety of forms—reviewing the annual estimates, exhorting the bureaus and agencies to effect greater efficiency and economy in their handling of public funds, supporting the estimates with statements to Congress, and, in some cases, encouraging revisions in the estimates.[7] That early Presidents appreciated the tactical and programmatic implications of budgetary decisions is apparent. John Quincy Adams, for example, advised his Secretary of the Treasury that some padding of department estimates might be necessary given Congress' tendency to cut the estimates regardless of justification: "If some superfluity be not given them to lop off, they will cut into the very flesh of the public necessities."[8]

Nevertheless, there was no clear presidential responsibility for budget leadership nor any effective budget centralization within the executive branch. There was for a time, however, a degree of centralization in Congress. Up until the Civil War, the Ways and Means

Committee in the House and the Finance Committee in the Senate handled both revenue and appropriations (spending) bills. However, this centralization soon disappeared. Appropriations Committees were established to handle spending bills, but they quickly lost their exclusive jurisdiction over spending to the legislative committees. By the 1880s, there was no budget system in any real sense.[9] Spending and revenue decisions were not considered comprehensively, and control over spending decisions was divided between the Appropriations and legislative committees.

The lack of a national budget system, however, was not perceived as unduly serious, since the United States enjoyed continuing budget surpluses during this period (as indeed it had during much of the century). Most federal revenue was generated by customs tariffs, which generally were more than sufficient to cover government expenditures. Since protectionist sentiment was strong, Congress was in the enviable position of reaping the political benefits of both higher spending and higher tariffs.[10] There was, nevertheless, occasional conflict between the President and Congress over spending. This was especially true of presidential vetoes of the more popular forms of congressional largesse—rivers and harbors bills and pension bills. President Cleveland, for example, vetoed 304 bills during his first term in office, nearly three times the total for all his predecessors combined, and 241 of these were pension bills.[11]

One practice that gained increasing use at this time was the granting of deficiency or supplemental appropriations.[12] Agencies that had received smaller appropriations than had been requested or considered necessary (by those in the agency) spent their allotted funds before the fiscal year was completed and then went back to Congress for additional monies. Congress customarily acceded to these "coercive deficiencies," although just how coercive the practice was remains unclear. One critic charged that Congress often consciously underappropriated:

> One of the vicious party devices too often resorted to for avoiding responsibility for extravagance in appropriations is to cut down the annual bills below the actual amount necessary to carry on the government, announce to the country that a greater reduction has been made in the interest of economy, and after the elections are over, make up the necessary amount by deficiency bills.[13]

As might be expected, congressional committees often competed for appropriations, "the one striving to surpass the other in securing greater recognition and more money for its special charge."[14]

Beginning in fiscal 1904, increased spending resulted in several budget deficits after more than a quarter century of surpluses. This generated pressure in the government and from the private sector to balance spending and revenues and to establish an effective budget system. Congress moved slowly to meet these demands. In 1906 it passed legislation to curb the use of deficiency appropriations by executive departments and agencies. A 1909 appropriations act provided that when the Secretary of the Treasury found that departmental spending would exceed estimated revenues, the President could propose appropriations reductions or revenue increases in his State of the Union message.[15] Congress was still not prepared, however, to concede to the President formal authority to review and amend department estimates before they were submitted. Attempts during the Taft administration to establish a national budget, with presidential review of departmental requests and recommendations concerning revenues and spending, in addition to the customary Book of Estimates were unsuccessful.[16]

In 1910, President Taft appointed, with Congress' concurrence, a Commission on Economy and Efficiency to study the financial. management of executive departments. While the Commission's recommendations for a national budget system were later ignored by Congress, it did focus attention on critical aspects and deficiencies of the existing process. The Commission stated that effective presidential involvement in the formulation of the budget was necessary to provide needed administrative centralization and political responsibility in the executive branch. In addition, it suggested that an executive budget needed to be truly comprehensive, covering not only expenditures and revenue under existing legislation but also examining the budgetary consequences of new or proposed legislation.[17] According to the Commission, an annual executive budget combined with a systematic budget process would assist Congress by providing "expert advice in thinking about policies to be determined"; allow administrators to prepare well supported, clearly defined, and carefully considered budget requests; and enable the President to "bring together the facts and opinions necessary to the clear formulation of proposals for which he is willing actively to work as the responsible officer."[18]

Executive formulation was thus identified as a necessary element in an effective budget system. To its proponents, it promised greater efficiency and economy in government spending by fixing initial responsibility for reviewing departmental estimates with the head of the executive branch, the President. But it also represented, as the Commission on Economy and Efficiency recognized, an acceptance of the policy-making role and responsibility of the Chief Executive. The opponents of executive budget formulation viewed it as an erosion of Congress' power of the purse and as a long-term threat to legislative authority.[19]

While World War I diverted immediate attention from budget reform, it also generated spending levels and financial pressures that actually strengthened the case for revising the budgetary process. Spending rose from its prewar level of $700 million to over $18 billion in fiscal 1919, and the national debt increased from slightly over $1 billion in 1916 to over $25 billion in 1919.[20] The prewar impetus for economy and efficiency and for administrative management was supplemented by the postwar need for debt management. In 1919, after various proposals for more limited changes had been considered by Congress, the Wilson administration called for the establishment of a national budget. Two years later President Harding signed into law the Budget and Accounting Act, which gave the President formal responsibility for preparing a national budget and established a Bureau of the Budget, located in the Department of the Treasury and headed by a director appointed by the President, to assist in this preparation.

Post-1921 Developments

Since 1921, several developments have strengthened the Presidency's budget leadership capabilities and broadened the scope of budget decision making. There have been, for example, periodic changes in the roles, influence, and organization of the Bureau of the Budget and other staff institutions having major budgetary responsibilities. While these changes will be covered in detail later in this chapter, it is sufficient to note at this point that presidential staff and support systems for budgetary and other purposes are important characteristics of the contemporary Presidency, and Congress has recently sought to match this presidential capability by establishing a counterpart budget staff for its own use—the Congressional Budget Office.

Moreover, the political and policy implications of presidential budget leadership have been broadened considerably. During the 1920s and

1930s, for example, there was increasing recognition of the federal budget's role in economic stabilization. For the Republican administrations of Harding, Coolidge, and Hoover, this meant balancing the budget, rigid controls on expenditures, and reduction of the federal debt.[21] When the Roosevelt administration took office in 1933, there was no firm conception that these emphases need be altered, yet during his first year Roosevelt admitted that deficit spending would be necessary for at least several years because of the economic emergency. By his second term, Roosevelt was defending the necessity for short-term deficits in order to achieve economic recovery and stability. In his 1937 budget message, Roosevelt declared:

> The programs inaugurated during the last four years to combat the depression and to initiate many needed reforms have cost large sums of money, but the benefits obtained from them are far outweighing all their costs. We shall soon be reaping the full benefits of those programs and shall have at the same time a balanced budget that will also include provision for reduction of the public debt.[22]

While this particular approach ran counter to traditional theories concerning government spending (and remains controversial even today), Roosevelt accepted a positive federal responsibility for managing the economy.

In 1946 legislation was enacted that ratified this federal responsibility:

> The Congress hereby declares that it is the continuing policy and responsibility of the Federal Government to use all practicable means consistent with its needs and obligations and other essential considerations of national policy . . . to promote maximum employment, production, and purchasing power.[23]

Under the 1946 Employment Act, the President was made responsible for presenting to Congress an annual economic report covering current and projected levels of prices, employment, and production, along with reviews of current or recommended policies related to achieving the objectives of the act. In preparing this report, the President was to be assisted by a newly established Council of Economic Advisers, to be located in the Executive Office of the President. Congress also created its own Joint Economic Committee to study and make recommendations concerning the President's economic report.

The Employment Act of 1946 therefore established a federal government role in economic management and assigned a central position to the President as what has been termed the "Manager of Prosperity."[24] Of course, it is likely that Presidents would receive the blame for poor economic conditions regardless of the 1946 legislation. The state of the economy, fairly or unfairly, is a potential albatross around a President's neck.[25] But the President's budget is now an important element in his general economic program.

This does not mean that the President's attempts to manage the economy are restricted to budget decisions or that budget decisions are strictly governed by fiscal policy determinations. There are a variety of legislative and administrative options available to affect the economy, including wage and price controls, antitrust policies, trade policies, and regulatory practices. But at least since the Kennedy administration, there has been an emphasis on the fiscal policy intentions and potential economic consequences of the President's budget. John Kennedy defended an active presidential role in economic planning and attempted to convince the business community that budget decisions, especially tax policies, could be used effectively to stimulate the economy and that under appropriate conditions budget deficits would be salutary. While Kennedy had difficulty in convincing Congress as well as the business community that budgets should be assessed in terms of fiscal policy, this view has since become generally accepted.[26]

Of course, what the President's fiscal policy intentions are and what is politically feasible are not always the same. It appears to be much easier to gain support for tax cuts and spending increases than for tax increases and spending cuts. Even as the costs of the Vietnam war escalated, for example, there was considerable reluctance to increase taxes, and the result was substantial deficit spending. It is necessary to recognize, therefore, that the fiscal policy effects of budget decisions are not always readily manipulable nor is the utilization of fiscal policy an exact science. In many instances, an administration's budget planning may be frustrated by Congress or by changing economic conditions. But it is clear that the President's political responsibility for economic management has become firmly established in recent years, and as a consequence Presidents must pay attention to the economic impact of budget decisions. This means that budget aggregates—total spending and total revenues—are a key element of an administration's economic policy.

Finally, there has emerged a widespread perception, reflected in Congress' major revision of its internal budgetary process, that the President has achieved dominance in budgetary decision making and that the executive budgetary process is more "rational" than Congress'. Whether these assessments are correct—and there is a considerable amount of contrary evidence and interpretation[27]—the Presidency does appear to have a public relations advantage over Congress concerning budgetary matters. The background to the passage of 1974 Congressional Budget and Impoundment Control Act reflects some of these advantages.

The 1974 legislation was in large part a reaction against the spending prerogatives claimed by the Nixon administration and against the practices, such as impoundment, used to support these claims. During 1972, President Nixon along with a number of administration spokesmen attacked the Democratic-controlled Congress for allegedly excessive spending, and in July Congress was asked to establish a $250 billion spending ceiling for FY 1973 and to give the President discretionary authority to cut spending wherever needed in order to preserve that ceiling. While the House agreed, the Senate was unwilling to give the President unlimited discretion, and the proposal ultimately died in conference committee. The administration subsequently announced its intention to impound funds to achieve the spending ceiling.

An interesting aspect of this controversy was that many legislators apparently were convinced that Congress had been irresponsible.[28] This was evidenced by the House of Representatives, traditionally the most zealous guardian of the power of the purse, agreeing to total executive discretion over spending cuts. As in 1921, there was a widely shared assumption, inside Congress and among the public, that the President was better able and certainly more willing than Congress to impose the required discipline on government spending and that the Presidency was a more effective budget-making institution than Congress.[29] Two years later, Congress decided to remedy the situation by approximating the budget centralization that had developed in the executive branch.[30] This provides a useful commentary on just how effectively presidential budget leadership has been established over the past half century. From a time in which Congress would not grant the President authority even to submit his budget recommendations along with the Book of Estimates, we have in recent years come to a point where Congress fears it has lost much of its power of the purse and thus attempts to counter the budget leadership of the President. At this stage, then, it might be helpful to examine the executive's budget system and to see how the President affects budget decisions.

Stages of the Budgetary Process

Under the 1974 Congressional Budget and Impoundment Control Act, the President is required to prepare and submit to Congress two annual budgets. The first, a current services budget, is submitted on November 10, approximately 11 months prior to the beginning of the fiscal year that it covers. The second budget, the President's *Budget of the United States Government*, is submitted 15 days after Congress convenes in January, more than eight months prior to the beginning of the fiscal year that it covers.

Current Services Budget

The information provided in the current services budget provides a basis for determining the overall size and direction of existing budget commitments and for assessing and evaluating subsequent budget proposals, such as the President's budget. The current services budget includes the "proposed budget authority and estimated outlays that would be included in the budget for the ensuing fiscal year . . . if all programs and activities were carried on at the same level as the fiscal year in progress . . . and without policy changes."[31] It also includes the administration's projections about economic conditions that affect spending, such as the rate of inflation, rate of economic growth, the level of unemployment, and so forth. Congress' Joint Economic Committee is then responsible for studying and evaluating these estimates and projections.

Preparation of the current services budget is supervised by the Office of Management and Budget (OMB), which provides the executive departments with the appropriate guidelines to be used in developing estimates. For example, since estimates should reflect anticipated costs without policy changes, the effects of all pending legislative proposals are excluded, regardless of the stage of the legislative process at which a proposal might be or of a proposal's likelihood of passage. Presidential requests for rescissions—that is, for cancellation of spending authority previously enacted—require congressional approval; thus pending rescission requests are not counted in the estimates. Pending deferrals, on the other hand, go into effect unless the House or Senate votes to disallow the request, so these deferrals are reflected in the estimates. Expiring programs that are clearly temporary are not carried forward. Where factors such as inflation, federal pay increases, and unemployment rates must be taken into account in preparing the estimates, the OMB provides the economic assumptions to be followed.[32]

There is limited discretion in determining current services estimates, but there is still a certain degree of imprecision. Since it is very difficult for the executive branch or Congress to estimate precisely what it is spending in the current fiscal year, leading to continued revisions of spending and receipts throughout the year, it is not surprising that estimates for subsequent years are sometimes treated with skepticism. Whatever the economic utility or accuracy of the estimates, however, they can be used for political purposes. The Ford administration, which prepared the first current services budget under the 1974 legislation, submitted to Congress a $28 billion tax cut package in October 1975 and linked this to a proposed $395 billion spending ceiling for FY 1977. It then presented Congress with a current services budget that estimated spending for FY 1977 at almost $415 billion. Congress was thus confronted with a tax program and spending ceiling designed to cut some $20 billion off the spending that would "automatically" occur without policy changes. While Congress refused to follow this program —as everyone no doubt anticipated—the presidential initiative was considered to be an effective political gambit.

The objectives of the current services budget—to provide an early indication of the cost of existing commitments and to serve as a guide for assessing subsequent budget proposals—are worthwhile. However, since the estimates can be substantially changed by legislative actions or by altered economic assumptions, it is probably the guideline objective that is best realized. As departments prepare their current services estimates, they are also developing their budgets based on presidential policies, and the comparisons between these sets of outlays provide a useful indication of the effective changes in the budget that the President wishes to accomplish.[33]

President's Budget

The President's annual budget reflects his decisions and recommendations to Congress about the size of the budget, its effects on the economy, and the allocations to various agencies and programs. It also contains projections of the budget authority and outlays required to fund agencies and programs in future years if presidential recommendations are followed. Unlike the current services estimates, this budget does contain suggested changes in current policies, projected new policies or programs, and presidential priorities with respect to spending. Planning on this budget generally begins some 18 months before the beginning of the fiscal year. For example, budget planning for FY 1979 (the fiscal period October 1, 1978, through September 30, 1979) began in the early spring of 1977. There are several stages in the planning and formulation process: (1) budget policy development, beginning in March (or earlier) and continuing through June; (2) compilation and submission of agency estimates, covering the period from July through September; and (3) OMB review and final presidential decisions. The process is illustrated in Figure 2.1.

Budget Policy Development. At this stage, preliminary decisions are made about general budget policy and major program issues. These decisions take into account projections of economic conditions and estimated revenues, and the review and evaluation of agency programs. Projections of economic conditions are prepared jointly by the OMB, the Council of Economic Advisers, and the Department of the Treasury. Economic models are developed that show the effects of alternative policy choices. These projections and models are then reviewed by presidential advisers and advisory groups that make their recommendations to the President concerning economic assumptions and general budget policy.

During this period, the executive agencies are going through the spring planning review. This involves evaluations of current policies and operations, assessments of major policy issues that have developed, and projections of future plans and costs. On the basis of this review, the OMB prepares recommendations on spending levels and programmatic emphases for the President. It is at this point that the President, in consultation with his advisers, establishes the general

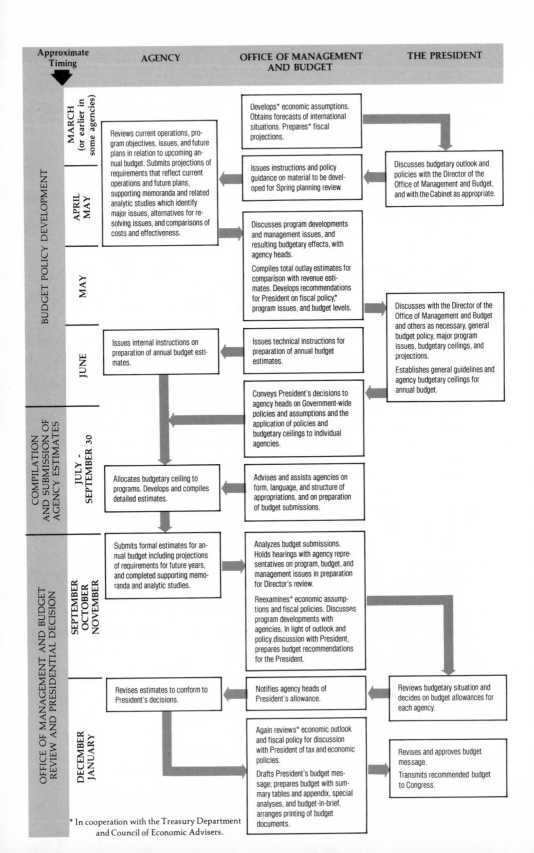

Approximate Timing	AGENCY	OFFICE OF MANAGEMENT AND BUDGET	THE PRESIDENT

BUDGET POLICY DEVELOPMENT

MARCH (or earlier in some agencies)

Develops* economic assumptions. Obtains forecasts of international situations. Prepares* fiscal projections.

Reviews current operations, program objectives, issues, and future plans in relation to upcoming annual budget. Submits projections of requirements that reflect current operations and future plans, supporting memoranda and related analytic studies which identify major issues, alternatives for resolving issues, and comparisons of costs and effectiveness.

APRIL MAY

Issues instructions and policy guidance on material to be developed for Spring planning review.

Discusses budgetary outlook and policies with the Director of the Office of Management and Budget, and with the Cabinet as appropriate.

MAY

Discusses program developments and management issues, and resulting budgetary effects, with agency heads.

Compiles total outlay estimates for comparison with revenue estimates. Develops recommendations for President on fiscal policy,* program issues, and budget levels.

Discusses with the Director of the Office of Management and Budget and others as necessary, general budget policy, major program issues, budgetary ceilings, and projections.

JUNE

Issues internal instructions on preparation of annual budget estimates.

Issues technical instructions for preparation of annual budget estimates.

Establishes general guidelines and agency budgetary ceilings for annual budget.

COMPILATION AND SUBMISSION OF AGENCY ESTIMATES

JULY - SEPTEMBER 30

Conveys President's decisions to agency heads on Government-wide policies and assumptions and the application of policies and budgetary ceilings to individual agencies.

Allocates budgetary ceiling to programs. Develops and compiles detailed estimates.

Advises and assists agencies on form, language, and structure of appropriations, and on preparation of budget submissions.

OFFICE OF MANAGEMENT AND BUDGET REVIEW AND PRESIDENTIAL DECISION

SEPTEMBER OCTOBER NOVEMBER

Submits formal estimates for annual budget including projections of requirements for future years, and completed supporting memoranda and analytic studies.

Analyzes budget submissions. Holds hearings with agency representatives on program, budget, and management issues in preparation for Director's review.

Reexamines* economic assumptions and fiscal policies. Discusses program developments with agencies. In light of outlook and policy discussion with President, prepares budget recommendations for the President.

Revises estimates to conform to President's decisions.

Notifies agency heads of President's allowance.

Reviews budgetary situation and decides on budget allowances for each agency.

DECEMBER JANUARY

Again reviews* economic outlook and fiscal policy for discussion with President of tax and economic policies.

Drafts President's budget message; prepares budget with summary tables and appendix, special analyses, and budget-in-brief, arranges printing of budget documents.

Revises and approves budget message.

Transmits recommended budget to Congress.

* In cooperation with the Treasury Department and Council of Economic Advisers.

Figure 2.1

Formulation of the executive budget. [Source: Office of Management and Budget, *Major Steps in the Budget Process* (Washington, D.C.: Government Printing Office, 1972).]

budget policy and program priorities to be followed. Much of the emphasis necessarily focuses on aggregates—what revenue levels and spending levels can be anticipated and what the balance between revenue and spending should be. Since most agencies and programs are unlikely to warrant presidential attention, changes in existing spending levels are likely to be marginal. However, the President can recommend large increases or decreases in those policy areas that he considers to be especially important. Budget policy development, then, is a mechanism for general rather than detailed presidential supervision of the budgetary process. There are important choices to be made about the potential economic impact and programmatic emphases of the budget, but much of the budget will necessarily reflect past commitments and policies, and the President's discretion about the remainder is limited by what is politically feasible.

Agency Estimates.   General budget policies must be translated into detailed information on programs, financing, personnel, and other costs. On the basis of the technical instructions, policy and budgetary guidelines, economic assumptions, and budget ceilings provided by the OMB, the executive agencies must prepare their budget estimates. Decisions are first made about allocations to various programs—for example, how much the Forest Service in the Department of Agriculture will allocate to forest protection and utilization, construction and land acquisitions, forest roads and trails, construction and operation of recreation facilities, assistance to the states for tree planting, and so forth. Then detailed estimates are developed on the funding requirements of current and proposed programs. The estimates and program proposals represent an effort to integrate an agency's legislatively established programs and responsibilities with presidential policies, and it is up to the agency to provide necessary justifications—such as program or performance studies—for its programs and financing and to explain increases (or decreases) in budget estimates as compared with current and past spending.[34]

OMB Review and Presidential Decisions.   The final stage of budget formulation includes a review of the economic assumptions and fiscal policy decisions made earlier in the year, an examination of agency budget estimates, and final decisions on budget totals and allocations. Specialists (budget examiners) at OMB conduct a full-scale analysis of the budget estimates submitted by the agencies. Agency representatives meet with their OMB counterparts, formal presentations and hearings are conducted, and the OMB then decides what funding levels it will recommend to the President. At the same time, economic conditions and projections and fiscal policy alternatives are reviewed by presidential advisers. On the basis of recommendations from the OMB and other advisory groups, the President makes his final decisions on budget totals and budget allocations. Once this occurs, the OMB and the agencies prepare the estimates and supporting information for the President's budget, which is then submitted to Congress shortly after it convenes in January.

Formulation of the executive budget usually does not involve detailed presidential superintendence, but the President can significantly shape the general outlines and press for selected policy initiatives. His decisions about budget totals are especially important, since they provide the context in which detailed judgments about program increases or decreases are made, and these decisions also reflect the fiscal policy preferences of the administration. Presidential decisions and their implementation do not, however, take place in isolation. There are other key participants in the executive budget process, including the staff and advisory groups that assist the President in budget decision making and the executive agencies that are directly affected by these decisions. There are important differences between these participants not only in terms of their relationship to the President but also in the roles and functions that they perform in budget decision making. By examining these differences in roles and functions, it is possible to gain some insights into the politics of the executive budgetary process.

Executive Budget
Participants and Their Roles

The formulation of the executive budget is in part, of course, a highly technical exercise with a peculiar and largely inaccessible language. The decision stages in executive formulation described above must inevitably be translated into a financial accounting of what agencies do and how much their activities cost. At the same time, these decision stages are a highly political negotiations process in which the judgments, interests, roles, and influences of the various participants may differ substantially. The process is not nearly as centralized, the decisions not as rational, nor the President's lines of control as strong as a diagram of the process might suggest. It is important, therefore, to understand the general division of labor and the effects of this division on budget decisions. This can be accomplished by examining the roles of the departments or agencies on the one hand and of the OMB along with other presidential staff and advisory groups on the other.

Departments and Agencies

The impact of budget decisions is specific and direct within the bureaucracy, so it is not surprising that the departments and agencies "are expected to be advocates of increased appropriations."[35] In order to continue or expand existing programs or to establish new programs, budget support is essential. Thus, there is competition between as well as within departments for available funds. At this level, the primary concern is not how departmental or agency budget requests will affect the President's fiscal policy or general program preferences. These considerations are more appropriately the concerns of presidential staff and advisory groups, such as the OMB or the Council of Economic Advisers. Rather, the overriding objective is to obtain support for those particular policies and interests that fall within a department's or agency's domain.

Department heads and their staffs are responsible for representing and advocating their department's interests when initial allocations and ceilings are being worked out by the OMB and the President. Generally, the President's concern early in the budgetary process is with the fiscal policy implications of the budget—and thus with the overall spending and revenue levels—together with selected policies and programs. Departmental leadership must attempt, where possible, to encourage presidential attention to their programs or at least to insure that presidential emphasis on the programs of other departments does not adversely affect their own budgets. As the budgetary process unfolds, continued advocacy and negotiation with the OMB might be necessary to protect or increase departmental allocations. As final budget decisions are made, department heads must protect their allocations when these are considered adequate or perhaps press appeals with the OMB or the President to increase these allocations.

There is, of course, a degree of tension in all of this. A department secretary is the President's appointee and owes, as a consequence, at least some loyalty to the President and his programs. At the same time, a secretary has a duty to subordinates within his department, to the interests or groups that the department serves, and to the general goals and purposes of his department. The selection process usually insures that this type of sympathy or commitment does characterize Cabinet appointments, as Presidents attempt to satisfy geographical, clientele group, or ideological interests. That the Cabinet has usually not served as a significant high-level advisory group for the President is at least in part a reflection of the particularistic interests and loyalties of individual secretaries.[36] Thus what the President and his advisers believe to be adequate for a particular department need not be, indeed probably will not be, perceived as adequate by the leadership of that department. Occasionally this results in a secretary "going public" with his case and seeking to develop support outside the executive branch to challenge budget decisions.

In November 1975, for example, President Ford fired his Secretary of Defense, James R. Schlesinger, reportedly as a result of a lack of "personal compatibility" and of Schlesinger's publicly stated dissatisfactions with cuts in the defense budget. Schlesinger had carried his attack on defense spending cuts outside the administration and had denounced House Appropriations Committee reductions in the defense budget as "deep, savage, and arbitrary," also suggesting that some members of the committee had been "driven by political considerations."[37] It was reported that the President "also disliked what he regarded as Schlesinger's political disloyalty . . . in arguments over reducing the fiscal 1977 defense budget to conform with Ford's over-all plan to cut $28 billion in federal spending."[38] While the Schlesinger case was unusually dramatic and controversial, it does reflect the inherent problems that a department head faces in trying to be both an advocate of his department's interests and a member of the President's "team." It also suggests that Presidents do expect their Cabinet members to temper their advocacy, particularly in public debate.

Within the department, moreover, agencies are expected to be advocates for their specific programs and interests. This means that there will usually be competition for resources between agencies in the same department. One would expect the career civil servants in an agency to support as a matter of course the programs and interests for which they have worked.

A man who has spent many years working in, say, the natural resources area can be expected to believe that his programs are immensely worthy of support. (He may try to eliminate programs he deems unworthy but there are always others to take their place.) Indeed, he would hardly be worth having as a governmental employee if he did not feel this way in this position. One can only imagine what the reaction would be if such a person intimated that soil conservation, reforestation, or recreation must just possibly be all right but that he was more than ready to believe that many, many other things were equally or more important, and that his projects could easily be postponed or eliminated. By serving as an advocate in the real world he sees to it that important values in his area are not neglected if he can help it.[39]

In serving this advocacy function, there are several points at which the agency must attempt to exercise its influence. First, there is the intradepartmental allocation in which agencies can draw on outside support, such as that in Congress or among influential clientele groups, to support their shares of departmental funds and to guard against departmental or OMB pressures that could challenge these shares. Second, the agency must justify its programs to the OMB as effectively and vigorously as possible when initial ceilings and guidelines are being adopted and then as negotiations concerning final budget decisions take place. Third, the agency is expected to be equally vigorous in justifying budget recommendations before the Appropriations Committees in the House and Senate. Indeed, it is considered acceptable for agencies to press for upward revisions as long as this is done with the appropriate degree of subtlety and with the necessary declarations of support for presidential decisions.

Agency advocacy is not directed solely at securing the highest possible appropriation in a given year. Agencies must be realistic in what they ask for, or they risk losing the confidence of the OMB and congressional committees. Agencies also have a vested interest in long-term stability for their programs. For most agencies, therefore, advocacy is tied to an incremental budget strategy, in which (1) the budget decisions of one year are affected primarily by the decisions of previous years, (2) most changes are marginal, and (3) much of what has been done in the past no longer needs to be justified or examined in any great detail. Thus, most agencies seek to establish a base—that is, programs that are continued from year to year without much scrutiny—

and also to have their share of increases or decreases tied to what other agencies receive.[40] In this context, advocacy is still necessary, but the stakes are relatively limited. It is not a case of an agency getting all that it wants as opposed to receiving nothing at all but rather of assuring a satisfactory, if not perfect, level of funding with continuity and the possibility for expansion and innovation over time.

The pressure from the departments and within the departments, naturally enough, is to receive budget support for specific programs and interests, to press their needs when dealing with the OMB or the President, to develop and maintain clientele group and congressional support (and on occasion to utilize that support to reverse or alter presidential decisions without showing disloyalty), and to insure a high degree of stability and continuity in budget decisions. A department's perspective is not presidential, and there is no reason why it should be, since enforcing and articulating the President's interests and preferences is more appropriately the province of other participants in the budgetary process, particularly the OMB and other presidential advisory groups.

The Presidential Perspective

A number of staff and advisory groups have been created to assist the President in making and implementing decisions. This development is part of a broader contemporary phenomenon—the repeated attempts to improve presidential access to advice and information in order to strengthen presidential policy leadership. Some of the major institutional changes in the Presidency have directly involved the budgetary process, since this process has generally been viewed as a central resource in the President's attempt to implement his policy preferences and to supervise and direct the federal bureaucracy. Traditionally, the most prominent of the budget staff institutions has been the OMB (formerly the Bureau of the Budget), but other important participants include the Council of Economic Advisers and, in recent administrations, the Domestic Council and the Economic Policy Board.

Other staff and advisory groups do influence budget decisions. For example, the National Security Council and staff have substantial influence over the defense budget, since they serve as the President's central advisory group on national security affairs. Policy-making groups and individual presidential advisers, therefore, often have a significant impact on budget decisions, since they affect the policy choices an administration makes. The responsibility for actually translating presidential policy preferences into budget choices, however, falls to a small group of staff institutions. These staffs assist the President in making his budget decisions and insure that the presidential perspective is maintained as these decisions are implemented. They are, in effect, representing the President in the budgetary process.

Office of Management and Budget

The Bureau of the Budget was established in 1921 under the Budget and Accounting Act to assist the President in preparing the budget. Since that time, the Bureau (now the OMB) has occupied a central position in the budgetary process, and its several functions, as well as the problems it has faced in performing them, illustrate the relationships between budget decisions and policy leadership. The Bureau was initially placed in the Treasury Department and empowered to "assemble, correlate, revise, reduce, or increase the estimates of the several departments or establishments." Its role was to act as a presidential agent in budget matters, which was emphasized by the decision to have the President appoint its director without Senate confirmation. In 1939, the Bureau was transferred to the newly established Executive Office of the President, and since that time it has become one of the largest and most important parts of this important advisory system. The switch in name and to some extent in function occurred in 1970, when President Nixon established the Office of Management and Budget along with a cabinet-level Domestic Council, which was to assume major domestic policy making responsibilities. Four years later, after a series of acrimonious battles between the President and Congress over impoundments and other budget matters, legislation was passed requiring Senate confirmation for the director and deputy director of the OMB. Both the Bureau of the Budget and OMB, however, have performed functions vital to presidential interests—control of spending, program planning, and administrative management.

Budget Review. The Bureau of the Budget was established to provide central budget review, but the scope and purposes of budget review have changed markedly, reflecting the Bureau's adaptation to what different Presidents seek to achieve through the budget. Initially, the

Bureau's focus was on spending control—forcing greater economy and efficiency in the expenditure of public funds. During this period, agencies were still responsible for preparing their budget estimates with little or no policy direction—beyond the exhortations concerning economy and efficiency—from the President or the Bureau. The Bureau served its first three Presidents by cutting agency requests and supervising the actual spending of funds to prevent deficiencies and to effect savings.[41]

With the New Deal, the emphasis on budget cutting declined as the President's responsibility for and attention to policy initiation and policy leadership became firmly established. Exclusive attention to spending control no longer served the President's interests; the focus of budget decision making shifted to the financing of necessary or politically popular programs and to the effects of budget totals on the economy. Thus, the Bureau began to use the budget as a means to satisfy the President's "concerns about the relative priorities of domestic and foreign policy programs, his beliefs about the desirability of a balanced budget, his preferences, in the areas where he has them."[42] With its transfer to the Executive Office and the rapid expansion of its staff from approximately 40 to some 600 shortly thereafter, the Bureau of the Budget became a central presidential agency in using the budget to promote policy leadership.[43]

As central budget review became increasingly tied to program planning, however, the Bureau encountered serious difficulties, not the least of which was the difficulty of reconciling its budget-cutting ethic with presidential demands for program innovations. Recent Presidents have responded to this by changing the focus of budget review. Thus in the mid-1960s President Johnson attempted to establish a program budgeting system throughout the executive branch that would enable the Bureau to combine budgeting and program planning. The Bureau would utilize this system in determining the cost-effectiveness of various domestic programs and thereby be able to use budgetary criteria to assess and compare these programs. This attempt met with little success, and in 1970 President Nixon reorganized the Bureau, creating the OMB and giving it the responsibility of implementing and evaluating legislation and policies. At the same time, a Domestic Council was established to advise the President on policies outside the defense and foreign policy areas. As the reorganization message stated: "The Domestic Council will be primarily concerned with *what* we do; the

Office of Management and Budget will be primarily concerned with *how* we do it and how *well* we do it."[44]

Despite this attempt at separating budgeting from program planning, it appears that the OMB has gradually regained much of its former responsibility for program planning as it relates to budgeting.[45] Under President Carter, the OMB has a major role, since the President has pledged to achieve a balanced budget by the end of his first term. This means that program planning must be tied directly to budget criteria and choices. As long as the presidential emphasis on spending control remains, the OMB will be able to use its budget review capability for its most effective purpose.

Legislation and Programs. A second area in which the Bureau of the Budget became active involved legislative clearance. At first, the Bureau exercised clearance only over those legislative proposals that would require immediate or future appropriations. Any such proposal from an executive department was required to be submitted to the Bureau for approval before it could be transmitted to Congress. This limited type of clearance gradually expanded to encompass all legislative proposals developed by the departments. The Bureau determined if the proposal was in accord with the President's program and could thus be sent to Congress. In addition, the Bureau was given responsibility for coordinating departmental responses (such as testimony, reports, or analyses) to legislation originating in Congress and to legislation passed by Congress in order to advise the President on signing or vetoing enrolled bills.

Under President Truman, the Bureau's role became more positive as it was given the responsibility for soliciting legislative proposals as well as budget estimates and for incorporating these proposals into a comprehensive presidential program. This responsibility was, however, curtailed during the Kennedy administration, as presidential policy advisers on the White House staff gained increased responsibility for developing major program initiatives and as the legislative liaison office in the White House coordinated executive relations with Congress on important policy questions.

The Bureau has maintained its clearance function, but its purview is now generally limited to matters that do not command presidential attention. Major program initiatives are usually handled elsewhere—by White House staff acting as policy advisers or by advisory groups, such as the Domestic Council under Richard Nixon or cabinet-level bodies under Gerald Ford.

Administrative Management and Improvement.   When it was relocated in the Executive Office of the President, the Bureau became heavily involved in making new agencies and their programs work. Budgeting and administration responsibilities were thus combined in the Bureau, and for a time the administrative management section was a large and prominent component of the Bureau, dealing with agency reorganization and internal management techniques. Beginning in the early 1950s, however, the reliance on the Bureau for this type of assistance declined as special study commissions, intradepartmental management staffs, and private management consultant firms gained widespread use.[46]

The 1970 reorganization was, in part, an attempt to reestablish the Bureau's administrative management responsibilities, especially with respect to the coordination of interdepartmental and intergovernmental programs. The OMB now has a major role in determining how such programs can be implemented and evaluated and in advising on administrative changes to improve implementation. Here also the Carter administration has assigned increased responsibility to the OMB for utilizing the budget process to improve administrative efficiency.

From a limited role at its inception, then, the Bureau of the Budget-OMB has developed into one of the Presidency's most important advisory and support staffs. It has acquired a variety of functions designed to utilize the budget as a means of strengthening policy leadership in the White House. While it has lost its exclusive or nearly exclusive jurisdiction over these functions, it remains a central participant in the task of translating the President's preferences and intentions into budgetary decisions.

Council of Economic Advisers

The Council of Economic Advisers was established as part of the Executive Office of the President in 1946. It consists of three members, appointed by the President with the advice and consent of the Senate, along with a career staff, which now numbers around 45 persons. The Council's primary function is to assist the President by analyzing economic developments, appraising current economic programs and policies, and recommending policies to achieve economic growth and stability. The Council is also responsible for preparing the President's annual economic report to Congress.

While the Council is a professional advisory group, its members also have, as part of the Executive Office, a responsibility for explaining and defending administration policy. This is especially true of the chairman, who in recent years has been a prominent administration spokesman on economic policy matters. Of course, the effectiveness of the Council is tied to its members' recognition that economic advice, no matter how professionally sound, must take cognizance of political realities, such as public opinion or congressional opinion.

The Council's responsibilities necessarily involve it in the budgetary process. Here its function is to develop, along with the OMB and the Department of the Treasury, the economic projections and assumptions that must be taken into account in estimating revenues and spending. But it is also responsible for advising the President, throughout the budgetary process, on the fiscal policy strategies available in the budget and on the economic implications of current or future programs.

Economic Policy Board

Recent administrations have attempted to establish advisory groups to coordinate and implement economic policy. The Nixon administration, for example, established a Council on Economic Policy. In September 1974 the Ford administration created an Economic Policy Board with broad responsibilities to provide advice to the President on national and international economic policies and to oversee the formulation, coordination, and implementation of economic policy. This specific structure has been abandoned by President Carter, but the general functions that the Board performed are worth examining.

Although the full Board included all of the Cabinet members (except the Secretary of Defense and the Attorney General) along with virtually all high-level government officials involved in economic policy, its work was carried out by an executive committee that met daily and was responsible for its major advisory activities. The chairman of the Board and of the executive committee was the Secretary of the Treasury. The original executive committee included the director of the OMB, the chairman of the Council of Economic Advisers, the Assistant to the President for Economic Affairs, and the executive director of the Council on International Economic Policy. Subsequently, the Secretaries of State, Commerce, and Labor were added. The President generally met with the executive committee once or twice weekly.

The Board's purview was extremely broad. It reviewed, for example, the economic projections prepared by the Council of Economic Advisers, OMB, and the Treasury, and advised the President on budgetary strategies. The Board had, in effect, superseded the "Troika"—the chairman of the Council of Economic Advisers, the director of the OMB, and the Secretary of the Treasury—as the final review board for economic projections. While it was not involved in the detailed superintendence of budget decision making, the Economic Policy Board did consider the budgetary impact of major policy decisions. President Carter's decision to replace the Board with an Economic Policy Group does not represent a major change in function. His advisory group will also coordinate economic policy making and advise the President on the budgetary implications of policy choices. However, the Economic Policy Group will meet less frequently, will not have a permanent staff, and will operate more flexibly and informally than did the Economic Policy Board.

Summary

There is no set purpose with or method by which Presidents approach the budget; as a consequence, there have been periodic changes in the functions of budget staff and advisory groups. Fiscal policy, for example, has been largely set by the President after consultation with a variety of groups—the OMB, the Council of Economic Advisers, the Department of the Treasury, and the economic policy advisory groups in recent administrations. Legislative clearance, which traditionally was handled by the Bureau of the Budget, is now shared by the OMB and White House policy staffs. Detailed superintendence and implementation of budget decisions is conducted by the OMB. The groups that the President relies on to perform particular functions or the relative importance he places on these functions, however, should not obscure the central point about these budget staff groups—their role is to assist the President in deciding on and implementing his objectives. It is up to the President to decide what he wants to achieve through the budget. It is then up to these staff and advisory groups to insure that his purposes are carried out in the development of the executive budget. If this is successful, attention then turns to Congress, where the President must attempt to protect his objectives and policy preferences against congressional attack.

Presidential Budget Policies and Controversies

An administration must ultimately be concerned with the fate of its budget recommendations in Congress. In recent years, the annual budget confrontations have usually been intense, reflecting in large part the strains between a Democratic-controlled Congress and Republican Presidents. But even during the Kennedy and Johnson years, when the Democratic party controlled both branches, there were serious budget controversies over spending ceilings and budget priorities, and the Carter administration has also had its problems with Congress.

The scope of presidential-congressional budget controversies, however, has been enlarged by increased attention to budget aggregates. Under its new budget system, Congress acts on budget totals and fiscal policy. In 1975 and 1976, for example, Congress adopted spending levels substantially above administration recommendations, but in both instances spokesmen for the congressional Budget Committees explained that the resulting higher deficits were necessary for greater economic stimulus. This was an unprecedented situation, for Congress was explicitly considering the fiscal policy effects of the budget and challenging administration budget policy. As might be expected, administration spokesmen were not enthusiastic about Congress' challenge—President Ford's budget director characterized Congress' work on the fiscal 1977 budget as "appalling"[47]—but at least presidential-congressional differences on fiscal policy will be considerably easier to assess in the future than they have been in the past. Previous elements of controversy, moreover, are likely to remain, even when control of the government is not divided. Thus, debates over spending ceilings, vetoes of appropriations bills, and program priorities reflect a persistent tension between the President and Congress, a tension that has been unusually evident during recent administrations.

The Johnson Presidency

The Presidency of Lyndon Johnson produced a classic budgetary di-
lemma—"guns versus butter"—as he attempted to finance the war
in Vietnam as well as the ambitious social programs of the Great Society. For a time the administration argued that the nation could afford to
meet war costs without slighting its domestic needs, increasing taxes,
or running unacceptable risks with inflation. But by 1967 it was apparent that this was not possible.

The pressures were extraordinary. The administration's commitment
in Vietnam escalated rapidly in 1965, and the costs of this commitment
were not accurately forecast. As defense spending was growing, political support for the war was eroding, making it difficult for the administration to argue publicly that the traditional priority assigned to war
expenditures should be followed. At the same time, not only the Great
Society's philosophical commitments but also urban riots made it difficult to ignore demands for increased spending on education, health,
welfare, housing, and employment. President Johnson finally proposed that taxes be increased and that spending reductions then be considered. Congress was committed, however, to a reversal of these
priorities, with congressional spokesmen arguing that tax increases
should follow, not precede, expenditure reductions. For almost one
year the two branches fought over these issues, while the inflationary
effects of previous budget policy became even more serious. (Delays
such as this evidence the inherent difficulty in using the budget to
control the economy, leading to proposals for standby presidential authority to raise or lower taxes in order to use the budget in a more
effective and timely manner.)

In President Johnson's first budget message in 1964, he stressed the
need for controlling expenditures and presented a budget that was considerably below forecasts.[48] The next year's budget, however, emphasized increased spending for health, education, and welfare programs and proposed cuts in defense spending. Indeed, Mr. Johnson
stated that although government spending would continue to rise, it
would rise more slowly than GNP and thus decline in relation to total
output. While the budget estimate for defense spending was about $6
billion below actual outlays, the budget problems were still in their early
stages, and Congress passed, with little serious controversy, appropriations only slightly less than what the administration had requested.[49]

For FY 1967 the administration proposed substantial increases in defense spending and much more moderate increases for domestic social programs. There was little congressional alteration of the defense requests, but a major battle developed in Congress over domestic spending. Congressional liberals tried to increase appropriations for social programs above administration requests, leading President Johnson to criticize the inflationary impact of these increases and to press for limits on appropriations totals. On the other side, conservative Democrats and Republicans focused on spending cuts. While this was not a new pattern, it became a major issue as the financial pressures from the war increased. During 1966, however, attempts to reduce spending by substantially cutting administration requests in seven non-defense-related appropriations bills were unsuccessful, and total appropriations of $130.3 billion were less than $1 billion below administration requests.

However the 1966 elections reduced administration support in Congress, and during President Johnson's last two years in office, Congress continued to press spending cuts and spending ceilings. It refused the administration's request for a tax increase, cut appropriations requests by almost $6 billion, and directed federal agencies to limit spending on controllable expenditures by some $4 billion. For a time House-Senate differences over budget cuts became so serious that even some continuing resolutions—which are routinely used to provide funds for agencies until final appropriations bills are passed—were delayed, leaving some agencies without funds.

The budget conflict continued in 1968, when the administration was unable to win congressional approval of its tax surcharge proposal without expenditure control commitments. In June the tax increase was passed, but Congress added provisions to the bill mandating a $6 billion reduction in federal spending during FY 1969. It also cut administration appropriations requests by more than $14 billion.[50] The result was that President Johnson was unable to "hold the line" on domestic spending and was forced to accept serious cuts in a number of social welfare programs.

The legislative innovations of the Johnson years were in large part frustrated by the inexorable budgetary pressures of the war. The budget battles with Congress were intense and protracted, and the administration was finally forced to accept a spending ceiling and appropriations cuts that it had resisted for almost one year. The President's political vulnerability resulting from Vietnam gave Congress an unusual opportunity to challenge successfully the executive's budget leadership, a challenge that was repeated when the Nixon administration became mired in the Watergate controversy. With Nixon, however, it was Congress that fought to protect spending for social welfare programs and the President who sought to limit that spending.

The Nixon Presidency

The tax surcharge passed in 1968 resulted in a budget surplus for FY 1969, the first surplus after eight consecutive years of budget deficits, including a deficit of more than $25 billion in FY 1968. But the Nixon administration soon was embroiled with Congress in continuing budget battles over deficit spending, spending ceilings, impoundments, and vetoes, all accompanied by unusually heated rhetoric.

The budget that the outgoing Johnson administration submitted for FY 1970 projected a $3.4 billion surplus. The Nixon administration, committed to lowering federal expenditures, revised the Johnson budget, recommending reductions in defense and domestic spending to achieve a $5.8 billion surplus. While Congress voted almost $6 billion in defense cuts, it also increased spending for a number of domestic programs and refused to enact administration proposals for additional revenues. In early 1970 a recession struck the economy, reducing revenues from existing taxes. This, coupled with increases in uncontrollable spending, turned the projected surplus into a $2.8 billion deficit. While Congress adopted a spending ceiling early in the year that was $1 billion below the administration's spending projections, it also added provisions to adjust the ceiling to accommodate subsequent congressional actions and even to allow the President to increase the limit by up to $2 billion to reflect increases in uncontrollable spending. When this cushion proved insufficient, Congress simply raised the ceiling later in the year. Actual spending for the year turned out to be almost $4 billion more than the administration had requested.

For his fiscal 1971 budget, Mr. Nixon again projected a slight surplus; this time the deficit was $23 billion. During 1970 the budget disputes over spending and spending priorities became more heated. Congress enacted a spending ceiling of $200.8 billion—the same as projected by the administration—but like the previous ceiling this had cushions for uncontrollable spending and allowances for congressional action. As anticipated, both of these factors contributed to spending increases, resulting in a $211.4 billion total for the year. Congress also challenged the administration on priorities, cutting requests for defense, foreign aid, and space spending and increasing the amounts for a variety of domestic social programs. This led to presidential vetoes of five bills on spending grounds, with two of these vetoes overridden by Congress. When the first of these became law on June 30, it marked the first congressional override of a presidential veto in ten years. Administration attempts to cut $2.1 billion annually by reducing or terminating what it termed "low priority" programs, such as aid to federally impacted school districts, found little support in Congress.

In 1971 and 1972, President Nixon shifted his budget strategy markedly. Responding to a worsening economic situation, the administration proposed substantial deficit spending in both years, using what it termed "full-employment budgets" to suggest that the budget would be balanced if the economy were performing at full potential. However, the administration still insisted that federal spending be controlled and deficits limited. In 1971 three successful vetoes were cast for budgetary reasons. As in previous years, program reductions and terminations were proposed by the President, although largely ignored by Congress.

It was during 1972 and 1973, however, that the budget conflicts reached their zenith. In July 1972, the President sent a message to Congress proposing a spending ceiling of $250 billion for FY 1973, with presidential discretion to reduce or eliminate programs if outlays threatened to breach the ceiling. One month before the election, the President charged that excessive spending by Congress might necessitate a tax increase. While the House voted for the ceiling, the Senate placed restrictions on the nature and size of any cuts. The Senate continued to resist any broad presidential authority, rejecting a conference report containing a compromise version of the ceiling, and the final result was that no ceiling was enacted.

The administration responded with a series of vetoes and impoundments. On October 27, nine bills were pocket vetoed, with the President's veto message stating that they could not be financed without higher taxes. Funds for a variety of programs, including housing, agriculture, and water pollution control, were then impounded as the administration announced that the President would hold outlays to the $250 billion figure.

After its landslide victory in the 1972 presidential election, the administration pressed Congress once again on federal spending. The fiscal 1974 budget called for a $268.7 billion spending ceiling and proposed the reduction or elimination of more than 100 programs, with many of these concentrated in the Department of Health, Education and Welfare. The administration further proposed that 70 existing federal grant programs be consolidated into special revenue-sharing funds to be given to state and local governments for education, law enforcement and criminal justice, and manpower training and urban development. The budget message also took the unusual step of providing Congress with several suggestions about improving its budgetary process.

The fiscal 1974 budget message thus presented a clear challenge to the Democratic Congress, and it also showed that much of the conflict was not actually over spending but rather over programs. The administration had, for example, previously pushed for passage of a five-year, $30 billion general sharing program, and it was now proposing a $6.9 billion special revenue-sharing program. It also sought increases in defense spending and Social Security payments totaling more than $10 billion.

The anticipated confrontations over the budget were, however, diminished if not eliminated by the growing attention to Watergate. Congress succeeded in passing legislation revising its internal budget process and also strictly limiting the President's power to impound funds. Program reductions and terminations were largely ignored, and no spending ceiling was adopted. While vetoes of appropriations bills continued, the Nixon administration's fiscal 1975 budget message was "conciliatory to Congress and conventional in direction. Few innovations were offered but neither were the administration's attempts to dismantle federal social programs on a wholesale basis renewed."[51]

While Congress was able to resist any significant curtailment of its budgetary authority during the Nixon years, the 1972 battle over the spending ceiling showed that Congress was unable to defend itself effectively against the charge of excessive spending. Even some members of Congress who opposed the President's request for unlimited discretion in enforcing the spending ceiling suggested that Congress had forced the request by behaving irresponsibly on spending legislation.[52] While there is limited evidence to support this charge, it is apparent that it had enough superficial credibility to be used effectively as a political tactic by the Nixon administration.

The Nixon years, then, provided a series of sharp confrontations over the budget. The President was able to mount an effective political attack on Congress' spending actions and to engage in an unprecedented series of impoundments and vetoes. While Congress was finally able to protect most of the programs challenged by the administration, it was sufficiently convinced of its budgetary failings to revise its internal procedures.

The Ford Presidency

After August 1974, relations between Congress and the executive improved considerably in tone. While there were important differences in budgetary policies and priorities, the rhetorical excesses of the Nixon years were generally absent. Indeed, the new congressional budgetary process allowed reasonable public debate about fiscal policy and spending priorities.

In its fiscal 1976 budget, presented to Congress on February 3, 1975, the Ford administration proposed $349.4 billion in spending and a $51.9 billion federal deficit. Despite the large deficit, Congress first voted a total outlays ceiling of $367 billion with a planned deficit of $68.8 billion. In October the administration submitted revised spending projections of $366.5 billion with a $68.5 billion planned deficit, but Congress then raised its spending ceiling to $374.9 billion with a $74.1 billion deficit. The congressional debates on the spending ceilings reflected special concern over the economic stimulus of the deficit, as did the administration's presentations of its original and revised budgets. Moreover, the President resorted to the veto in an attempt to enforce a lower deficit, but on two of the major actions—an education appropriations bill and a Labor–Health, Education and Welfare appropriations bill—Congress overrode the vetoes.

Congress was also able to effect cuts in programs that the administration favored. The biggest decrease was in the defense appropriations bill, where the administration's request was reduced by over $7 billion in budget authority and almost $3 billion in outlays. For FY 1976, then, Congress was able to force a higher spending ceiling than the administration requested and also to impose its own priorities on spending programs within that ceiling. On the administration side, there was some satisfaction that the continuing attention to spending had effectively restrained Congress from even greater spending.

A similar pattern characterized the fiscal 1977 budget. The Ford administration, as noted earlier, requested a spending ceiling that Congress refused to accept. In adopting its first and second concurrent resolutions setting spending ceilings, Congress projected more spending and a larger deficit than the administration had requested, and again the congressional justification was that a greater stimulus was necessary to continue the economic recovery. The President vetoed the Labor–Health, Education and Welfare appropriations bill, which was $4 billion over his budget, but Congress overrode the veto. His veto record on authorization bills was mixed.[53]

The pattern that emerged during the Ford administration was, of course, unusual, reflecting the effects of the new congressional budgetary process as well as partisan and ideological differences between President and Congress. But it is clear that a President now faces potential congressional challenges over the fiscal policy implications as well as the program preferences of the budget. On the other side, Congress has become increasingly sensitive to charges of excessive spending, providing the President with considerable leverage in budget debates. Thus, Ford was able to resist any major new spending programs in 1975 and 1976 despite being faced by a two-to-one Democratic majority in Congress.[54]

The Carter Presidency

Democratic party control of both the White House and Congress has by no means eliminated serious budget conflicts. Early in his Presidency, for example, Jimmy Carter nearly sabotaged the congressional budget process, publicly threatened Congress with vetoes if spending bills exceeded his recommendations, and sought to cut spending for one of Congress' favorite programs—water resources projects. There was not much of a "honeymoon," and the prospect is for even more intense battles as Carter attempts to achieve a balanced budget by 1981.

The difficulties with the budget process occurred when Carter recommended changes in the fiscal 1977 budget and presented his revisions for the fiscal 1978 budget (which the Ford administration had sent to Congress just before leaving office). The fiscal 1977 changes were part of an economic stimulus package—tax cuts and job programs— that the Carter administration presented to Congress several weeks after taking office. Congress responded promptly, amending the budget that it had adopted the previous September—and that had been in operation since October 1—to allow for the revenue cuts and spending increases contained in the stimulus package. While Congress did increase the size of the package above the President's recommendations, it had reacted to the administration's initiative quite favorably. Shortly thereafter, however, the President withdrew his support for the tax rebate proposal that had been a key part of his stimulus program. Congress once again amended the fiscal 1977 budget, although this time there was considerable discontent over the administration's handling of the rebate issue and its attitude toward Congress.

In February the President sent Congress his budget recommendations for FY 1978. His defense spending request included budget authority of approximately $120 billion and outlays of just under $112 billion. The House Budget Committee, however, recommended to the House a defense spending target more than $4 billion below the budget authority request and $2.3 billion below the outlay request. The House Armed Services Committee then announced its intention to challenge the spending target on the floor by sponsoring an amendment to increase defense spending in line with administration requests. Harold Brown, Carter's Secretary of Defense, lobbied members of the House to urge support for the amendment, despite complaints by the House Democratic leadership that administration intervention was jeopardizing the entire resolution. The amendment was passed, raising the defense spending target, but the House then rejected the entire budget resolution by a vote of 87–320.

After the House defeat, the Democratic leadership met with Carter to explain the purposes of the congressional budget process and to caution against similar intervention in the future. A second budget resolution was prepared by the House Budget Committee (with a small increase over the first defense spending total). This time the House rejected the same defense spending amendment it had approved earlier and then adopted the budget resolution.

President Carter thus faced the same problem with defense spending that confronted his predecessor. His comments on spending controls, vetoes, and "pork barrel" spending have not been dissimilar either. Ford's 1978 budget message, for example, stated that "we need to overcome the idea that Members of the Congress are elected to bring home Federal projects for their district or State."[55] Carter's stand on water resources projects conveyed the same theme—that federal spending should not be used to insure the reelection of members of Congress.

But while disputes over particular programs have been important, the most serious problem that Carter faces with Congress is his intention to balance the budget by the end of his first term. As part of this, President Carter conducted agency-by-agency budget reviews in the spring of 1977 and then sent "guidance letters" to all department and major agency heads announcing a $500 billion ceiling for FY 1979. The "real growth"—that is, spending discounted for inflation—in the budget was projected at less than 2 percent. Unless there is an unanticipated improvement in economic growth between 1978 and 1981, there will also be little room in future budgets for major new spending programs. It is doubtful that the majority of Mr. Carter's fellow Democrats in Congress will respond enthusiastically to these constraints on spending, particularly since Carter has also indicated that defense spending cannot be cut over the next several years.

President Carter and Congress, then, are involved in several major budget disputes. There is disagreement over the economic effects of limiting future deficits, with Congress likely to resist any major stimulus reduction unless there is a marked drop in the unemployment rate. There is also a persistent tension over the relative desirability of balancing the budget as opposed to enacting new programs. While the President is committed to eliminating the deficit—which his advisers consider a key to his reelection—liberal Democrats in Congress appear more interested in a comprehensive national health insurance program and other program innovations. As a result, Mr. Carter may find himself in 1980 running against the spending programs sponsored by his own party.

Presidents Versus Congress

The institutional and policy disputes that have occurred between recent Presidents and Congress highlight several important points about budgetary politics. There has developed, for example, a clear split between Congress and the President over the direction and growth of federal spending. The executive has become a leading advocate for defense spending, with Presidents Ford and Carter both fighting hard in Congress for substantial increases in the defense budget. At the same time, Congress has become the leading defender of social welfare spending and has strenuously resisted executive attempts to limit domestic spending growth.

Moreover, there has been a reversal of roles with respect to the budget. Congress has largely abandoned its role of guardian of the Treasury, a role that it performed vigorously from the beginning of the New Deal through the mid-1960s. Instead, Congress has directed its efforts to expanding existing spending programs and establishing new ones. Recent Presidents, on the other hand, have apparently decided that there is more political credit to be gained in protecting the Treasury than in program innovations. Much of this, of course, reflects ideological changes. Since the end of the Johnson Presidency, the Democratic majorities have been more liberal than the Presidents they faced, a situation that helps to explain the congressional pressures for domestic spending. At the same time, there appears to be an institutional distinction. The President appears less vulnerable than Congress to the multiplicity of spending pressures contained in the budget and can therefore focus his attention on controlling the total. Members of Congress, however, are faced with specific spending demands by their constituents, and Congress has reacted to these demands—and to the reelection interests of its members—by increasing total spending. The present situation corresponds in some important respects to the budgetary situation earlier in the century. As Congress proved unable or unwilling to control spending and to practice fiscal responsibility, pressure developed to place these responsibilities in the hands of the President. Congress may find that the President can once again exploit this sentiment to gain leverage in budget disputes.

It is also important to recognize that Congress now confronts the President directly on fiscal policy. During the Ford Presidency, Congress challenged successfully the administration's budget aggregates and raised the planned deficit substantially. Congress has also voted higher deficits than President Carter has recommended, and it will be interesting to see how Congress reacts to the Carter plan for significant deficit reductions in future years.

Finally, largely as a result of the Nixon impoundments, Congress has restricted the President's discretionary spending authority. The President can no longer use impoundments to frustrate congressional spending preferences. Rather, he must gain congressional consent to any alterations in spending commitments once funds have been appropriated.

Summary

Over the past half century, the President has assumed a major and sometimes dominant role in the budgetary process. Presidential budget participation can involve a variety of purposes and objectives—administrative control, economic management, policy innovation, and partisan or institutional advantages. In addition, the contemporary Presidency is characterized by a number of prominent staff and advisory groups that assist the President in budget planning and budget decision making. The budget represents, then, an opportunity for Presidents to achieve certain objectives. What these objectives are and how successfully they are achieved have varied from administration to administration, reflecting in part presidential emphases and skill and also the practical and political constraints that affect budget planning and formulation at a given time. What is consistent over time is that a President cannot ignore the economic and programmatic implications of his budget recommendations. Budget leadership is now a major responsibility of the Presidency.

In recent years, the budget controversies between the President and Congress have involved serious differences over spending ceilings, program priorities, and the efficacy of recommended fiscal policy alternatives. At times these specific differences have been translated into broader issues of presidential versus congressional powers and prerogatives. As a result, Congress has attempted to increase its influence in the budgetary process through changes in procedure and organization. While the President retains the advantage of initiative, Congress is now able to present in a coherent fashion alternatives to his fiscal policy and spending recommendations. This provides greater parity between presidential and congressional influence over federal economic policy and the broad range of government activities and programs. In attempting to exercise budget leadership, Presidents must necessarily confront a Congress less dependent than in the past on executive advice and information and better equipped to challenge executive recommendations.

In addition to dealing with Congress, however, the President must confront executive departments and agencies whose interests differ from his and whose loyalties he must share with Congress and clientele groups. Presidents have attempted to overcome this diffusion of interests and loyalties by employing budget staffs and advisory groups that can provide assistance in developing budget strategies, making budget choices, and implementing budget decisions. Thus, the budget represents one mechanism through which the President can attempt to control the executive branch.

The President, therefore, can use the budget to achieve policy or institutional goals, but he must also act within recognized constraints imposed by Congress, interest groups, and executive agencies. The changes that a President is able to accomplish in any one year are likely to be marginal. But the cumulative, long-term impact of even marginal changes over the course of an administration can be substantial. The stakes, then, are significant, and a President must be able to develop and utilize political support to achieve his budgetary objectives. The President must, in other words, be adept at the politics of the budgetary process if he is to challenge successfully the other participants.

Notes

1. See Edwin L. Dale, "Can Congress at Last Control the Money Tree?" *New York Times Magazine*, August 22, 1976, pp. 10–11, 69–76.
2. There is the argument that these constraints limit the budget's utility as an instrument of presidential power. See Allen Schick, "The Budget Bureau That Was: Thoughts on the Rise, Decline and Future of a Presidential Agency," *Law and Contemporary Problems*, 35 (Summer 1970), 519–539.
3. See Louis Fisher, "Congress, the Executive and the Budget," *Annals of the American Academy of Political and Social Science*, 411 (January 1974), 102–113.
4. Allen Schick reports that "in preparation of his 1971 budget, President Nixon is reported to have invested approximately 40 hours and to have been displeased by what he regarded as an unproductive use of so much of his time." "Budget Bureau That Was," p. 521. President Ford, on the other hand, was more active in detailed budget decision making, and President Carter has also devoted considerable attention to budget matters.
5. Arthur Smithies, *The Budgetary Process in the United States* (New York: McGraw-Hill, 1955), p. 53.
6. Louis Fisher mentions Presidents John Quincy Adams, Van Buren, Tyler, Polk, Buchanan, Grant, and Cleveland as examples of this involvement. *Presidential Spending Power* (Princeton, N.J.: Princeton University Press, 1975), p. 10.
7. Ibid., chap. 1.
8. Quoted in Fisher, *Presidential Spending Power*, p. 16.
9. Smithies, *Budgetary Process*, pp. 60–62.
10. Ibid.

ial Spending Power, p. 26.

ımerding, Jr., The Spending Power (New Haven, Conn.: Yale
ess, 1943), chap. 7.

arfield, quoted in Wilmerding, Spending Power, p. 141.

g, Spending Power, p. 143.

, Budgetary Process, p. 62.

Presidential Spending Power, pp. 30–31.

ies, Budgetary Process, pp. 68–71.

ıted in Smithies, Budgetary Process, p. 68.

her, Presidential Spending Power, p. 33.

oid., p. 32.

See Lewis H. Kimmel, Federal Budget and Fiscal Policy, 1789–1958 (Washington, D.C.: Brookings Institution, 1959), pp. 89–98, 143–174.

Quoted in Kimmel, Federal Budget, p. 182.

3. On the background and passage of this legislation, see Stephen K. Bailey, Congress Makes a Law: The Story Behind the Employment Act of 1946 (New York: Columbia University Press, 1950).

24. See Clinton Rossiter, The American Presidency, rev. ed. (New York: New American Library, 1960), pp. 32–36.

25. For example, presidential popularity appears to be very susceptible to economic downturns, such as increases in the unemployment rate. See John E. Mueller, War, Presidents and Public Opinion (New York: Wiley, 1973), chap. 9.

26. Even the Nixon administration accepted this midway through its first term, although the President sought to gloss over the planned deficit by using the "full-employment budget" to show that the budget would have been balanced if there had been no recession. The fact that Republican administrations no longer feel compelled to treat unbalanced budgets as anathema is a substantial change, although Republicans still appear to be much more uncomfortable with deficits than are Democrats.

27. See Aaron Wildavsky, The Politics of the Budgetary Process, 2nd ed. (Boston: Little, Brown, 1974), pp. 209–216.

28. Fisher, "Congress, the Executive and the Budget," p. 103.

29. Ibid., pp. 110–112.

30. The new process is described in detail in Chapter Three.

31. Office of Management and Budget, Preparation and Submission of 1977 "Current Services" Budget Estimates, Bulletin No. 76-4 (Washington, D.C.: August 13, 1975), p. 1.

32. Ibid., pp. 2–4.

33. It is this comparison that the Ford administration continually stressed.

34. See Office of Management and Budget, Preparation and Submission of Budget Estimates, Circular No. A-11 (Washington, D.C.: June 16, 1976), pp. 9–33.

35. Wildavsky, Politics of the Budgetary Process, p. 18.

36. See Richard F. Fenno, The President's Cabinet (Cambridge, Mass.: Harvard University Press, 1959).

37. *Congressional Quarterly Weekly Report, 33,* no. 45 (November 8, 1975), 2356.

38. Ibid., p. 2352.

39. Wildavsky, *Politics of the Budgetary Process,* p. 162.

40. Ibid., chap. 2. For a refinement of this concept, which distinguishes between mandatory increases and programmatic increases, see John Wanat, "Bases of Budgetary Incrementalism," *American Political Science Review, 68* (September 1974), 1221–1228.

41. See Fisher, *Presidential Spending Power,* pp. 37–39.

42. Wildavsky, *Politics of the Budgetary Process,* p. 35.

43. Fisher, *Presidential Spending Power,* p. 44.

44. Quoted in Schick, "Budget Bureau That Was," p. 536. On foreign policy and national security matters, the National Security Council has been the key advisory group, and budget review of the Department of Defense has usually been less stringent than for the domestic departments. When the Bureau was reorganized in 1970, there were suggestions that one purpose was to strengthen "the budget planners' hand in questioning the expenditure requests of the Department of Defense—a function that had fallen into virtual disuse during the Kennedy and Johnson administrations." *Congress and the Nation, Vol. III, 1969–1972* (Washington, D.C.: Congressional Quarterly Service, 1973), pp. 68–69.

45. The Domestic Council's potential to influence domestic policy making was not achieved under either Nixon or Ford. For an analysis of its first two and one-half years, see John H. Kessel, *The Domestic Presidency: Decision-Making in the White House* (North Scituate, Mass.: Duxbury Press, 1975). President Carter's reorganization of the White House staff and the Executive Office has replaced the Domestic Council with a small staff, headed by a top White House aide, that will perform more limited domestic policy-planning functions than those originally envisioned for the Council. The domestic policy staff will develop policy positions for the President on issues that he considers of major importance and occasionally mediate jurisdictional or policy disputes between departments.

46. Schick, "Budget Bureau That Was," pp. 529–530.

47. Office of Management and Budget director James T. Lynn also said that he could not recommend that Republicans in Congress vote for the fiscal 1977 budget resolution, since it was far too different from presidential policy. *National Journal, 8,* no. 19 (May 29, 1976), 743.

48. The administrative budget used until 1968 did not include a substantial portion of federal spending, primarily transactions of the federal trust funds. Thus the emphasis in Johnson's first year was on keeping this budget below $100 billion. After being recommended by a 1967 presidential study commission, a unified budget was introduced, providing a much more accurate and comprehensive picture of federal financial transactions.

49. The appropriations bills passed totaled $107 billion compared with administration requests of $109.4 billion.

50. Reductions in existing spending authority and in the numbers of federal employees were also legislated, but most agencies were able to avoid these restrictions.

51. *Congressional Quarterly Almanac, Vol. XXX, 1974* (Washington, D.C.: Congressional Quarterly Service, 1975), p. 936.

52. See Fisher, "Congress, the Executive and the Budget," p. 103.

53. In all, Congress overrode 12 of 61 Ford vetoes of public bills, the highest override rate in over a century.

54. James E. Connor, staff secretary to President Ford and secretary to the Cabinet, argued that Ford's success in resisting new spending programs indicated that presidential budget powers were not weakened by the new congressional budget process. *National Journal, 8,* no. 19 (May 29, 1976), 741.

55. *The Budget of the United States Government, Fiscal Year 1978* (Washington, D.C.: Government Printing Office, 1977), p. M6.

Three

The Power of the Purse: Congressional Participation

The power of the purse has traditionally been the basis of congressional authority, "underpinning all other legislative decisions and regulating the balance of influence between the legislative and executive branches of government."[1] But while the reach of the taxing and spending authority is substantial, Congress has been frustrated in recent decades by its inability to exercise this authority with maximum effectiveness. Since the early 1920s there have been several congressional attempts to organize, reorganize, and revise its budget process and procedures as well as those of the executive, with the latest and one of the most extensive efforts being the 1974 Congressional Budget and Impoundment Control Act. In this instance, as well as in the previous, unsuccessful attempts to establish legislative budgets, omnibus budgets, and budget ceilings in the post–World War II period, Congress has sought to achieve several objectives: (1) to provide comprehensiveness and coherence in budget decisions by relating spending decisions to revenue decisions; (2) to enforce congressional program preferences and priorities by relating spending decisions to each other within an overall spending limit; and (3) to limit executive influence and independence in budget decisions.

During the nineteenth century, there was no elaborate budget system in either the executive branch or Congress. Government spending and revenues were usually quite limited, and presidential participation in the budgetary process was minimal. Therefore, the major developments in the budgetary process were essentially limited to congressional decisions concerning the jurisdiction and influence of committees. In 1802, for example, the House vested jurisdiction over spending bills and revenue bills in the Ways and Means Committee, and in 1816 the Senate created a Finance Committee with similar jurisdiction. It was not until 1865 that the House transferred jurisdiction over spending legislation to an Appropriations Committee, with a counterpart committee established in the Senate two years later. However, these committees did not retain exclusive control over spending legislation for very long. In the period 1877 to 1885, the House removed 8 of the 14 annual appropriations bills (accounting for approximately one-half of total spending) from its Appropriations Committee and transferred them to the legislative committees. This apparently reflected growing dissatisfaction with the independence and emphasis on economy displayed by the Appropriations Committee.[2] While these transfers allowed the legislative (or authorizing) committees greater influence over spending decisions affecting their programs, the result was a diffusion of responsibility for financial policy.

The increases in spending and the debt resulting from World War I led Congress once again to revise its spending procedures and also to establish a budgetary system for the executive. In 1920 the House returned exclusive spending controls to its Appropriations Committee, and in 1922 the Senate followed the House lead. Moreover, as part of the Budget and Accounting Act of 1921, Congress established the General Accounting Office (GAO) to strengthen its supervision of spending by executive agencies. But with the establishment and development of executive responsibility and influence in the budget process and with the dramatic spending increases that have occurred since the New Deal, Congress has been under continuing pressure to centralize its budget procedures in order to counter executive influence. Attempts to do so, however, have generally failed, in part because centralization has been resisted by the legislative committees. The difficulty of reconciling these internal and external pressures is enormous even under the best of circumstances, and Congress has not been blessed with favorable circumstances very often. There is a considerable body of opinion both in and out of Congress that the executive has been allowed to achieve unwarranted influence in a variety of policy areas since the New Deal period, and in this context the 1974 reform of the budgetary process can be viewed as part of a broader effort to redress an imbalance in executive and congressional relations.[3] Whether this budget reform succeeds would appear to depend more on its internal suitability for Congress than its planned rationality in dealing with the President, but the outcome will undoubtedly affect the relative authority of Congress and the President over national policy.

Development and Exercise of Congressional Authority

The powers to tax, spend, and borrow are essential elements in financial control and in the determination of fiscal policy. Over the past several decades, the scope and impact of these powers have increased as federal budgets have grown and federal responsibility for economic management has become established. These changes have necessarily affected the standing committees with primary responsibilities for taxing and spending decisions—the House Ways and Means Committee, the Senate Finance Committee, and the Appropriations Committees of the House and Senate.

Taxing Power

The constitutional basis for the power to tax and spend is found in Article I, Section 8, clause 1: "The Congress shall have power to lay and collect taxes, duties, imposts and excises, to pay the debts and provide for the common defense and general welfare of the United States." With the exception of the Supreme Court's 1895 decision invalidating the income tax[4]—which was superseded by the adoption of the Sixteenth Amendment in 1913—the power to tax has been liberally interpreted, and the "general welfare clause" has provided a broad authority for the exercise of the taxing power. Until the passage of the income tax amendment, federal revenues were drawn primarily from tariffs (duties on imported goods) and excises (taxes on the manufacture, transfer, or sale of domestic goods).[5] But it has been the taxes on individual and corporate incomes along with the payroll taxes established during the 1930s (to finance programs such as social security and unemployment compensation) that have provided a steadily expanding revenue base to finance federal activities. Thus, the importance of tax policy for revenue purposes, regulation, and economic stimulus or restraint has grown substantially during this century.

The Committee on Ways and Means.   The Constitution specifies that revenue bills must originate in the House of Representatives. This means that the House must complete action on a tax bill before the Senate can begin its deliberation, and this initiative has traditionally been reflected in the power of the Ways and Means Committee. Prior to 1975, when it was affected by a series of personnel, party, and procedural changes, Ways and Means had long been acknowledged as one of the most powerful and prestigious committees in Congress.[6] While it retains considerable power because of its jurisdiction, its ability to adapt to these changes and maintain its effectiveness will substantially affect the power of the House to determine tax policies as well as the more general operations of the new congressional budget process.

Until the recent changes, Ways and Means was a relatively small, senior, and strongly led committee. Its jurisdiction was broad, covering trade, debt, customs and trade, social security, and general revenue-sharing legislation. Its 25 members were House veterans whose professional approach to legislation and restrained partisanship contributed to the Committee's high status and influence in the House.[7] The Committee worked closely with Treasury Department officials and staff and with the highly expert staff of the Joint Committee on Internal Revenue Taxation in drafting its complex and technical bills,[8] and its legislation was generally reported to the floor under a closed rule. This meant that the bill was not open to amendments from other House members, and as a result Ways and Means was usually successful in having its legislation accepted as written.[9]

The standing and influence of the Ways and Means Committee can be traced to a variety of factors, some peculiar to the Committee and others reflecting congressional or at least House characteristics. Its broad jurisdiction coupled with the extremely effective leadership of Wilbur Mills, who served as chairman from 1958 through 1974, was certainly important. Mills, for example, was considered to be "one of the most influential committee chairmen in recent years, if not in history."[10] In addition, the strong consensus within the Committee on

maintaining its influence in the House and preserving its independence and that of the House in relationships with the President or the
Senate contributed substantially to the decision-making autonomy of
Ways and Means.[11] Indeed, the influence of the House on tax policy
rested in large part on the power of Ways and Means. As John Manley
concluded in his study of the Committee through the mid-1960s:

> A study of the relationship between the Ways and Means Com-
> mittee and the executive branch shows that the Committee and
> Congress generally are by no means subservient to executive
> branch policies. Ways and Means, particularly in the area of taxa-
> tion, is an independent force in policy-making that is responsive
> to demands not aggregated by the Treasury Department, that is
> well-equipped to compete on equal terms with the expertise of
> the executive, and that stands as a formidable challenge to presi-
> dents and their programs.[12]

By 1976, however, it appeared that Ways and Means had lost much
of its status and effectiveness. As one lobbyist commented, "Ways and
Means has now become like any other committee."[13] Wilbur Mills had
resigned his chairmanship in 1974 under pressures resulting from his
highly publicized personal problems. The Committee had survived
major challenges to its jurisdiction, but it was greatly increased in
size—from 25 to 37 members—in 1975, with many of the new and
liberal members disinclined to accept or support strong leadership
within the Committee.[14] The Committee was forced to form subcommittees (under Mills, all business was considered by the full committee), and along with other House committees, to conduct most of its
business in public rather than executive session. The Democrats on the
Ways and Means Committee, who had previously served as the committee on committees for the House Democrats, lost their assignment
function to the Democratic Steering and Policy Committee. Perhaps
most important, the Democratic caucus took an aggressive stance toward Ways and Means. It effectively foreclosed the Committee's ability to get a closed rule by indirectly sponsoring floor amendments.
Throughout 1975 the Ways and Means Committee found it difficult to
develop legislation, to pass legislation on the House floor in recogniza-
ble form, and to present a united front in conference with the Senate
Finance Committee.[15] While the Committee has since managed to
overcome these problems to some extent, its members remain divided

over whether its more "democratic" internal procedures and the open floor procedures have adversely affected its legislative product and its effectiveness.[16]

The Finance Committee.   The Senate counterpart of the Ways and Means Committee—the Committee on Finance—often exercises very liberally its power to propose amendments to House-passed revenue bills. Indeed, much of the Senate's participation on tax legislation involves the sponsorship of amendments reflecting the constituency interests or personal policy preferences of individual Senators.[17] The Committee has been characterized in the past as less cohesive, less specialized, and considerably less concerned with having its bills pass intact on the floor than Ways and Means has been.[18]

Senate rules do not allow the Finance Committee the floor protection once available to Ways and Means. Even when a tax bill emerges from the Finance Committee in much the same form as it passed the House, it may be substantially amended on the floor. While this does not always occur, there are some legendary examples. In 1966 the Foreign Investors Tax Act—originally fairly narrow legislation dealing with the balance of payments—was amended in the Finance Committee and on the Senate floor with provisions affecting the financing of presidential candidates, self-employed businessmen, mineral ore entrepreneurs, large investors, hearse owners, and an aluminum company.[19] Among the various "Christmas tree bills"—so named because of the special tax benefits for numerous groups—the 1966 bill remains a classic. In 1969 a House-passed measure on tax reform provisions emerged from the Finance Committee relatively intact only to be heavily amended on the floor. Provisions were included on medical deductions for the elderly, social security minimum benefits, tax credits for college expenses, and investment tax credits for small businesses and economically depressed areas (which included the entire state represented by the sponsoring Senator).[20] Several years later, a House bill on import duties was "revised" with Senate amendments involving charities, a life insurance company, state-run lotteries, flood disaster victims, family farming, low-income housing, and medical studies for servicemen.[21]

In the Senate, the Finance Committee has not performed the control function that traditionally characterized Ways and Means in the House. Rather, the Committee has allowed its members as well as other Senators to pursue specific and particularistic benefits in dealing with tax legislation. Participation in determining tax legislation has been more widespread in the Senate than in the House. As a result, the Finance Committee's relations with its parent chamber have tended to be less adversarial than relations between the Ways and Means Committee and the House.

The Conference. The difference between the House and Senate versions of a bill are resolved by a conference committee, with the conferees normally chosen from those committees that originally considered the bill. In the case of Ways and Means and Finance, the conference generally consists of ten conferees (three majority party members and two minority party members from each committee), with the chairman of Ways and Means presiding. As in all conferences, the House and Senate sides each vote as a unit with the majority vote controlling on each side.

In the past, the House conferees have been successful in removing many of the Senate amendments (as with many of the amendments noted above), but the Senate conferees have often won important disputes on tax, social security, and trade legislation.[22] It is not at all clear that either side has usually dominated, but it is apparent that considerable bargaining and compromise do occur between the Senate and House positions.[23] As during the committee stage, the conferees work with congressional staff and Treasury tax experts, and the result is usually a highly technical document. The conference report is then presented to each chamber and, if passed, goes to the President for his signature.

Over the past several years, the secrecy and discretion of conference committees have been curtailed. Unless a majority of either the House or Senate conferees vote publicly to close a session, conferences are now open. Also, the appointment of House conferees—formerly the prerogative of committee chairmen although formally exercised by the Speaker—has come under increasing scrutiny by the Democratic caucus. The desired result is conferees who will be responsive primarily to the House-passed bill rather than to the committee that first considered it. The effect of these changes on the revenue committees, particularly Ways and Means, is not altogether clear, but it is doubtful that such changes will enhance committee autonomy.

In the past, then, the Ways and Means Committee has not necessarily dominated the conference, but its general role in financial decision making has benefited greatly from its advantages of initiation and autonomy. With changes in the latter, the influence of Ways and Means in relation to both the Senate Finance Committee and the executive branch would appear to be diminished, and this loss of influence may be especially evident during the conference stage.

Relations with the Executive.   While the executive branch has generally taken the lead in proposing major changes (and has usually worked very closely with the revenue committees), Congress has occasionally initiated tax legislation. In 1969, for example, Congress initiated and developed a major revision of the tax code with minimal executive participation. Moreover, Congress has frequently revised or rejected executive proposals for changes in the tax codes. The context within which tax policy has been considered, however, has been considerably broadened since the early 1960s. Up until that time, consideration of tax legislation was governed primarily by revenue requirements. The Kennedy administration, however, adopted the argument of many professional economists in emphasizing the economic policy effects of tax increases and tax reductions. According to this view, the economy can be stimulated by tax cuts, while tax increases can be utilized when restraint is needed. While the 1964 tax cut was credited with assisting economic expansion, later attempts to use tax increases to reduce inflationary pressures were considerably less successful, particularly the delay in enacting a surtax to cover increasing war costs in 1967 and 1968. In 1975 and 1976, however, Congress again was receptive to temporary tax cuts.

One of the problems in the exercise of this type of policy is timing. Congress often does not or cannot act quickly enough to provide the stimulus or restraint at the "proper" time—that is, when the administration or economists think necessary. President Kennedy accordingly proposed in 1962 that Congress grant the President standby authority to adjust tax rates temporarily (and to initiate public works spending). This request was ignored by the revenue committees, as were similar administration requests in 1963 and 1964 and a 1966 recommendation by the Joint Economic Committee. Thus, while there has usually been executive-congressional cooperation with respect to the more technical aspects of tax legislation, Congress has guarded its authority with respect to tax policy.

Taxation and the Budget. A major consideration in budget decision making is, of course, the availability of resources, resulting in a direct relationship between revenue decisions and spending decisions. This does not mean that actual or potential revenues represent an absolute constraint on spending, since the federal budget has run quite large deficits in recent years. It also does not mean that such an absolute constraint would necessarily be desirable. As has been noted, planned deficits and tax cuts have often been utilized to stimulate the economy. Inevitably, however, revenue decisions do serve to define in large part what the government will have available for financing its agencies and programs, thereby focusing attention on budget aggregates—revenue totals and spending totals. Just as those responsible for spending decisions cannot entirely ignore the limits on available revenues, those who are responsible for determining tax policy cannot escape the budgetary implications of their decisions. Since 1974 Congress has explicitly recognized this by adopting revenue and spending targets to guide the decisions of its revenue and spending committees.

Revenue decisions, then, are an integral part of the budgetary process. The revenue committees play a major role in effecting the fiscal policy choices made by Congress and providing the resources to implement congressional spending decisions. At the same time, however, the Ways and Means Committee and the Finance Committee must deal with tax policies in other contexts. For example, certain tax legislation—such as protective tariffs or certain excise taxes—has a regulatory rather than a revenue-raising purpose. Moreover, the methods and sources of raising revenues are intensely political issues in their own right. The House and Senate have frequently been in conflict with each other and with the executive branch not only over how much revenue should be raised but also over how a given revenue level should be derived. In 1975 and 1976, for example, the Ways and Means and Finance Committees differed sharply over tax code revisions despite the fact that they were attempting to effect similar total revenue levels. The concerns of the revenue committees, then, extend beyond the budgetary process, and many of their most important decisions may be made primarily in response to pressures or issues only indirectly related to the budget. Nevertheless, the revenue side of the budgetary process represents a major vehicle for implementing congressional priorities and fiscal policy choices.

Spending Power

Congressional spending decisions are made through a multistep process that has become increasingly complicated in recent years. As discussed in Chapter One, spending first requires an authorization. This means that a law must be passed establishing a program or agency, specifying the objectives or aims involved, and in most cases setting a maximum amount on the monies that can be used to finance the program or agency. Authorization bills are handled by the substantive legislative committees. For example, legislation authorizing the Department of Defense to initiate a weapons research and development program would be required in advance of the actual appropriation of funds for that purpose. This legislation would be handled by the House and Senate Armed Services Committees.

Subsequent to the passage of authorizing legislation, the appropriations stage is initiated to grant the actual monies that have been authorized (although the maximum amount authorized need not be appropriated). By tradition, and despite occasional Senate challenges, appropriations bills originate in the House.

House Appropriations Committee.   Like the Ways and Means Committee, the House Committee on Appropriations has been generally recognized as extremely powerful and influential. Also as in the case of Ways and Means, there have been some recent challenges to its independence and authority. Appropriations is a large committee (55 members during the 95th Congress, comprising 37 Democrats and 18 Republicans), which operates through 13 subcommittees, each of which has in the past exercised substantial discretion within its jurisdiction (see below). Thus when the President's budget is received, the complex and detailed work of examining and deciding on appropriations requests is conducted within these House subcommittees.

Jurisdictions of House and Senate Appropriations Subcommittees
95th Congress (1977–1978)

Agriculture and Related Agencies

Defense

District of Columbia

Foreign Operations

Housing and Urban Development—Independent Agencies

Interior

Labor—Health, Education and Welfare

Legislative

Military Construction

Public Works

State, Justice, Commerce and Judiciary

Transportation

Treasury—Postal Service—General Government

In the past, the subcommittees have worked independently of each other, and the full committee has generally approved without major modification the appropriations bills and reports prepared by its sub-committees. At least a partial measure of committee influence is pro-vided by its success rate on the House floor. A study of decisions from 1947 through 1962 found the House accepting Appropriations Committee money recommendations without change in approximately 90 percent of the cases.[24] Since the subcommittee leadership is respon-sible for managing its bill on the House floor, it is apparent that the reputation that the subcommittees have acquired for diligence, dedica-tion, and expertise are an effective component of their influence in the House.[25]

One source of the Appropriations Committee's influence is the per-ception that its strength and unity help the House of Representatives to maintain its independence and power against the executive branch and to a lesser extent the Senate. The Committee has also benefited from its decision-making initiative, which allows it to set the "direction and magnitude of most congressional appropriations decisions. . . . It cherishes the appropriations function more dearly and defends it more strenuously than does any other group."[26]

In recent years, however, the Appropriations Committee has been challenged. Most important for both the Senate and House Commit-tees are the series of budgetary process changes incorporated in PL 93-344, the 1974 Congressional Budget and Impoundment Control Act, and the developments in nonappropriations spending discussed later in this chapter. In addition, the House Appropriations Committee has been particularly affected by procedural changes, such as those requiring open committee and subcommittee sessions (during the 1950s and 1960s the Committee usually conducted its important business in executive sessions), earlier circulation of committee reports and bills, and recorded votes in the Committee of the Whole. As part of their 1974–1975 internal reforms, House Democrats required that Appropriations subcommittee chairman nominations be submitted to the caucus for approval.[27] This was an attempt to increase responsiveness to the caucus and to decrease the control of the committee chairman, George Mahon of Texas. As the disputes over the relationship between the caucus and the standing committees multiplied during the first months of 1975, Mahon suggested that committee chairmen "ought to be responsive to the caucus on big issues. We ought to let legislation come out so it can be considered. But instructing committees on specifics is out of the question. That would destroy the committee system."[28]

Senate Appropriations Committee.   The Senate and House Committees differ in several respects. The Senate members have additional committee assignments, sometimes serving on both the authorizing committee and the appropriations subcommittee for an agency or program.[29] Senate subcommittees generally do not engage in the lengthy or detailed work of the House subcommittees. Like other Senate committees, Appropriations is "permeable"—not exclusive in its membership, less autonomous in its procedures, closely interlocked with other committees, and more responsive to the policy preferences of nonmembers. The decision-making process on appropriations legislation is much less committee-dominated than it is in the House; as a consequence the independent influence of the Senate Appropriations Committee is considerably less than that of its House counterpart.[30]

Particularly important is the greater emphasis that the Senate Committee has placed on financing programs and projects as opposed to the House emphasis on economy. This reflects the broader "policy environment" in which the Senate subcommittees operate—a context in which the executive branch, colleagues on other committees, and various clientele groups come independently to them.[31] As Richard Fenno describes it:

The Senate Committee prescribes for itself the tasks of an appellate court, which makes decisions on the basis of agency appeals for the restoration of the incremental reductions made by the House Committee. This goal expectation—which contrasts with the House Committee's expectation of budget reduction—is primarily a result of the fixed appropriations sequence. . . . By prescribing an appeals court task for itself, the Senate Committee makes it very likely that it will, in fact, grant increases.[32]

Because the Senate Committee is usually able to accommodate this broader policy environment and to emphasize the need for financing programs that the Senate membership supports, its success on the floor has been impressive. In a study of 36 bureau appropriations recommendations covering a 15-year period, the Committee's recommendation was upheld in 88.5 percent of the cases (as compared to 89.9 percent for the House Appropriations Committee).[33] There are, as in the case of the House, relatively few successful amendments.

Conference.   Differences between the House and Senate versions of an appropriations bill are usually substantial enough to require conference committee reconciliation. As with revenue bills, bargaining and compromise are characteristic of the process. The House's advantage stemming from decision-making initiative in the appropriations process is countered, at least partially, by the greater support that Senate conferees have within their chamber. The more widespread participation in appropriations decisions in the Senate means that the Senate bill is usually more representative of the policy preferences of the chamber than is the House bill. In addition, the Senate usually benefits from defending the higher appropriation:

The demands for increased appropriations become more concentrated and intense as appropriations decision-making moves from stage to stage and as the controversial increment of the budget progressively narrows. Individuals and groups have more time to mobilize, have more information, and have fewer issues to contest at each succeeding stage—from House to Senate, from Senate to conference. Conversely, economy sentiment (unless maintained by extraordinary external events) tends to take the form of evanescent moods, to become progressively weaker with the passage of time and with the intrusion of new legislative events.[34]

Thus, the House does not clearly dominate the conference stage,[35] although its influence in the entire appropriations process is more pervasive than that of the Senate.[36]

Limits on Appropriations Control.   The Appropriations Committees have traditionally had to contend with executive pressures in the budget decision-making process, but since the early 1950s they have also been faced by challenges within Congress, particularly the use of annual authorizations and various forms of backdoor spending. The first of these, annual authorization, has been aimed at the House Appropriations Committee. It represents an attempt by the authorizing committees to maintain their influence over agencies and programs by requiring the same annual review as that provided by the appropriations process.

In part, the double review—first by the authorizing committee and then by the Appropriations Committee—provides the House with information and judgments from more than one source, lessening its dependence on the Appropriations Committee. In addition, the double review encourages the development of program and financial expertise among authorizing committee members. Two of the persistent complaints about Appropriations—its lack of communication with nonmembers and its excessive involvement in legislative matters (since it is difficult to distinguish in many cases where the line between financial and programmatic judgments should be drawn)[37]—have thus been manifested in the increasing emphasis on annual authorization. Since the authorizing and Appropriations committees in the Senate are more closely linked, these complaints have not been as widespread as in the House, but the House has managed to gain the Senate's acquiescence to annual authorizations in most instances.

The second challenge—backdoor spending—reflects some of the same authorizing committee versus Appropriations Committee antagonisms, except that here the authorizing committees attempt to establish exclusive or dominant control over spending decisions. Budget authority is usually in the form of appropriations, but the latter term has been broadened to include not only measures that pass through the Appropriations Committees but also other legislative actions that create obligations or make funds available for obligation or expenditure.[38]

The earliest examples of backdoor spending involved contract authorization and loan authority. Under the first, an authorizing commit-tee sponsored legislation creating statutory authority for a department or agency to enter into contracts or obligations before specific appro-priations were approved. Once contracts had been entered into or obli-gations incurred, appropriations were necessary to liquidate the obliga-tions, but neither the Appropriations Committees nor Congress had much discretion about providing the necessary funds. With loan au-thority, certain agencies were allowed to borrow funds directly from the Treasury rather than having to go through the appropriations pro-cess. Here, too, the jurisdiction was with the authorizing committees.

Both these approaches thus allowed programs to circumvent effec-tively the Appropriations Committees, and their increasing use by au-thorizing committees during the 1950s finally resulted in a legislative battle in the House. The House Appropriations Committee challenged both these practices and succeeded, during the early 1960s, in gaining the authority to review the granting of loan authority and to set annual maximum limits on contract authorizations.[39] This has cut down, al-though not eliminated, these forms of backdoor spending. In 1975, for example, approximately $11.5 billion in contract authorizations and $1.5 billion in loan authority were available without current action by Congress.[40]

At the same time, however, other forms of backdoor spending have emerged and become an extremely significant portion of annual spend-ing. In recent years "mandatory entitlements" have become especially important. These are payments to persons or to state and local gov-ernments that the federal government is obligated to make when the legal requirements for receiving payment are fulfilled. The costs of such entitlements are determined by the pool of eligible recipients. As the size of this pool increases (or decreases), costs fluctuate and au-tomatically affect spending. For example, the eligible pool of food stamp recipients grew substantially during the early 1970s—3.5 million persons were added between June 1974 and December 1974, bringing estimated participation to 17 million people. But because of the lack of clarity in the legislative and administrative guidelines, it was still un-clear as to how many persons were actually eligible but not participat-ing or participating but not actually eligible. Some studies estimated that the program's "target population" was between 27 and 39 million people, with additional fluctuations possible if economic conditions changed.[41] Thus, for programs of this type, spending decisions are a product of eligibility requirements, economic conditions, and administrative efficiency rather than appropriations decisions made in advance of spending.

A related type of effect occurs when payments are tied to various indexes. For example, retirement benefits can be linked to changes in the cost of living. As the consumer price index changes, program costs automatically change. Here again, actual spending will result from economic conditions that are not always predictable in advance. The authorizing committees, by sponsoring legislation that establishes an automatic increase in payments or benefits under various programs, can evade effective review by the Appropriations Committees for programs within their jurisdiction.

The result of these types of backdoor spending is that many budget decisions are made outside the regular, annual appropriations process. Spending control is therefore fragmented between the authorizing committees and the Appropriations Committees. The growing seriousness of this problem led Congress to set certain controls on backdoor spending as part of the broader revision of the budgetary process in 1974.

Controlling Spending—Attempted Reforms

Throughout its history, Congress has had considerable difficulty in designing budget procedures that could resolve the competing goals and claims of its standing committees. One persistent tension has been that between the authorizing committees, with their emphasis on support for programs within their respective jurisdictions, and the Appropriations Committees, with their relatively greater emphasis on economy and other financial considerations. When Congress has moved to centralize spending control in its Appropriations Committees, as it did after the Civil War and during the 1920s, the authorizing committees have inevitably challenged this centralization (as they successfully did between 1877 and 1885) or have developed backdoor spending methods to circumvent the appropriations process (as they have done for the past several decades). A second area of tension involves the relative influence of Congress and the President with respect to government spending. As discussed in Chapter Two, the executive budget process has become increasingly important and influential since its establishment in 1921, and this has presented a continuing challenge to Congress' budget capabilities. Prior to 1974, Congress was unable to resolve fully either of these tensions, much less to find a method of reconciling both satisfactorily.

Since the mid-1940s, Congress has made several attempts to revise and improve its budgetary process, with the most recent and elaborate revision being the 1974 Congressional Budget and Impoundment Control Act. Some perspective on this latest effort can be gained by surveying the fate of two earlier attempts.

Legislative Budget.   As part of the 1946 Legislative Reorganization Act, Congress established a legislative budget. Four committees (Ways and Means, Finance, and the Appropriations Committees) were to meet as the Joint Budget Committee at the beginning of each session and to prepare estimates of total receipts and expenditures. By February 15 their report, along with a concurrent resolution setting the maximum amount to be appropriated for the following fiscal year, was to be sent to the House and Senate for consideration. Further, the appropriations limit could not exceed estimated receipts unless the resolution specified a necessary increase in the public debt; if a surplus was estimated, a reduction in the debt was to be recommended.

Congress unsuccessfully attempted to develop a legislative budget in 1947, 1948, and 1949. Estimates on revenues and spending were inaccurate, spending ceilings were violated, and the Senate and House had continual disagreements.[42] One major problem was the February 15 deadline for reporting a spending ceiling. This did not allow the Committee adequate time to study the President's budget in detail or to specify where budget cuts were to be made. Since there was no provision for amending the ceiling, the procedure did not allow Congress to take into account changes in economic conditions or other circumstances as it made its spending decisions.[43] Moreover, the feasibility of operating such a large committee (the Joint Budget Committee had more than 100 members) as well as the perceived inadequacy of available staff presented serious problems, which were complicated by policy disagreements between the congressional parties and by the hostility of the House Appropriations Committee.[44] In 1947 the Senate and House could not come to agreement on the size of the cut in the President's budget or on the disposal of the unspent funds, and no legislative budget was adopted. In 1948 both chambers agreed on a

$2.5 billion cut in the executive budget, but there was no specification of what form this cut would take. Congress then violated the spending ceiling by appropriating $6 billion more than specified in the concurrent resolution. The following year Congress finally changed the date for adopting the concurrent resolution to May 1, but since most appropriations bills had been passed by that time, no legislative budget was adopted. By 1950 the concept had been effectively dropped.[45]

Omnibus Appropriations Bill. In 1950 Representative Clarence Cannon, chairman of the House Appropriations Committee, tried to establish a different type of expenditure control by combining all of the separate appropriations bills into one measure. The assumption was that acting on separate bills one by one made it quite difficult to control total outlays, but that a comprehensive consideration would allow for an effective check on total outlays. During its 1950 trial, the omnibus bill cut the President's budget requests significantly, although large supplemental appropriations were soon necessitated by the Korean war.[46] More important, the subcommittee chairmen of the House Appropriations Committee viewed the omnibus approach as a threat to the power and autonomy of their subcommittees. In 1951 the omnibus approach was abandoned, and Senate-sponsored attempts to revive the practice have not been supported by the House. Subsequently, additional revisions—such as separate budget sessions, expenditure ceilings, and Joint Budget Committees—have been proposed, but these have not been both acceptable and effective.

1974 Congressional Budget and Impoundment Control Act

Congress has, then, periodically if unsuccessfully attempted to revise and improve its budgetary organization and process. Both the legislative budget and omnibus appropriations bill experiments reflected a concern with controlling expenditures, which became pronounced once again with the expenditure increases of the early 1970s. In addition, however, Congress was faced in 1972 with a sharp executive challenge to its budget authority. When Congress did not agree to the Nixon administration's request for a $250 billion ceiling on fiscal 1973 expenditures, the President accelerated the use of impoundments to impose the ceiling.[47] This presidential challenge was perceived by some observers as extremely effective politically, since it played on the electorate's growing concern with federal spending. Louis Fisher, for example, suggested that congressional budgetary reform was necessary if Congress was to retain control over national policy making:

> Unless Congress can improve its budget capability it will remain a patsy, forever being bulldozed around by executive assaults and encroachments—no matter how factually unsound or spurious in design they are. Such capability is needed not merely to restore a balance between the two branches and to protect congressional spending prerogatives, but to raise the level of public debate and the quality of public policy.[48]

As part of its 1972 debt limit legislation, Congress therefore established a Joint Study Committee on Budget Control and directed it to provide recommendations for improving congressional control and coordination of budget outlays and receipts. The Committee's report was issued in April 1973; after significant modifications of its recommendations, budget reform legislation was signed into law July 12, 1974. Within a relatively short period, Congress had instituted the most substantial budget reform in over half a century, and the overwhelming support for this reform reflected widespread agreement about the severity of the problems that had developed under the old process.[49]

The Problems

During congressional consideration of budget reform legislation, attention focused on a series of major problems that characterized Congress' handling of the budget.[50]

1. The lack of coordination in the budget process made it difficult to relate taxing and spending actions to fiscal policy needs. Because taxing and spending measures were considered by numerous committees with no required coordination, congressional taxing and spending decisions were often unrelated to each other. This meant that Congress had no mechanism for setting fiscal policy and thus for challenging the executive's dominance over fiscal policy decisions. In addition, it meant that members of Congress were not forced to make conscious and explicit decisions about total spending and to relate them to available revenues.

2. The lack of coordination in the budget process had negative effects on Congress' ability to manage programs—many of the outlays in a given year were removed from the regular appropriations process or represented long-term commitments over which control was limited. The budget was increasingly inflexible and resistant to congressional policy preferences. Since Congress was unable to control substantial amounts of short-term spending, its ability to use the annual budget as a means for implementing its policy preferences was circumscribed.

3. The traditional budgetary process did not provide a mechanism through which Congress was forced to make necessary but difficult choices on priorities. Indeed, under the traditional process, appropriations bills were passed at different times, and Congress was able to avoid direct confrontations about competing priorities. Moreover, there was growing concern about the massive spending increases and deficits in previous years, indicating that Congress would inevitably be forced to consider spending decisions not only in relation to each other but also in relation to their cumulative impact on the budget.

4. There was no staff organization responsible to Congress to provide fiscal policy and program analysis. Congress was accordingly too reliant on information and analyses provided by the President and the Office of Management and Budget (OMB).

5. The timing of congressional budget actions was unsatisfactory— action on appropriations bills was seldom completed by the beginning of the fiscal year. One result was that many agencies operated with stopgap funding (continuing resolutions) for part or all of a fiscal year.

6. Executive claims of impoundment authority challenged Congress' appropriations powers and threatened its exercise of the power of the purse. The unprecedented use of impoundment by President Nixon and the expansive claims of federal authority that accompanied it could not be continually tolerated if Congress was to preserve its institutional integrity and authority.

The problems, then, were serious, since they ultimately affected Congress' capacity to make and control policy. At the same time, however, there were differing expectations about the effects of budget reform. Conservatives, for example, supported budget reform, since they viewed it as the means to limit the growth in federal spending and to eliminate budget deficits. Liberals, on the other hand, focused on those aspects of reform that would allow Congress to challenge the President on fiscal policy and to enforce its spending priorities and policy decisions. Thus, there were questions from the first about the survival of the new budgetary process, given these differing expectations and the partisan and ideological battles that would inevitably occur.[51]

Under PL 93-344, the Congressional Budget and Impoundment Control Act, Congress enacted a number of important procedural and organizational changes. New Budget Committees were created, and a congressional budgetary staff organization was established. The fiscal year was changed as was the fiscal year timetable for congressional consideration of the budget. Elaborate and complex procedures were adopted that governed executive and congressional budget participation. Major revisions were made to deal with backdoor spending and impoundment.

Budget Committees and Staffs

A standing Committee on the Budget has been established for each chamber, and these committees have broad jurisdiction over the congressional budget process. They are responsible for reporting to Congress each year at least two concurrent resolutions that allow Congress to set its fiscal policy choices and to adopt guidelines to be used in its actions on revenue, spending, and debt legislation. The Committees are also responsible for studying the budgetary effects of existing and proposed legislation and for overseeing the operations of the Congressional Budget Office (CBO). Each committee also has its own staff.

There are differences in the rules governing selection and tenure on the Budget Committees. As initially set up in 1975, the Senate Committee included 16 members selected by normal committee selection procedures—that is, by the Democratic and Republican conferences. There is no required rotation for Senate Budget Committee members, although they are restricted in the number of additional committee and subcommittee positions they can hold. Under new Senate rules adopted in 1977, each Senator can serve on two major committees and one minor committee. The Budget Committee was designated as a minor committee for the 95th Congress and as a major committee beginning in 1979. For members newly appointed to the Committee in 1977, however, the Committee was classified as a major committee. In addition, members of the Senate Budget Committee were allowed to serve on three subcommittees, as opposed to the limit of two applied to other minor committees. Membership on the Committee has been set at 16, with the party ratio for the 95th Congress being 10 Democrats and 6 Republicans. Senator Edmund Muskie (D-Maine) has served as the Committee's chairman since its establishment.

The House Committee is larger and has more elaborate rules governing its membership. Rules adopted in 1975 set total membership at 25, with 5 seats assigned to Ways and Means Committee members, 5 seats to Appropriations Committee members, and the remainder apportioned among the legislative committees and party leadership. Tenure on the panel is restricted, with each member limited to serving four years in any ten-year period. For the 95th Congress, the party ratio was set at 17 Democrats and 8 Republicans with Representative Robert Giaimo (D-Conn.) being selected as chairman.[52] He succeeded Brock Adams, who had been appointed as Secretary of Transportation by President Carter.

Congressional Budget Office. The CBO is a major innovation. It is an attempt to develop a professional budget staff in Congress that will combine certain functions performed by the OMB, the Council of Economic Advisers, and the Treasury Department in the executive budget process. The CBO is to provide the Budget Committees and Congress with a variety of budget and policy analysis information.[53] Certain CBO functions are prescribed by the 1974 act. These include: (1) preparation of an annual report on budget alternatives, including fiscal policy options, levels of tax expenditures, and budget priorities; (2) issuance of five-year budget projections; (3) estimates of costs, when possible, of bills reported by House and Senate committees; and (4) issuance of periodic "scorekeeping" reports—tracking the effect of specific congressional budgetary actions on the overall budget targets established by Congress. In addition, the CBO assists the Budget Committees and, to a lesser extent, other committees by preparing commissioned research reports on economic and budgetary issues. It has also developed data management systems to support the congressional budget process.

Timetable, Process, and Procedures

The revised budgetary process includes a new fiscal year timetable and a number of procedural requirements. The beginning of the fiscal year has been moved from July 1 to October 1 to provide an additional three months for congressional consideration of the budget. Moreover, since presidential budget estimates are now due approximately eleven months in advance of the beginning of a fiscal year, the budget sequence on the congressional side now covers almost one full year. Figure 3.1 lists the various deadlines involved in the development of the congressional budget.

1. The first step is submission of the current services budget by the President on November 10. This budget estimates the budget authority and outlays required to continue government policies and programs under existing legislation and current economic assumptions. It is intended to provide, therefore, an estimate of the spending levels required without program changes or new programs. The current services budget is reviewed by Congress' Joint Economic Committee, which is directed to assess its estimates and economic assumptions and to report these assessments to the Budget Committees.

2. Within 15 days after Congress convenes in January, the President submits his budget for the upcoming fiscal year. This contains the usual information and recommendations concerning economic assumptions, revenues and outlays, budget authority, and fiscal and program policy choices. There are additional requirements that it provide estimates of and recommendations for changes in tax expenditures and five-year estimates of federal spending under existing commitments.

3. By March 15 the Budget Committees are to receive reports on budget recommendations and proposals from other congressional committees. The CBO report on budget options and priorities is due April 1. On the basis of these reports, the President's budget proposals, and hearings or other sources of information, the Budget Committees are required to develop and report to Congress the first concurrent resolution on the budget.

4. April 15 is the deadline for reporting the first concurrent resolution. This resolution sets targets for expenditures and revenues to guide subsequent congressional budget decisions. The resolution

October-December: Congressional Budget Office submits five-year projection of current spending as soon as possible after October 1.

November 10: President submits current services budget.

December 31: Joint Economic Committee reports analysis of current services budget to budget committees.

Late January: President submits budget (fifteen days after Congress convenes).

Late January-March: Budget committees hold hearings and begin work on first budget resolution.

March 15: All legislative committees submit estimates and views to budget committees.

April 15: Budget committees report first resolution.

May 15: Committees must report authorization bills by this date.

May 15: Congress completes action on first resolution. Before adoption of the first resolution, neither house may consider new budget authority or spending authority bills, revenue changes, or debt limit changes.

May 15 through the 7th day after Labor Day: Congress completes action on all budget and spending authority bills.

• Before reporting first regular appropriations bill, the House Appropriations Committee, "to extent practicable," marks up all regular appropriations bills and submits a summary report to House, comparing proposed outlays and budget authority levels with first resolution targets.

• CBO issues periodic scorekeeping reports comparing congressional action with first resolution.

• Reports on new budget authority and tax expenditure bills must contain comparisons with first resolution, and five-year projections.

• "As possible," a CBO cost analysis and five-year projection will accompany all reported public bills, except appropriation bills.

August: Budget committees prepare second budget resolution and report.

September 15: Congress completes action on second resolution. Thereafter, neither house may consider any bill or amendment, or conference report, that results in an increase over outlay or budget authority figures, or a reduction in revenues, beyond the amounts in the second resolution.

September 25: Congress completes action on reconciliation bill or another resolution. Congress may not adjourn until it completes action on the second resolution and reconciliation measure, if any.

October 1: Fiscal year begins.

Figure 3.1

Congressional budget deadlines. [Source: *Congressional Quarterly Almanac, Vol. XXXI, 1975* (Washington, D.C.: Congressional Quarterly, Inc., 1976), p. 918.]

specifies total outlays and revenues and the projected surplus or deficit. Within the outlays total, spending is broken down by the functional categories used in the President's budget.[54] Congress has until May 15 to debate this resolution and to adopt a final version.

5. May 15 is also the deadline for reporting most authorizing legislation that will be required for the upcoming fiscal year.[55] (Administration requests for authorizing legislation are due one year in advance of this date.)

6. From May 15 through early September, the regular appropriations process proceeds with initial consideration by the House Appropriations subcommittees. However, spending decisions as well as tax proposals being considered by the revenue committees are to take into account the guidelines established in the first concurrent resolution. Each appropriation bill will go sequentially through the traditional route; after final House and Senate agreement, the individual bills can be sent separately to the President or all can be held until September.

7. After action has been completed on spending and revenue bills, but on or before September 15, Congress must adopt a second concurrent resolution. This second resolution will either affirm or revise the targets set in May for spending, revenues, and the debt limit. It will also review the spending and revenue decisions that Congress has taken in the interim (on appropriations, entitlements, tax legislation, and so forth). If ceilings have been exceeded, estimated revenues are insufficient, or the debt limit must be revised, the second resolution will direct those committees with the appropriate jurisdiction to make and report the necessary legislative changes. This could include revising appropriations or other spending legislation, raising or lowering revenues, adjusting the debt ceiling, or any combination of these. If the changes are confined to one committee in each chamber (for example, a tax bill revision by the Ways and Means and Finance Committees), then the changes are reported directly to the floor. If the necessary changes are more extensive, the Budget Committees are responsible for combining the changes in a reconciliation measure that is then reported to the House and Senate. This measure is to be adopted by September 25 and is then sent to the President. If Congress has withheld all appropriations and other budget-related bills, this measure then becomes the final budget legislation. If individual bills have been passed, this measure—if signed by the President—supersedes all previously passed legislation.

By October 1, then, the budgetary process is to be completed, although congressional delays or presidential vetoes could obviously carry the process past the deadline. Indeed, the specified deadlines can be waived by the House and Senate. Moreover, Congress can also pass additional budget resolutions and revise its earlier decisions once the fiscal year has begun.[56] Nevertheless, the process envisions an orderly congressional review of budget measures and provides for the comprehensive consideration of revenue and spending measures and fiscal policy choices in a four-stage process (see Figure 3.2).

This elaborate procedure has several objectives. First, Congress is able to make explicit decisions on fiscal policy by voting on budget aggregates—total spending and total revenues—and thus setting a budget deficit or surplus level that it believes appropriate. Second, the concurrent resolution that Congress adopts in the spring establishes expenditure and revenue targets to guide subsequent authorization, appropriation, and revenue decisions. If congressional spending or revenue decisions do not fall within these targets, the second concurrent resolution forces Congress to make the necessary adjustments in its budget totals. Third, since the concurrent resolutions include expenditures by functional categories, Congress must consider its spending decisions in relation to each other, which provides for congressional determination of priorities. And fourth, the new budgetary process is designed to insure passage of budget legislation before the beginning of the fiscal year to which it applies. If the deadlines are met, the funding for agencies and programs should be firmly established once the fiscal year begins. Moreover, since the beginning of the fiscal year has been advanced to October 1, Congress has almost eleven months—beginning with submission of the current services budget—to work on its budget.

Budget Controls

In addition to changes in congressional organization and in the budget process, the 1974 law also contained provisions designed to strengthen congressional budgetary controls. These included new procedures for dealing with backdoor spending, estimating and reporting tax expenditures, and most important, establishing a congressional check on presidential impoundment.

Stage 1. November 10 - April 15	Information gathering, analysis, preparation and submission of congressional budget by Congressional Budget Office and Budget Committees.
Stage 2. April 15 - May 15	Debate and adoption of congressional budget by both houses; establishment of national spending priorities.
Stage 3. May 15 - Early September	Enactment of spending bills.
Stage 4. September 15 - September 25	Reassessment of spending, revenue, and debt requirements in second budget resolution; enactment of reconciliation bill.

Figure 3.2

Four stages of the budget process. [Source: House Committee on the Budget, *Congressional Budget Reform*, 93rd Congress, 2nd Session (Washington, D.C.: Government Printing Office, 1975), p. 16.]

Backdoor Spending. With certain exceptions, new backdoor spending in the form of contract or borrowing authority and entitlements was made subject to increased control by the Appropriations Committees. Most new contract or borrowing authority, for example, was made dependent on prior appropriations. This changed new contract or borrowing authority into a standard authorization subject to the funding recommendation of the Appropriations Committees. In addition, the Appropriations Committees were given the authority to review new entitlement legislation, but only if the legislation provided budget authority in excess of the latest budget resolution allocation for that function. More important, spending for certain trust funds, such as social security, was exempted from review.

Tax Expenditures. Provisions relating to tax expenditures dealt primarily with reporting. In the case of any committee reporting tax expenditure legislation, estimates must be prepared (in consultation with the CBO) that detail the effects of the proposed legislation on the existing level of tax expenditures and project the costs for a five-year period. Since the CBO is also required to furnish five-year projections for all existing tax expenditures, Congress can more adequately assess the short- and long-term revenue effects of new tax expenditure legislation.

Impoundment.   Title X of the 1974 act established impoundment controls and represented a major check on executive spending discretion. This section established two categories of impoundments—deferrals and rescissions. If the President wishes to defer the actual spending of appropriated funds during a fiscal year, he must inform Congress by special message of the amount, time period, justifications, and estimated program effects of the proposed deferral. Either the Senate or the House can disapprove the deferral by adopting an impoundment resolution, in which case funds must be made available for obligation. If funds are to be rescinded permanently—that is, if budget authority is to be eliminated—the President must notify Congress by special message of the amount, justification, and estimated program impact of the rescission. Unless Congress adopts a rescission bill within 45 days of continuous session after receipt of this message, the President must release the funds proposed for rescission.

Policy Evaluations

Congress also recognized the necessity for program review and evaluation in budget decisions. It authorized committees to exercise their oversight responsibilities by contract or by requiring federal agencies to conduct evaluations. In addition, the GAO was directed to assist committees in their evaluations and in developing statements of legislative objectives or intent, and the GAO was authorized to establish an Office of Program Review and Evaluation. Finally, the Budget Committees were directed to study proposals for improving budget decision making, including time limitations for program authorizations, pilot testing of programs, and other testing and evaluation techniques. The 1974 act did not provide a great deal of specificity relating to program evaluation and review, but it did signal a growing congressional awareness of the need to expand committee oversight and thereby to improve Congress' ability to evaluate its past budget decisions and make more informed future choices.

The Budget System—Performance and Potential

The new budget system is elaborate and detailed, representing an unusual degree of centralization in congressional decision making. It tests Congress' ability to challenge executive decisions and to maintain the cohesion and discipline necessary to make unified budget decisions. The budget system focuses congressional attention on fiscal policy and program priorities. This requires that Congress consider total spending and total revenues. In addition, spending measures cannot be dealt with separately, nor can they be divorced from decisions on tax measures. If Congress wishes to increase spending for specific programs, it must raise additional revenues, accept a larger deficit, or balance the increase by reducing spending elsewhere. But while the process requires that Congress act in a comprehensive and coordinated fashion, it is unclear that Congress either wishes to exercise or can exercise this type of control. In assessing the future prospects and impact of the budgetary process, then, it is helpful to examine its actual operation.

Budget Resolutions

The first year of the new budget system (1975 for the fiscal 1976 budget) was designated as a trial run in order that committees and staffs could be established and members of Congress could become acquainted with the new procedures. The fiscal 1976 budget was therefore the first attempt by Congress to coordinate taxing and spending decisions and to set fiscal policy through the concurrent budget resolutions. While the deadlines were not met (the second resolution was not adopted until December, almost three months late), there were noteworthy developments during the first year.

Congress challenged the Ford administration on fiscal policy and spending priorities. The President's budget had recommended a deficit of $51.9 billion and total outlays of $349.4 billion. In its first budget resolution, Congress set the deficit at $68.8 billion, which it then raised to $74.1 billion in its second resolution. There was, as might be expected, considerable controversy over the size of this planned deficit, but Congress had finally attempted to determine fiscal policy. In addition, Congress differed with the administration over spending priorities. In most instances, Congress adopted higher spending levels than the President had recommended, but it also cut executive requests for national defense and international affairs.[57] Congressional spending decisions were significantly higher in areas such as health; commerce and transportation; and education, training, employment, and social services.

On the other hand, the trial run uncovered some political obstacles. Support for both budget resolutions was extremely shaky in the

House, with only bare majorities voting for passage and only then after the Democratic leadership intervened. There was fundamental disagreement in the house, and even in the Budget Committee, over the purpose of budget control. For many conservatives, the purpose of budget control was to limit federal spending, not to program deficits on the order of $74 billion. This was the view of many House Republicans, only a handful of whom voted for the budget resolutions. For others, such as Senator Muskie and Representative Adams, the chairmen of the Budget Committees, the purpose of budget control was to allow Congress to establish fiscal policy and to set spending priorities. Even this approach ran into difficulty, however, when attempts were made to enforce ceilings for programs that had broad support in Congress. During 1975, for example, there was substantial pressure within the Democratic party to increase spending for social programs, education, and jobs beyond the levels recommended by the Budget Committees. Indeed, some members who had voted in favor of the budget resolution targets also wound up supporting amendments to spending bills that would breach the ceilings. The difficulty of reconciling the goals of the various ideological blocs with the discipline necessary to enforce budget controls was apparent in 1975, and it still represents one of the most serious problems affecting the budget system.

The second year of operation began positively. On May 13, two days before the deadline, Congress adopted its first concurrent resolution for the fiscal 1977 budget. The resolution called for $17.5 billion more in total spending than the President had recommended, but it also set revenue targets $11.2 billion above administration recommendations. The resolution passed by more than a two-to-one margin in the Senate and by a comfortable 224–170 vote in the House. Moreover, following adoption of the resolution, the appropriations process moved very quickly, and all but one of the major appropriations bills had passed the House and the Senate by July 1. Indeed, conference committee reports on three appropriations bills had passed by that date.

Congress also met the September deadline. On September 15 the Senate approved the second concurrent budget resolution by a vote of 66–20, and final action was completed the following day when the House voted 234–143 for adoption. In contrast to the 1975 trial run, the new budget procedures worked very smoothly in 1976. Differences between the House and Senate versions of the budget resolutions were minor and easily resolved by the conference committee, and the votes for adoption in both chambers were substantial.

Moreover, the congressional budget resolutions again differed significantly from administration recommendations in several respects. The $413.1 billion limit on expenditures for FY 1977 was almost $20 billion above the original budget requests submitted by President Ford, with the major spending increases concentrated in the areas of health, education and social services, and community and regional development. The projected deficit, however, was only some $7.6 billion more than the administration had recommended, since Congress approved tax reductions well below those suggested in the President's budget. According to the conference committee report accompanying the second resolution, the $50.6 billion deficit was a necessary stimulus to achieve higher employment and output.

The 1977 budget resolution, however, came to an unusual and confusing end. Soon after taking office, the Carter administration proposed a two-year economic stimulus package. Part of the package called for increased spending and reduced taxes during the 1977 fiscal year (which had, of course, begun the previous October). Congress reacted positively to the broad outlines of the plan, and in March both Houses adopted an unprecedented third budget resolution, which altered the spending ceiling, revenue floor, and deficit set by the second budget resolution. On April 14, however, the administration withdrew major tax portions of its stimulus package—including the $50 tax rebates and payments to individuals. Congress then was forced to revise once again its fiscal 1977 budget levels—increasing the revenue floor, decreasing the outlay ceiling, and lowering the planned deficit.

The revised binding levels for fiscal 1977 were adopted on May 17, the same day that Congress completed action on the first budget resolution for FY 1978, which had also followed a tortuous path. On April 28 the House rejected, for the first time, a resolution reported by its Budget Committee. The resolution's rejection, moreover, was overwhelming—only 84 members voted in support of the resolution, while 320 members opposed it. Budget Committee leaders attributed much of the blame for the defeat to the Democratic administration. When the resolution was reported, Carter officials, notably Secretary of Defense Harold Brown, lobbied members in support of an amendment to raise defense spending to the level recommended by the President in his February 22 budget. When this amendment was adopted, it opened the door for other amendments to increase domestic spending. The balance between defense and domestic spending that the Budget Committee had proposed was quickly upset, and the result was a bill that had little support in the House from either liberals or conservatives.

The problems encountered over the 1977 revisions and 1978 resolution did nothing to improve executive-congressional relations. The Speaker of the House, Thomas P. O'Neill, Jr. (D-Mass.), suggested that administration officials did not understand congressional procedures. The chairman of the House Budget Committee, Robert N. Giaimo (D-Conn.), was especially incensed, declaring that "this is the United States Congress where the Democratic majority is going to write the legislation. It is not the Georgia legislature." Other members argued that Congress had been ill-advised in the first place to accommodate the Carter administration so readily on the revisions for 1977 and should instead have made independent judgments about budget policy regardless of the political party occupying the White House.[58]

Following the April 28 debacle, the House Budget Committee prepared and reported a "compromise" resolution, which cut some three-fourths of the funds that had been added through floor amendments to the first resolution. When an admendment to increase defense spending was offered on the floor, the House defeated it 233–176. A week earlier the same amendment had passed 225–184. The House then adopted the resolution by 213–179. The Senate had meanwhile adopted its version of the budget resolution, adding $400 million in outlays and $7.2 billion in budget authority to the Budget Committee's recommendations. In conference, after disagreements over spending and revenue estimates, the Senate version largely prevailed, and both chambers accepted the conference report—the Senate approving it by 54–23 and the House by 221–177. The second budget resolution was adopted on September 15 but only after another floor fight in the House and a serious conference dispute over economic growth estimates. Moreover, several appropriations bills did not clear Congress by the September deadline, adding to the problems and confusion surrounding the fiscal 1978 budget.

The budget resolutions are the key to the congressional budget process, providing Congress with a mechanism to make comprehensive and coordinated budget decisions. Passage of the resolutions has sometimes been difficult, because partisan and ideological pressures present formidable obstacles to making such decisions in Congress. Conservatives have opposed the large, programmed deficits in previous resolutions. Liberals have attacked the resolutions for increasing defense spending at the expense of domestic programs. At the same time, it has been possible in the end to pass the resolutions, in part because some members have supported the budget process if not the content of the resolutions.[59] Whether Congress can continue to make unified budget decisions, particularly as pressures build to limit deficits or balance the budget, is questionable unless members emphasize such support for the process, which requires in turn that members perceive the survival of the process as necessary to protect Congress' independence and authority.

Budget Committees

As stated earlier, House and Senate Budget Committees have been established to develop and report the concurrent resolutions, to study the effects on spending of current and proposed legislation, and to oversee the CBO. While this approach differs markedly from the Joint Budget Committee that was set up in 1946 to implement the legislative budget, each Budget Committee faces the problems of withstanding challenges from existing committees and developing sufficient support to enforce its decisions. The House and Senate approaches to solving these problems have been significantly different.

The Senate Budget Committee has been much more aggressive in attempting to cut spending and in confronting the authorizing, revenue, and appropriations committees on the floor in order to enforce spending cuts. The Committee has been especially active in attempting to enforce the spending and revenue targets of the first budget resolution by opposing legislation that would breach the targets. In 1975 it even convinced the Senate to reject two conference reports—one a military construction authorization bill and the other a school lunch authorization bill—on the grounds that they exceeded the spending targets contained in the first budget resolution for FY 1976. Even though these bills were authorizations rather than appropriations, the Budget Committee leadership argued that budget control could not be achieved without effective restraints over authorizing legislation.[60]

The Senate Committee has not always succeeded in its confrontations. It has had, for example, particular difficulties with the Senate Finance Committee and its chairman, Senator Russell Long (D-La.). During the summer of 1976 the Budget Committee chairman, Senator Muskie (D-Maine), and its ranking minority member, Senator Henry

Bellmon (R-Okla.), challenged provisions of the tax reform bill reported by the Finance Committee on the grounds that the bill violated the fiscal and tax policies contained in the first budget resolution. Muskie argued that the tax cuts contained in the bill missed the revenue targets by $2 billion and, if enacted, would increase the planned deficit. After losing two key procedural votes, however, Muskie conceded defeat.[61]

The Budget Committee also suffered a setback during Senate action on the first budget resolution for 1978. The Banking, Housing and Urban Affairs Committee sponsored two amendments to the resolution, increasing new budget authority for low-income housing assistance and community development by almost $7 billion over the Budget Committee's recommendation. Muskie fought the amendments, stating that while they would not appreciably affect actual spending in FY 1978, they would have a significant impact in future years, making it even more difficult to achieve a balanced budget by the early 1980s. The Senate, however, passed both amendments.[62]

On appropriations bills, the Senate Budget Committee has made a major effort to enforce the spending targets. During the first year, it clashed with the Senate Appropriations Committee at several points over how the targets set for functional categories should affect actual spending bills. The appropriations bills Congress considers do not correspond to the functional categories used in the executive budget or in the budget resolution. The "crosswalk" procedure that the Budget Committee used to convert the functional category targets into targets for the specific appropriations accounts contained in appropriations bills led to complaints by the Appropriations Committee chairman, Senator John McClellan (D-Ark.), that his committee's jurisdiction was being infringed. While Muskie rarely opposed appropriations bills actively on the floor, he repeatedly forced the Senate to consider how a spending bill affected the targets and also how passage of a particular bill would affect remaining bills in the same functional category.[63]

The House Budget Committee, on the other hand, has usually avoided floor confrontations. Its first chairman, Representative Brock Adams (D-Wash.), worked closely with Appropriations subcommittee chairmen as spending bills were being drafted and attempted to protect the targets by operating behind the scenes. Adams believed that this was the most effective approach for influencing spending legislation, stating that "we've already done our work before the bills get to the floor."[64] In addition, the House Budget Committee has not challenged the authorizing committees by insisting that authorizations as well as appropriations be subject to budget resolution targets. Indeed, the House Committee has usually deferred to the authorizing committees and has resisted attempts to "dictate" action to these committees.[65]

This cautious approach, however, has been as much a result of necessity as of choice. The House Budget Committee has not been able to develop the cohesion or independence of its Senate counterpart. The tenure limitations in the House, for example, limit the Budget Committee's attractiveness, since members cannot build a career around service on the Committee.[66] Almost one-half of the House Budget Committee members hold mandated seats assigned to the Ways and Means Committee and the Appropriations Committee. As representatives from these committees, their primary loyalties and long-term interests are likely to remain with their original committees.[67]

In addition, the House Budget Committee has been continually tested by internal ideological and partisan pressures. Budget Committee members have not been at all reticent about taking battles that were lost in committee to the House floor. Indeed, floor opposition to the budget resolutions has frequently been led by Republicans, outraged over large deficits and too much spending, and Democratic liberals, equally outraged over too little spending for social programs and jobs, serving on the Budget Committee. Members of the Senate Budget Committee, on the other hand, have protected and supported their committee on the floor. While there have been divisions in the Committee over deficits and program priorities, the members have closed ranks once a budget resolution was reported. A key element in this has been the support that Muskie has received from the ranking minority member, Senator Bellmon, who has been emphatic about holding the Committee together and protecting the budget process.

As a result, the Senate Budget Committee has not faced serious problems in gaining Senate passage of its resolutions. The House Committee, however, has had difficulty in reporting out resolutions as well as in passing them. Its difficulties have not disappeared. In voting on the first budget resolution for FY 1978 (which the House finally passed by 221–177), four Democratic liberals and six Republicans from the Budget Committee voted against the resolution that their Committee had developed in conference with the Senate. While Republican backing for the resolution was higher than in past years, the overwhelming majority of Republicans voted against it (107–29). By way of contrast, the Senate adopted the resolution by 54–23, with a majority of Democrats and a majority of Republicans supporting passage. In September, the House Budget Committee again encountered difficulties, as its proposed second budget resolution was passed by a narrow 199–188 margin, and only after several floor amendments were adopted to increase spending.

The budget process, then, appears to be more firmly entrenched in the Senate than in the House. The Senate Budget Committee has managed to develop internal agreement over its role, and it has been active and influential throughout the budgetary process. The House Committee has not achieved a comparable level of internal agreement, and its members are not committed to protecting the Committee or insuring the survival of the budget process, which may reflect more serious problems in the House's approach to the budget process. Pressures for increased spending have been considerably more intense in the House than in the Senate, as reflected in the higher outlay levels in House versions of budget resolutions. In the final budget resolution for FY 1977, for example, the Senate adopted an outlay ceiling more than $5 billion lower than that of the House; the outlay target for FY 1978 was again more than $5 billion lower on the Senate side. Moreover, the conference versions adopted in each instance have been much closer to the Senate figure, although this has been due in part to technical disputes over estimates rather than policy differences. Nevertheless, the Senate has been generally successful in defending lower spending and smaller deficits. This pattern not only reflects a reversal in the traditional House and Senate approaches to spending but also limits the House's incentive to support the budget process, a major objective of which is to limit spending increases and reduce deficits. As traditional guardian of the Treasury, originator of spending legislation, and supporter of an independent and powerful Appropriations Committee, the House could effectively contest the Senate on money matters and preserve the essential element in its power and influence. The budget process now provides the Senate with a major benefit in its emphasis on fiscal policy. The House derives no advantage from its detailed study of budget requests when the debate is over budget totals or aggregates. Nor do budget resolutions originate in the House, which removes the advantages accruing from initiative. But most important, the House cannot expect to abandon its role of guardianship and at the same time convince its members to maintain a process that is predicated on guardianship. The new process, then, probably provides the Senate with greater influence over budget decisions than it had previously, while the House has thus far not been able to develop widespread agreement about its budgetary role.

Impoundment

One of the primary objectives of the 1974 budget reform was to place congressional controls over executive spending discretion. Under the procedures established by Title X, Congress can block presidential attempts to delay or cancel spending. During the Ford administration's tenure, Congress repeatedly rejected rescission and deferral requests when the President attempted either to eliminate spending appropriated in excess of his budget requests or to effect major policy changes. Congress was, however, willing to ratify routine impoundments.[68]

At the same time, questions have been raised about other effects of Title X. The House and Senate, for example, have disagreed over whether Title X creates new withholding authority. The House has maintained that the President can propose deferrals for policy reasons as well as for purely managerial reasons, while the Senate has argued that withholding for policy reasons is not allowed. The House position has been upheld by the Comptroller General, who is charged with overseeing the implementation of the impoundment control provisions. There has also been criticism that the rescission procedures allow the President to withhold spending for 45 days without congressional assent and that this represents a new and undesirable form of executive spending discretion. On the other side, some executive officials have argued that Title X will inevitably destroy presidential budget control over executive agencies, since these agencies can be protected by congressional committees who support their spending. According to this interpretation, Congress has no incentive to limit spending after it has appropriated funds, while the President is heavily dependent on spending discretion for administrative control. There is, however, one point that elicits widespread agreement. Since Title X requires that the executive report all impoundments, regardless of purpose or amount, the volume of paperwork that has resulted has been enormous and largely unnecessary, and has consumed valuable staff time in both branches.

Title X has had a significant effect, then, on executive-congressional relations. As originally conceived, Title X was aimed at placing congressional checks on presidential spending discretion and was a direct response to the acrimony surrounding the Nixon impoundments. While President Ford continually disagreed with Congress over spending, this type of hostility did not recur, and Congress was able to deal in a reasonably orderly fashion with a massive number of impoundment requests. It should be noted, however, that Title X provides a unique opportunity for the President and Congress jointly to monitor and reconsider spending decisions. This would allow spending to be adjusted as economic conditions or programmatic requirements change. It will also force Congress to deal more rigorously than it has in the past with the implementation of its spending decisions.

Summary

Congress has traditionally found it difficult to exercise the power of the purse effectively. During the past several decades this difficulty has been magnified by the growing influence of the executive over budget decision making. Thus, many efforts at reforming the congressional budget system have been aimed at redressing a perceived imbalance in executive-congressional relations. The 1974 revision of the budget system is no exception.

A second source of difficulty, however, has been internal. What is meant by effective exercise of the power of the purse is not necessarily a matter of agreement between the House and Senate or among the appropriations, revenue, and authorizing committees in each chamber. Just as the power of the purse is a source of institutional power in executive-congressional clashes, pieces of that power are sources of individual and committee influence in Congress. Thus, a workable budget system in Congress must provide benefits for individual members as well as promote the collective benefit of a "more effective Congress."

The 1974 Congressional Budget and Impoundment Control Act is an unusually far-reaching attempt to resolve these difficulties, and it might be helpful to offer some tentative assessments of its effects. First, the new budget process provides Congress with the mechanism to act on fiscal policy and to challenge executive dominance in economic management. Second, Congress can use the budgetary process to make priority choices by considering spending decisions in relation to each other. The budget resolutions therefore also make it possible for Congress to specify how its priorities differ from those of the President. Third, Congress has developed budgetary staff and information resources that reduce considerably its reliance on the executive for budget data and analysis. Fourth, the impoundment control provisions of the 1974 legislation establish clear congressional checks on the President's discretionary spending authority. Thus, where the objectives of budget reform relate directly to congressional versus executive influence over budget decision making, Congress' institutional authority has been enhanced.

The accomplishment of other major objectives appears less certain. The provisions affecting backdoor spending and entitlements are relatively weak and do not place these and other forms of uncontrollable spending under strict, centralized control. There is also some question about Congress' willingness to use the budget system to curtail overall spending increases and deficits. This is especially true in the House, where pressures for increased spending pose a potential threat to the budget process. If President Carter does attempt to achieve a balanced budget by the end of his first term, congressional spending pressures can no longer be absorbed by planned deficits, and Congress will be faced with much more difficult either/or choices on policy than it has faced thus far. Based on its recent approach to budget decision making, the Senate appears more likely than the House to achieve the necessary fiscal discipline to make such decisions. The House has not been able to establish a clear role for its Budget Committee, nor has it really decided what its own role should now be in budget decision making. Thus, the potential for breakdown of the budget process in the House does exist, and it will tend to increase if either the President or Senate (or both) exerts serious pressure on the House to limit spending increases.

The budget process, then, still faces serious challenges in Congress. While Congress has been strengthened institutionally with respect to the President, it has also received increased responsibility. Congress has in effect stipulated that it has the discipline and judgment to deal with fiscal matters in a coherent and comprehensive fashion. The budget reform was in large part a response to presidential attacks that Congress was incapable or unwilling to act responsibly to control spending. Unless Congress shows that it is willing to contain the spending pressures of its members in exchange for its new influence over fiscal policy and program priorities, these criticisms will reemerge. Congress will thus run the risk of losing its new authority—and much of its power over spending—to a President whom the public regards as better able to guard the Treasury.

Notes

1. Richard F. Fenno, Jr., *The Power of the Purse: Appropriations Politics in Congress* (Boston: Little, Brown, 1966), p. xiii.
2. Ibid., pp. 43–44.
3. For a balanced discussion of these efforts and their possibilities for success, see Richard E. Neustadt, *Presidential Power: The Politics of Leadership with Reflections on Johnson and Nixon* (New York: Wiley, 1976), pp. 1–68. On the budget reforms, Neustadt (p. 66) states, "At least it can be said that in the budget process Congress has reached for a tool which—if it musters leadership to handle—does create a sort of parity with any President, across the board of governmental programs. . . . Of all details to watch with care in the years just ahead, none will convey more portents for the future than details of organization and procedure, whether strengthening or weakening, in the first few congressional budgets.
4. In *Pollock* v. *Farmer's Loan and Trust Co.*, 158 U.S. 601 (1895), the Court held that a 2 percent tax on incomes over $4000 was a "direct tax" that had to be apportioned among the states according to population (under Article I, Section 2, paragraph 3). This apportionment restriction was removed from income taxes by the Sixteenth Amendment.
5. During the first half of the nineteenth century, most federal receipts were generated by customs duties. After the Civil War, customs duties and excise taxes provided most federal revenue. Since the adoption of the income tax, however, the proportion of federal revenues generated by these sources has declined steadily. It should also be noted that beginning in the 1930s, Congress has delegated considerable authority over tariffs to the President.
6. See John F. Manley, *The Politics of Finance: The House Committee on Ways and Means* (Boston: Little, Brown, 1970).
7. Ibid. See also Richard F. Fenno, Jr., *Congressmen in Committees* (Boston: Little, Brown, 1973), especially chap. 3.
8. This joint committee was established in 1926. It includes ten members from the Ways and Means and Finance Committees. There are certain legal responsibilities that this committee has, but the most important aspect is its professional staff, which serves as the revenue staff of Congress and provides the necessary technical expertise in writing tax legislation.
9. From 1953 through 1964, the Committee won 94 percent of the roll calls on which its decisions were tested. As Fenno notes, "The Committee probably has the highest percentage of passed-and-unamended bills of all

the committees in the Congress." *Congressmen in Committees,* p. 203. See also Manley, *Politics of Finance,* chap. 5.

10. Manley, *Politics of Finance,* p. 100.

11. Fenno, *Congressmen in Committees,* especially pp. 202–212.

12. Manley, *Politics of Finance,* p. 379.

13. "Ways and Means in 1975: No Longer Pre-Eminent," *Congressional Quarterly Weekly Report, 34,* no. 2 (January 10, 1976), 40.

14. The Ways and Means Committee did lose jurisdiction over revenue-sharing and export control legislation, but it retained control over tax, welfare, trade, Social Security, unemployment, and health legislation.

15. "Ways and Means in 1975," pp. 40–44.

16. The loss of the closed rule, or at least its diminished use, might prove to be a major blow against Ways and Means' ability "to put a damper on particularism in tax and tariff matters and to protect what members call the 'actuarial soundness' of the social security program." According to this interpretation, Ways and Means serves as a "control committee" for the House, insulating it from demands and pressures that members would otherwise find difficult to resist. In return for their contributions toward this institutional maintenance, members of the Committee are accorded prestige and influence in the House. David H. Mayhew, *Congress: The Electoral Connection* (New Haven, Conn.: Yale University Press, 1974), pp. 154–156.

17. Fenno, *Congressmen in Committees,* pp. 181–187.

18. Ibid. See also Manley, *Politics of Finance,* chap. 6.

19. *Congressional Quarterly's Guide to the Congress of the United States: Origins, History and Procedure* (Washington, D.C.: Congressional Quarterly, 1971), p. 182.

20. Ibid., p. 183.

21. *Congressional Quarterly Weekly Report, 32,* no. 36 (September 7, 1974), 2433.

22. See Manley, *Politics of Finance,* pp. 269–294.

23. Ibid. In 1975 the Senate did unusually well in conferences on tax and energy legislation, and the Senate Finance chairman, Russell Long, was able to dominate the bargaining. This perhaps reflected the weakened status of Ways and Means and the less forceful leadership style of Representative Al Ullman, the successor to Wilbur Mills as chairman of Ways and Means. *Congressional Quarterly Weekly Report, 34,* no. 2 (January 10, 1976), 40–44.

24. Fenno, *Power of the Purse,* p. 450.

25. Fenno, *Congressmen in Committees,* pp. 193–202.

26. Fenno, *Power of the Purse,* p. xv.

27. See Lawrence C. Dodd and Bruce I. Oppenheimer, "The House in Transition," in *Congress Reconsidered,* ed. Lawrence C. Dodd and Bruce I. Oppenheimer (New York: Praeger, 1977), pp. 21–53.

28. *Congressional Quarterly Weekly Report, 33,* no. 18 (May 3, 1975), 912.

29. This was limited by the 1977 Senate reorganization (S. Res. 4), passed February 4, 1977, which restricted each Senator to service on two major

committees and one minor committee. The Appropriations Committee was established as a major committee under this plan, but it was exempted from the provision that each Senator could serve on no more than three subcommittees of a major committee. The reorganization plan's limits on the committee and subcommittee memberships for each Senator eliminated also the practice of having members of legislative committees sit as ex officio members of the counterpart Appropriations subcommittee. See *Congressional Quarterly Weekly Report, 35,* no. 7 (February 12, 1977), 279–285. Prior to this change, about one-half of the Senate participated directly in the work of the Appropriations Committee, since three ex officio members were allowed for eight legislative committees. See Fenno, *Congressmen in Committees,* p. 149.

30. Fenno, *Congressmen in Committees,* pp. 146–149.

31. Ibid., pp. 154–155.

32. Fenno, *Power of the Purse,* p. 562.

33. Ibid., p. 597. However, one study of the Senate Appropriations Committee suggests that the Committee does not fully utilize its potential effectiveness in the Senate or in Congress generally. See Stephen Horn, *Unused Power: The Work of the Senate Committee on Appropriations* (Washington, D.C.: Brookings Institution, 1970). Horn argues that for most Senators on the Committee, the power of the purse is attractive primarily for its utility in serving their states rather than for more generalized policy control.

34. Fenno, *Power of the Purse,* p. 666.

35. According to Horn, however, Senate success in conference is often exaggerated by focusing simply on the dollar amounts in the final bill as compared with the original House and Senate versions. *Unused Power,* p. 213.

36. Fenno, *Power of the Purse,* p. 663. He states that *"dominance in the conference committee must never be confused with dominance in the appropriations process as a whole."* (Italics in original.)

37. Ibid., pp. 33–39.

38. Louis Fisher, *Budget Concepts and Terminology: The Appropriations Phase* (Washington, D.C.: Congressional Research Service, November 21, 1974), p. 22.

39. *Congressional Quarterly's Guide to the Congress,* p. 188. However, these limits apply only to the amount of annual payments, not to the total payments made over the life of a contract, which may run 40 or 60 years. See Fisher, *Budget Concepts and Terminology,* p. 24.

40. Fisher, *Budget Concepts and Terminology,* p. 25.

41. Comptroller General of the United States, *Report to the Congress, Observations on the Food Stamp Program* (Washington, D.C.: General Accounting Office, February 28, 1975), pp. 1–3.

42. Ralph K. Huitt, "Research Study Seven, Congressional Organization and Operations in the Field of Money and Credit," in Commission on Money and Credit, *Fiscal and Debt Management Policies* (Englewood Cliffs, N.J.: Prentice-Hall, 1963), p. 441.

43. See James P. Pfiffner, "Congressional Budget Reform, 1974: Initiative and Reaction" (paper presented at the 1975 annual meeting of the American Political Science Association, San Francisco, September 2–5, 1975), pp. 6–7.

44. On this last point, see Fenno, *Power of the Purse,* p. 122.

45. Pfiffner, "Congressional Budget Reform," pp. 7–8.

46. *Congressional Quarterly's Guide to the Congress,* p. 21.

47. The administration first requested that Congress allow it to cut spending in order to hold the ceiling. The House voted to allow this, but the Senate would not agree to do so without restrictions on the size of the cuts and the programs affected. The conference committee was unable to reach agreement, and the authority was subsequently withheld. Louis Fisher, "Congress, the Executive and the Budget," *Annals of the American Academy of Political and Social Sciences, 411* (January 1974), 104.

48. Ibid., p. 113.

49. The Congressional Budget and Impoundment Control Act passed the Senate by 75–0, and the House by 401–6.

50. For an informative discussion of these problems and the different ways in which they were perceived, see John W. Ellwood and James A. Thurber, "The New Congressional Budget Process: The Hows and Whys of House-Senate Differences," in *Congress Reconsidered,* ed. Lawrence C. Dodd and Bruce I. Oppenheimer (New York: Praeger, 1977), pp. 164–169.

51. Ibid.

52. In December 1976 the Democratic caucus changed the selection process for Budget Committee members. Previously the chairmen of the Ways and Means and Appropriations Committees had each nominated three members for designated seats on the Budget Committee (the other two designated seats for each committee were allocated to the Republican party). Under the revised rules, this responsibility was vested in the Democratic Steering and Policy Committee, which serves as the Democrats' committee on committees. This allowed the Budget Committee to be set up several weeks earlier than in the past. In addition, the Democratic Steering and Policy Committee does not nominate a chairman. Any member of the Budget Committee can seek it, with the choice being made by the Democratic caucus.

53. The CBO staff is under a director appointed for a four-year term by the Speaker of the House and president pro tem of the Senate upon recommendation of the Budget Committees. The first appointee was Alice M. Rivlin, an economist and senior fellow at the Brookings Institution, who had also served as an assistant secretary in the Department of Health, Education and Welfare during the Johnson administration. As originally set up, the CBO had budget analysis, tax policy analysis, and fiscal policy analysis sections, along with program divisions covering broad policy areas. As of early 1976, the program divisions included natural resources and commerce, human resources and community development, and national security and international affairs. In addition, a section was established on management programs.

54. These include categories such as national defense, international affairs, agriculture, and commerce and transportation. See Table 1.1 for presidential recommendations and congressional targets in these functional categories for the fiscal 1978 budget.

55. This deadline does not apply to social security and other entitlement programs.

56. It did so in the spring of 1977, when the new Carter administration requested an economic stimulus package with spending increases and tax reductions for the fiscal 1977 budget, which had gone into effect the previous October.

57. Because of certain technical problems, outlay totals by function were not part of the actual budget resolutions during the first year, but they were included in the reports accompanying the resolutions.

58. *Congressional Quarterly Weekly Report, 35,* no. 18 (April 30, 1977), 775–777.

59. See Ellwood and Thurber, "New Congressional Budget Process," p. 175.

60. Ibid., pp. 177–178.

61. *Congressional Quarterly Almanac, Vol. XXXII, 1976* (Washington, D.C.: Congressional Quarterly Service, 1977), pp. 51–52; see also Ellwood and Thurber, "New Congressional Budget Process," pp. 179–180.

62. *Congressional Quarterly Weekly Report, 35,* no. 19 (May 7, 1977), 843–844.

63. *Congressional Quarterly Almanac, Vol. XXXI, 1975* (Washington, D.C.: Congressional Quarterly Service, 1976), pp. 919–920.

64. Ibid., p. 919.

65. Ellwood and Thurber, "New Congressional Budget Process," pp. 178, 181–182.

66. Ibid., p. 184.

67. Ibid.

68. See Allen Schick, *The First Years of the Congressional Budget Process* (Washington, D.C.: Congressional Research Service, June 30, 1976), pp. 30–38.

Four

Budget Implementation: Execution and Review

After the President has prepared and submitted his budget estimates and recommendations and final action has been completed on authorization and appropriations legislation, there remains the actual obligation and expenditure of funds (budget execution). This part of the budgetary process is not always automatic or predictable. Sometimes the problems encountered during budget execution are simply the result of unanticipated changes in economic conditions or other circumstances that affect program spending. On occasion, however, executive officials have attempted to alter the budgetary decisions and priorities contained in spending legislation by refusing to spend appropriated funds or by using such funds for purposes other than those which Congress had intended. One of the persistent tensions affecting budget execution has been, therefore, a lack of agreement about the appropriate degree of executive spending discretion on the one hand and the form and extent of congressional checks on the other.

An interesting illustration of the conflict that sometimes arises over budget execution developed during the fall of 1976. In hearings before the House Budget Committee on November 22 and 23, administration witnesses testified that the government had spent less than predicted during FY 1976 and the three-month transition quarter from July 1 through September 30. The shortfall was then estimated at between $10 and $20 billion, although final figures showed the actual shortfall to be considerably less than $10 billion. The reasons for lowered spending were not entirely clear, although it was suggested that changes in economic conditions and uncontrollable factors, delays in obligating funds, and reduced grant spending by state and local governments had contributed. While the 1976 shortfall was neither exceptionally large nor unprecedented, there was considerable apprehension among Budget Committee members that the underspending had been a deliberate attempt by the Ford administration to lessen the economic stimulus that Congress had incorporated in the budget. Actually, the shortfall resulted from mundane errors in estimating inflation and expenditures, and it heavily affected defense spending, an area in which the Ford administration recommended even higher spending than that approved by Congress.[1]

While the budget execution problems encountered during 1976 were not unusual, they were highlighted by an increased congressional sensitivity concerning budget control. In this instance, the issue was economic management—the possible frustration of congressional fiscal policy decisions by the executive. In previous years other conflicts had arisen over spending for specific programs and agencies, which usually involved discretionary spending tools—such as impoundment, reprogramming, and transfers—that had been utilized by the executive branch to alter spending decisions made by Congress. In some cases, these tools were accepted as necessary components of administrative flexibility and discretion. In other instances, most frequently during the Nixon administration, there were charges by members of Congress that the executive branch was using its control over budget execution deliberately to frustrate congressional policies and spending decisions. There has been, then, continuing tension over the relative degree of presidential and congressional influence relating to budget execution, and Congress has moved in recent years to strengthen its authority.

A second aspect of budget implementation is the process of review, audit, and evaluation, designed to assure not only that funds have been spent in accordance with law but also that spending is economical and efficient and that programs are effective. Much of this is an internal process within the executive branch, involving the individual agencies and the Office of Management and Budget (OMB). In addition,

Congress is responsible for exercising oversight through its committees and through the review and audit functions of the General Accounting Office (GAO). Here, too, Congress has been attempting to exercise its oversight responsibilities more aggressively and thus to strengthen its power of the purse.

Budget implementation, then, is still another stage for presidential and congressional attempts at budget control. In this chapter the activities and responsibilities of executive and congressional participants regarding budget implementation will be examined, along with some of the more recent major developments affecting the discretionary authority of executive branch officials in budget execution, particularly with respect to impoundments, reprogramming, and transfers.

Budget Execution in the Executive Branch

The formal procedure for budget execution within an agency begins after the appropriation bill for that agency has become law. The Department of the Treasury and the GAO provide the agency with an appropriation warrant, which becomes the basis for the agency's operating budget for the coming fiscal year. If the appropriation bill differs from the original agency budget recommended by the President, it is necessary at this point for the agency to revise its original budget accordingly. One of the major benefits of the new congressional budgetary process is the emphasis on passing all appropriations bills prior to the beginning of the new fiscal year. This will eliminate or at least reduce the difficulties that agencies have faced in the past in revising operating budgets well into the fiscal year.

The next step is for the OMB to apportion budget authority and other budgetary resources to the agency. This apportionment is usually on a quarterly basis, although it can also be based on specific activities or programs that the agency administers. The agency is then limited in incurring obligations to the amounts specified for the time period or activity. The authority to apportion funds is actually delegated by the President to the director of the OMB, and one of its major objectives is to insure control of the rate of commitment of budget authority and thus to limit the need for additional or supplemental budget requests by the agency during the fiscal year. Moreover, the OMB can reserve funds from obligation in order to provide for contingencies or when changes in requirements or greater efficiency in operations subsequent to enactment of the appropriation bill allow savings to be effected.

Once an agency has received its apportionment, allotments are made to its bureaus and divisions. These allotments are for a specific time period and are an internal mechanism for controlling spending. During budget execution, the agency has the administrative responsibility for insuring that its obligation of funds does not exceed its apportionment, and it is required to report periodically to the OMB on its spending activities. It is at this stage of the budgetary process, then, that funds are actually spent or obligated for the goods and services needed by the agency. Most agencies, however, cannot issue checks directly to pay for these goods and services. Vouchers and invoices specifying payment are therefore prepared, certified by the OMB, and sent to the Treasury, which actually issues the checks to pay the agencies' bills.

Throughout this process, there are reviews of financial management and operations as well as program performance and effectiveness within an agency. Each agency has an internal review and control system to assure that obligations and outlays conform to the provisions of authorization and appropriation legislation and to other laws and regulations governing the obligation and expenditure of funds. In addition, the OMB periodically reviews agency programs and financial reports and monitors the attainment of program objectives.

The formal procedure for budget execution, then, is relatively straightforward. In practice, however, there is often room for executive discretion in determining whether appropriated funds will be spent and in specifying the actual purposes for which these funds will be spent. Such discretion can sometimes be used to alter the programs and priorities established by Congress. To the extent that the President and other executive officials attempt to achieve through budget execution what they were unable to achieve during the authorization and appropriation stage, the congressional power of the purse will be continually challenged.[2] Budget execution is an executive process, and there are justifiable reasons why actual obligations and outlays sometimes differ from appropriations. But the central question is whether executive officials will exercise discretion and judgment to promote or to frustrate the policy goals that have been established by law.

Within the executive branch, control of budget execution has been centralized, primarily in the OMB. Because OMB is active throughout the budgetary process—from the initial decisions on budgetary guidelines to the monitoring and evaluation of actual spending and performance—it provides the President with an effective mechanism for achieving spending and policy priorities. In many instances, however, administration goals and congressional goals have differed greatly. While the congressional approach to budget execution and implementation is less centralized, Congress has moved to strengthen its control over what happens after the budget has been approved. Congress does not execute the budget, but it can supervise budget execution to insure that its spending decisions are carried out. Moreover, it can also review ongoing programs to increase effectiveness and promote savings.

The Budget and Congressional Oversight

Congressional review of budget implementation is part of the broad process of congressional oversight or supervision of the activities of executive agencies and the operation of federal programs. Under the 1970 Legislative Reorganization Act, each standing committee of Congress is directed to "review and study, on a continuing basis, the application, administration, and execution of those laws, or parts of laws, the subject matter of which is within the jurisdiction of that committee."[3] As far as budget implementation is concerned, this responsibility is exercised directly by the Appropriations subcommittees and the authorizing committees for each agency. Further, the government operations committees of the House and Senate have jurisdiction over budget-related matters such as federal spending practices and efficiency, and accounting and management practices.

General Accounting Office

To assist its committees in conducting their oversight functions, Congress has periodically expanded the authority of the GAO to audit, review, and evaluate executive agency operations and to conduct cost benefit studies of government programs. The GAO was established in 1921 under the Budget and Accounting Act. Auditing and accounting functions that had previously been assigned to officers and divisions within the Department of the Treasury were transferred to the GAO.

Heading the GAO are the Comptroller General of the United States and the Assistant Comptroller General. These officers are nominated by the President for 15-year terms and must be confirmed by the Senate. They are removable, moreover, only by a joint resolution of Congress, and Congress has traditionally considered the GAO to be its agency.[4]

The initial function of the GAO was to review and audit expenditures to insure that they conformed to law. Over the years, however, the auditing of the operations and accounts of executive agencies has been broadened to allow the GAO to examine the efficiency of expenditures, evaluate program performance and effectiveness, and conduct investigations for and issue reports to Congress. The 1974 Congressional Budget and Impoundment Control Act directed the GAO to assist congressional committees in program evaluation and in developing statements of legislative objectives, and authorized the establishment within the GAO of an Office of Program Review and Evaluation. The law also provided the Comptroller General with authority to determine when the President had failed to comply with its impoundment control provisions and to bring suit to compel the release of improperly impounded funds.

The GAO has a staff of approximately 5100; its 1976 budget was almost $135 million. With some limited exceptions, such as the Internal Revenue Service and the Federal Reserve System, "the auditing authority of the GAO extends to all activities, financial transactions, and accounts of the Federal Government."[5] When the GAO issues a report containing recommendations regarding financial operations, management, or program performance to the head of any federal agency, the agency is required, under the 1970 Legislative Reorganization Act, to submit written reports to the House and Senate Appropriations Committees and government operations committees informing them of the actions taken in response to these recommendations.

The expanded role of the GAO reflects the necessary connections between oversight and the authorization and appropriation process. As the Comptroller General, Elmer B. Staats, stated in testimony before the House Select Committee on Committees in 1973, the primary objective of the GAO is "to recommend ways of making both proposed and ongoing federal programs work better and to make the results of our studies known before legislative decisions are reached."[6] While much of GAO's workload still consists of providing the Appropriations

Committees with audit information to be used in evaluating executive agency budget requests, it has become increasingly active in providing direct assistance to other standing committees. The GAO issues hundreds of reports each year—in 1975, for example, 1177 reports on audits or special studies were completed.[7] These reports often contain recommendations for legislation to increase economy and efficiency in public expenditures. Many of the reports are narrow and technical, and it is not always possible to measure precisely the savings that would result if GAO recommendations were followed. In its 1975 report, for example, the GAO estimated that savings primarily attributable to its work amounted to $503 million. It also noted, however, that many of its recommendations were aimed at increasing the effectiveness of federal programs rather than in accomplishing measurable savings, and that this focus on effectiveness was in some respects more important than actual savings.[8]

The audit work performed by the GAO usually consists of three phases. The first phase is a plan or survey of working information to be obtained and analyzed about the agency or program involved. This survey serves to identify areas that deserve greater scrutiny. A review stage is then conducted to provide detailed information about these areas. The final stage is the report that transmits the results of GAO's examinations and its recommendations for changes.

As indicated above, Congress does sometimes respond favorably to GAO recommendations, and resulting improvements in effectiveness or in savings are significant. Changes, however, are not always easy, even when the case seems unexceptionable. In its summary of recommendations for legislative action that were open at the end of 1976—that is, on which Congress had not yet acted favorably—the GAO included a 1972 recommendation to the Appropriations Committees and Agriculture Committees to change a minor provision of the Soil Conservation and Domestic Allotment Act. This provision, which was a 1938 amendment, required that farmers receiving cost shares of less than $200 per year for conservation practices be paid an additional nominal amount. The intent of this amendment was to provide additional assistance to small farms. By 1972 this program was costing about $7 million and the payments were truly nominal—ranging from $0.40 to $14.00 each. The GAO found that the payments did not further the objectives of the conservation program, that they were an administrative burden, and that the funds involved could be used to increase participation in

the program by thousands more farmers, thus providing greater conservation benefits.[9] Congress did not agree, however, to this recommendation, and at the end of 1976 it was still pending, along with
more than 100 other GAO recommendations for legislative action.

Oversight and Budget Execution

Through the "scorekeeping reports" issued by the Congressional
Budget Office, Congress is continually apprised of its actions regarding
budget requests; of course, the new budgetary system requires that
Congress reconcile its individual spending decisions with overall
spending ceilings. What has not been developed, however, is a parallel
procedure to inform Congress about the actions taken on money that it
appropriates. As Louis Fisher, a budget analyst in the Congressional
Research Service, has stated, information on budget execution is plen-
tiful but its utilization is often poor.

> Much of the material is already available. Hundreds of valuable
> agency reports are sent to Congress and parcelled out to commit-
> tees and subcommittees. The only public notice is a seldom read
> section in the Congressional Record called "Executive Communi-
> cations," which lists agency reports on transfers, deficiencies,
> contract modifications, use of contingency funds, etc. GAO re-
> ports are summarized in the Record each month. Still other
> studies are published by the committees, the Congressional Re-
> search Service, and private organizations. What is lacking is a
> central legislative body . . . to compile this information, analyze
> it, and present the results to all Members of Congress. . . . The
> structure and content of CBO reports would be sharpened by
> regular hearings on budget execution by the Budget Committees,
> the Appropriations Committees, the Government Operations
> Committees, and other committees devoted to oversight ques-
> tions.[10]

In the past, congressional oversight of budget implementation, like
congressional oversight of other executive agency activities, has been
neither systematic nor comprehensive. This has resulted from several
factors. First, members of Congress are unlikely to exercise energetic
oversight over agency activities and programs about which there are
high levels of satisfaction and agreement. Just as Congress' review of

the budget tends to be highly selective and not comprehensive, its attention to budget implementation has also tended to focus primarily on those areas where there are policy disagreements or where legislators perceive challenges to their individual or committee prerogatives. Second, the relationship between congressional oversight committees and administrative agencies is more frequently characterized by cooperation than by conflict.[11] Members of Congress often find that they can exert considerable influence over public policy by developing stable and compatible working relationships with agency personnel. Indeed, some major domestic policy areas are dominated by a cooperative arrangement that also extends outside the government to clientele and interest groups.[12] When ideological and personal conflict is low, there is little motivation for continued oversight of budget execution or other agency activities. Third, responsibility for oversight is, as noted above, diffused among a number of congressional committees. Members of each committee have considerable latitude in determining the extent and focus of oversight activities, and the result has usually been sporadic activity and high selectivity.

These and related factors mitigate against any wholesale changes in oversight activity. In recent years, however, there has been evidence of at least modest changes in the congressional attitude toward oversight activities. Broadened requirements for oversight activities, expanded staff and information resources, and specific controls on the discretionary authority of agencies and executive officials have been implemented. On the budgetary side, this has been evidenced by closer supervision of budget execution and more stringent checks on discretionary spending tools, as well as by an increased emphasis on the review and evaluation of spending programs. It is likely that much of the impetus for these changes was provided by the Nixon and Ford presidencies, as the Democratic majority in Congress sought to exert control over agencies against continual spending and program challenges by executive officials. Whether a comparable level of activity will be necessary under a Democratic President is not altogether clear, although Congress appears to have concluded that it still must jealously guard its budgetary and other prerogatives despite the change in party control of the White House. Indeed, the significance of the 1974 changes in the budgetary process depends on congressional control over actual spending. Unless Congress can enforce its spending decisions, the 1974 reforms will have a limited effect at best.

The increased attention that Congress now assigns to its spending decisions is therefore gradually being extended to budget implementation. A major part of this has thus far involved budget execution, with Congress attempting to control discretionary spending actions. In the following section, why and how this has occurred will be examined by focusing on impoundments, reprogramming, and transfers. The general point, however, is that more effective congressional supervision of budget implementation is recognized as a necessary element in Congress' utilization of the power of the purse.

Presidential Spending and Congressional Controls

The degree of discretion accorded executive officials during budget execution is, in many instances, a function of specific congressional delegation. Congress has, in the past, used a variety of means to increase discretionary authority. For example, in crisis situations and especially during wartime, Congress has often provided the executive with "lump sum" or very broadly defined appropriations, allowing executive officials to commit funds as they see fit within a specified ceiling. Over the past several decades, Congress has also reduced the number of specific appropriation items (line items) by using broader appropriations classifications.[13] While this has not meant unlimited spending discretion, it has increased budget flexibility to some extent and accorded executive officials wider latitude in the actual expenditure of funds.

Discretionary spending authority has also been evidenced by a long history of confidential and secret funding.[14] Confidential funding occurs when an appropriation is a matter of public record but the actual expenditure of funds is not. Such funding was once utilized chiefly for diplomatic and wartime expenses. By the early 1970s, it had been extended to numerous appropriations accounts, several of which (including the Special Projects Fund, which gained some notoriety during the Watergate investigations) were controlled directly by the President.[15] Secret funding, on the other hand, occurs when neither the appropriation nor the expenditure of funds is a matter of public record. Such funding was used, for example, during World War II to finance the atomic bomb project.[16] It has also been utilized for intelligence organizations, such as the CIA. The CIA budget has not been directly appropriated. Rather, CIA activities have been financed by transfers of funds from other appropriations accounts, primarily those within the Department of Defense. As a result, the CIA budget has been hidden not only from the public but also from many members of Congress.

In recent years Congress has moved to restrict the use of confidential and secret funds and to subject existing funds to greater congressional scrutiny. There has even been a move to make public the funding of the CIA and other intelligence organizations.[17] The essential point, however, is that Congress can limit or eliminate these types of budgetary practices. It can insure, as it has done with respect to the CIA, that more of its members participate in oversight activities. Congress can also provide for review and audit by the GAO to insure that confidential or secret funds are expended in accordance with legislative intent.[18]

It would be difficult and probably unwise for Congress to attempt to write authorization and appropriation legislation so detailed and specific as to eliminate all executive discretion in the expenditure of funds. There are legitimate purposes served by contingency funds to meet emergencies or unexpected expenses, and national security considerations might justify the limited use of confidential or secret funding. But it is also apparent that abuses have occurred because of both lack of good faith by executive officials in the expenditure of discretionary funds and inadequate congressional attention to how such funds are spent. Thus, it would be reasonable to expect that Congress will in the future establish more clearly the legislative intent governing the use of discretionary funds and provide the appropriate review and audit safeguards for checking that funds are spent in accordance with this intent.

A somewhat different set of issues is raised, however, by discretionary actions where legislative intent is clear. In particular, executive impoundments, reprogramming, and transfers have often been utilized in the past to challenge congressional spending decisions by cutting spending below funded levels or using funds for programs or projects that Congress has either refused to support or provided only limited support. It is worthwhile, therefore, to examine the problems that have arisen with respect to these discretionary spending tools and to analyze the congressional attempts to restrict their use.

Impoundment

The issue of spending discretion with respect to congressionally appropriated funds encompasses a variety of executive actions, but none has been as controversial or has involved such broad assertions of executive power as the practice of impoundment. In a technical sense, impoundment occurs when the executive refuses to obligate funds that have been provided by Congress. Impounded funds are then retained by the Treasury. The political significance of impoundment, however, relates to the basis of or justification for this refusal. For example, funds that are not obligated because a program can be run more economically or efficiently than anticipated do not represent a serious challenge to congressional appropriations powers. But where an administration refuses to spend funds because of policy or budgetary disagreements with Congress, the challenge is clear and direct. During the Nixon Presidency, refusals of this latter type were frequent, resulting in continuing clashes with Congress and culminating in the passage of legislation that imposed a congressional check on presidential impoundment.

Historical Development.   While extensive use of impoundment is confined to the past several decades, there are scattered nineteenth century examples. The most famous, or at least most frequently cited, was President Jefferson's refusal in 1803 to spend $50,000 appropriated by Congress for gunboats to be used on the Mississippi River. The appropriation was a response to the summary closing by France of the port of New Orleans to American trade. With the successful negotiation of the Louisiana Purchase, however, Jefferson reported to Congress that "the favorable and peaceful turn of affairs on the Mississippi rendered an immediate execution of that law unnecessary, and time was desirable in order that the institution of that branch of our forces might begin on models the most approved by experience."[19] Subsequently, funds were spent on different types of gunboats to be used elsewhere. Jefferson's message clearly indicated that changing circumstances and a more effective utilization of the appropriated funds were the bases for his "impoundment."

Another nineteenth century example involved public works projects contained in rivers and harbors appropriations bills. President Grant refused to spend funds that Congress had appropriated, arguing that the "very great necessity for economy of expenditures at this time" made it unwise to commit monies to "works of purely private or local interests in no sense national."[20] Grant subsequently blocked spending for public works projects to which he objected. A more restrictive view of presidential authority was expressed two decades later in an Attorney General's opinion which stated that the President was not required to obligate the total sum appropriated in a rivers and harbors bill if the objectives contained in the bill could be achieved with lesser amounts. This 1896 opinion foreshadowed subsequent legislation that allowed the executive to withhold funds from obligation for a period to prevent deficiencies or overspending in an agency or to effect savings where Congress had appropriated more than was necessary for a given purpose. These statutory procedures allowed for limited executive discretion with respect to spending, but they were aimed at promoting economy and efficiency, and assumed that congressional policy objectives would be carried out.

Beginning with the New Deal administration of Franklin D. Roosevelt, however, impoundments were utilized occasionally for budgetary or policy purposes. In certain cases, this was done with at least the implied consent of Congress. During the Depression, spending bills were sometimes treated as ceilings, allowing Roosevelt to impound monies that he considered unnecessary. During World War II, Roosevelt argued that his war powers provided a justification for cutting spending that was not essential to national security. The impoundments were not always acceptable to Congress—indeed, some were reversed because of adverse congressional reaction—but the assertion that these were necessary emergency measures provided at least an arguable justification and allowed Roosevelt to minimize the potential challenge to congressional prerogatives.

Post–World War II impoundments have been based on a variety of justifications. President Truman impounded $615 million that Congress had appropriated to increase the size of the Air Force, basing this on his authority as commander in chief but also noting the absence of mandatory language in the appropriations bill.[21] Impoundments were also used to cut spending for military programs during the Eisenhower administration. Funds were withheld from antiballistic missile system testing, manned bomber and submarine construction, and troop level support appropriations. The predominant use of impoundment in the defense area continued with John F. Kennedy. Against the advice of

Kennedy and his Secretary of Defense, Robert McNamara, the House Armed Services Committee added $320 million to the administration's budget request for development of a new manned bomber, the B-70. When the Committee attempted to insert language in the authorization bill to make the spending mandatory, Kennedy insisted that such language infringed on his authority as commander in chief. This position received sufficient support in Congress to force the Armed Services Committee to back down. The Kennedy episode and the defense-related impoundments of Truman and Eisenhower suggested that Congress was sensitive to the need for at least a moderate degree of executive discretion based on the President's constitutional responsibility as commander in chief.

Unlike his predecessors, Lyndon Johnson frequently employed impoundments to curtail spending for domestic programs. As Vietnam war spending created inflationary pressures, Johnson impounded funds for agriculture, conservation, education, housing, and transportation programs.[22] In most instances these actions were temporary deferrals, and funds were eventually released. Moreover, Johnson did not attempt to use impoundments to cripple or terminate programs that he opposed. Indeed, many of the programs from which funds were withheld had been sponsored by his administration. What was significant, however, was the claim that impoundment could be used on a widespread basis to combat inflation, a claim that was revived and expanded during the Nixon Presidency.

Impoundments directed by President Nixon were unprecedented in their scope and effects, with the challenges to congressional budgetary priorities especially severe in the several months following his reelection in 1972. Several agricultural programs, such as the rural environmental assistance program, the water bank program, and rural water and sewer grant programs, were terminated. When Congress passed the Federai Water Pollution Control Act Amendments of 1972 over a presidential veto, the administration impounded half of the $18 billion that had been allotted for fiscal years 1973 through 1975. Major impoundment reductions also were forced in low-rent housing construction, mass transit, food stamps, and medical research programs.[23] While administration spokesmen advanced a variety of justifications in support of these impoundments—including precedent, statutory responsibilities, and general executive authority—it was apparent that impoundment was being used to enforce the President's policy preferences and budgetary priorities. Moreover, the assertion that impoundment was necessary to check the inflationary impact of "reckless" congressional spending decisions was considerably weakened by the administration's sponsorship of major new spending programs such as general revenue sharing.[24]

The Nixon impoundments were challenged in Congress and in the courts. Congress, in addition to considering impoundment control legislation, inserted mandatory language in certain spending bills, eliminating the discretionary authority that executive officials had relied on in refusing to obligate funds. Numerous suits were instituted by state and local governments to force the release of impounded funds, and the federal courts generally decided against the administration. In a major decision following a series of cases at the district court and appeals court levels, the Supreme Court held, on February 18, 1975, that the impoundment of more than $9 billion in water pollution control funds was inconsistent with the language and intent of the 1972 Federal Water Pollution Control Act Amendments. Determining that the act required the full allotment of funds, the Court stated that it was unreasonable to argue that Congress had scuttled its "entire effort by providing the Executive with the seemingly limitless power to withhold funds from allotment and obligation."[25] Nonetheless, in this and other cases, the courts based their rulings on statutory language and did not reach the issue of the constitutionality of impoundment. Moreover, the water pollution cases dragged out for more than two years, providing the Nixon and Ford administrations with at least a partial victory in their attempt to limit congressionally directed spending. Indeed, by the time that the Supreme Court issued its ruling, Congress had already passed impoundment control legislation.

For more than four decades, Presidents had impounded funds. In most instances, the impoundments did not result in major confrontations between the executive and Congress. The language used by both sides when impoundments were contested was, until Richard Nixon, sufficiently moderate to allow compromises or at least face-saving. The Nixon administration managed to escalate the impoundment issue into a constitutional crisis, challenging directly Congress' authorization and appropriation powers. In so doing, Nixon's actions tended to obscure some important distinctions between types of impoundments, distinctions that are crucial in allowing a necessary degree of executive judgment and flexibility in budget execution.

Bases of Impoundment Authority.[26]   Not all impoundments represent threats to legislative prerogatives. Some impoundments are routine extensions of efficient management. Others are based on statutory responsibilities conferred on the President and other executive officials. Impoundments relating to national defense and foreign affairs raise questions about the President's constitutional authority in these areas. Finally, however, some impoundments are clear attempts to frustrate policy and budget decisions made by Congress. What constitutes necessary and appropriate executive spending discretion is therefore related to the particular basis of impoundment authority.

In a technical sense, impoundments occur whenever spending falls short of appropriations. It has traditionally been recognized by Congress, however, that efficient management may require the withholding of funds, either temporarily or permanently. Where economies can be effected, for example, it makes little sense to require that all appropriated funds be spent. As the House Appropriations Committee emphasized in a 1950 report, a given appropriation for a specific activity constitutes

> only a ceiling upon the amount which should be expended for that activity. The administrative officials responsible for administration of an activity for which appropriation is made bear the final burden for rendering all necessary service with the smallest amount possible within the ceiling figure fixed by Congress.[27]

If appropriations are to be regarded as permissive in this sense, it is necessary for executive officials to act in good faith. Efficiency and economy in spending are important managerial objectives, but if appropriations are to be considered as ceilings, it is essential that executive actions be consistent with congressional policy objectives. One of the unfortunate consequences of the Nixon impoundments was that Congress was forced to insert mandatory language in certain appropriations bills in order to insure that its policy objectives would be carried out. This eliminated or at least reduced the incentives for economy in budget execution.

Congress appropriates funds months and sometimes years in advance of actual expenditure, and its actions are usually predicated on a given set of circumstances or conditions. When these circumstances or conditions change, it might be unnecessary or even unwise for part or even all of an appropriation to be spent. In the case of Jefferson's temporary impoundment of the funds appropriated for gunboats, for example, there was a significant change in circumstance. With many of the recent impoundments, however, it is difficult to argue that such changes had occurred. Indeed, the extent of congressional opposition to the Nixon impoundments indicated that Congress remained convinced of the necessity for its original appropriations. Changing conditions can provide an appropriate justification for the exercise of executive discretion, but here again it is essential that the executive act in good faith and in response to the policies and priorities established by Congress.

It is also a basic executive responsibility to provide adequate administrative supervision of the expenditure of funds. Several times in recent years, federal grants to state and local governments or to private organizations have been suspended because of charges of fraud or poor administration.[28] In these and similar types of situations, executive discretion is being exercised to insure that funds are actually being spent in accordance with legislative objectives.

There are, then, a number of valid management objectives and responsibilities that might result in the temporary or permanent withholding of funds. Congress has traditionally recognized the necessity for executive discretion and judgment to insure that funds are not wasted. This type of action does not substitute the executive's programmatic preferences and priorities for those of Congress. It simply reflects the fact that an appropriate degree of administrative authority must be accorded executive officials if appropriations are to be spent economically and efficiently.

A second basis for impoundment involves statutory responsibilities. Congress has on occasion provided explicit statutory authority to allow the President to withhold funds. Under the 1964 Civil Rights Act, for example, federally financed programs were made subject to nondiscrimination requirements. Where state or local governments did not comply, the President was empowered to withhold funds. Congress has also acted to impose restrictions on the receipt of foreign assistance funds, highway funds, and various social welfare programs.[29] In these and similar cases, Congress has made the release of funds contingent on specified conditions and given the President the responsibility for insuring that these conditions are satisfied.

A different and more controversial statutory justification for executive impoundments was argued in support of the Nixon administration's impoundments. Frequently cited was a provision in the 1950 Antideficiency Act Amendments that authorized the setting aside of reserves "to provide for contingencies, or to effect savings whenever savings are made possible by or through changes in requirements, greater efficiency of operations, or other developments subsequent to the date on which such appropriation was made available."[30] According to administration spokesmen, the "other developments" clause was a broad grant of power, allowing impoundments to counter inflation and even extending to programs where the administration had proposed, but Congress had not acted on, legislation to terminate or phase out certain activities.[31] There was nothing in the legislative history of the 1950 amendments to suggest that this interpretation was valid. Indeed, a House Appropriations Committee report on the legislation had clearly noted that the authority to establish reserves was not to be construed as a justification for impoundments that would frustrate congressional policy.[32] Finally, in 1974, the dispute was resolved when the "other developments" clause was deleted from the act.

Similarly liberal interpretations of executive authority were advanced on the basis of the Full Employment Act of 1946 and the Economic Stabilization Act Amendments of 1971. While neither of these laws specifically authorized impoundments, Nixon administration officials asserted that the President had been granted a broad responsibility for economic management and that this required him to pursue actively policies that fought inflation, including, when necessary, the withholding of federal funds to reduce spending. Here again Congress reacted strongly against the administration's interpretation. In addition, the federal courts held that the discretion conferred on the President by these statutes was limited.[33]

It was also suggested that presidential impoundments were justified when government spending threatened to abridge the debt limit or when Congress voted spending ceilings. A legislatively directed spending ceiling could represent a statutory authority for impoundment, but in the 1972 controversy over the $250 billion spending limit proposed by the Nixon administration, Congress finally refused to impose such a ceiling when the House and Senate could not agree on provisions governing the exercise of impoundments. Moreover, the debt ceiling justification had been used in the past to defer spending, but prior to the Nixon Presidency, it had not been advanced as a broad authority to cut spending unilaterally. Indeed, Supreme Court Justice William Rehnquist prepared an analysis while serving as Nixon's Assistant Attorney General that argued that the debt limit could not serve such a broad purpose. He wrote that any conflict between the debt limit and existing appropriations needed to be "real and imminent" before the executive could order spending cuts.[34] Of course, the Nixon administration as well as previous administrations had usually handled this problem simply by requesting that Congress raise the debt limit.

It is possible, then, for Congress to provide the President with the statutory power to impound. Prior to the 1974 legislation governing impoundments, such authority had been explicitly conferred with respect to specific programs and appropriations. But claims that a broad and undefined impoundment authority was implied by the antideficiency, full employment, or economic stabilization laws or even by the permissive rather than mandatory language of most appropriations legislation were difficult to support. Such claims were especially weak when it was apparent that impoundments were to be employed selectively against programs that Congress supported and the President opposed.

Another area of contention concerning impoundment involves the possible constitutional basis for such actions. The defense of presidential impoundments on constitutional grounds relates to the general grant of executive powers and responsibilities to the President and to his specific authority in the areas of national defense and foreign affairs. The executive power rationale suggests that the President has a necessary discretionary authority in interpreting, implementing, and reconciling statutes. Whether an impoundment power is thus implied is a question that the courts have avoided. Even in the water pollution case decided in 1975, the Supreme Court focused on the specific legislation in deciding the issue and refused to define the circumstances, if any, in which a President might justify impoundments as a valid exercise of executive power. What is noteworthy, however, is that when faced with impoundment litigation, the courts have usually held that the appropriated funds must be obligated and spent. This suggests that there is no broad and overriding executive discretion that outweighs congressional intent as expressed in spending legislation, even when that intent is merely implied rather than explicitly stated.

As discussed previously, a number of presidential impoundments have been aimed at defense spending. As commander in chief and with the relatively broad constitutional authority granted him in the field of foreign affairs, the President's discretionary authority with regard to spending in these areas may be somewhat greater than in the case of purely domestic spending. However, Congress also has significant powers and specific responsibilities in defense and foreign policy making, and it is difficult to draw the line between valid executive discretionary acts and those that infringe directly on Congress' constitutional prerogatives. The episode involving the Kennedy administration and the B-70 bomber appropriation indicated that Congress can be sensitive to the constitutional distinctions between domestic affairs and national security affairs, but it is also apparent that this sensitivity does not extend to unlimited definitions of executive discretion. Moreover, Congress has in recent years used its legislative powers, including its authorizations and appropriations process, to limit presidential discretion in the conduct of defense and foreign affairs. This suggests that Congress may be less willing than in the past to grant any privileged status to impoundments, simply because they involve national security spending.

The most intense dispute about executive authority, however, concerns policy-based impoundment. While any impoundment action has policy implications, many impoundments are simply routine management actions, and others may be based on specific statutory authority. These examples of executive discretion do not ordinarily raise significant political or constitutional issues, but such issues do arise if impoundment is used to substitute presidential policy preferences and budgetary priorities for those that Congress has established. When, as occurred with President Nixon, Congress overrides a presidential veto of an appropriations bill and the Chief Executive still refuses to spend monies for programs covered in the bill, it is obvious that legislative powers are being challenged. Similarly, when impoundments are used to cripple or terminate programs that Congress has funded, the motives are unmistakable.

It is difficult to defend, on the basis of precedent or constitutional authority, policy-based executive impoundments. As the Rehnquist memorandum on the impoundment of education funds noted, it is "an anomalous proposition that because the executive branch was bound to execute the laws, it is free to decline to execute them."[35] Once Congress has appropriated funds, presidential impoundments that are not based on specific statutory authority or are not routine management functions amount to an item veto, and it is a peculiar construction of the Constitution that asserts that an item veto is somehow valid when spending legislation is involved.

1974 Impoundment Control Act.   The Nixon administration's impoundment actions and the broad claims of executive authority that accompanied them finally resulted in attempts by Congress to legislate controls over impoundments. In 1973 the House and Senate passed differing impoundment control bills. The House version allowed either the House or the Senate to disapprove any impoundment within 60 days after its proposal by the President. The Senate bill, on the other hand, provided that unless both houses affirmed a proposed impoundment within 60 days, funds would be released for obligation. It further provided that Congress could force the immediate release of funds at any time during the 60-day period by concurrent resolution. House and Senate conferees were unable to reconcile the differences between the two bills, and in 1974 it was agreed to incorporate impoundment control provisions into the budget reform legislation that Congress was developing. According to the House Rules Committee, this incorporation was essential to the major aim of the new budgetary process— strengthening the congressional power of the purse. A budgetary process without impoundment controls, the Committee stated, "would leave Congress in a weak and ineffective position. No matter how prudently Congress discharges its appropriations responsibility, legislative decisions have no meaning if they can be unilaterally abrogated by executive impoundments."[36]

As finally adopted, the impoundment control provisions of the 1974 Congressional Budget Act represented a compromise between the earlier House and Senate bills. Two types of impoundments are now defined—rescissions and deferrals. Rescissions are impoundment actions that cancel existing budgetary authority. For example, if the President determines that the objectives of a program or project can be achieved for less than the appropriated budget authority or that part or all of an appropriations should not be obligated for fiscal or other policy reasons, he is directed to submit to Congress a special message requesting a rescission of that budget authority. Within 45 days of receipt of this message, both houses must approve the rescission bill. A rescission bill can include several presidential actions and be approved in whole or in part. If approval is not granted, budget authority is made immediately available for obligation.

A deferral request, on the other hand, is required when the President seeks to withhold or delay the obligation of available budget authority but anticipates the need for funds in the future. Either the House or Senate can disapprove a deferral request, and no time limit is imposed on the exercise of this one-house veto. Once a deferral request is rejected, funds are to be released immediately.

Since distinctions between rescissions and deferrals are not always clear, the act also authorizes the Comptroller General to review each impoundment request and to reclassify rescissions as deferrals or deferrals as rescissions when necessary. Also, as discussed earlier, the Comptroller General is now empowered to bring suit in the federal courts if the President does not comply with the impoundment control provisions.

Implementation of the new law encountered some immediate difficulties. Major disputes arose concerning which congressional committees had jurisdiction over rescission and deferral requests and the extent to which the law created any new impoundment authority for the President. The issue of committee jurisdiction was finally resolved by granting the Appropriations Committees the broadest jurisdiction while reserving more limited review to the Budget Committees and other standing committees. The more important question, however, was the extent of the President's authority under the new legislation, particularly with regard to the use of impoundments for fiscal or other policy reasons. House and Senate spokesmen disagreed on this, and finally the Comptroller General issued an opinion on December 4, 1974, which concluded that impoundment control provisions did confer additional authority on the President to justify impoundment requests on the basis of fiscal or other policy considerations. This interpretation, which has not been successfully challenged, was used by the Ford administration as the basis for an unprecedented number of policy impoundments.[37]

Congress reacted to the Ford actions by refusing to approve most rescissions and by rejecting a significant number of deferral requests as well. During fiscal years 1975 and 1976, for example, Congress enacted rescission bills totaling approximately $530 million, while administration rescission proposals amounted to over $7.5 billion.[38] On the deferral side, many deferrals were not challenged, since they involved routine financial transactions. But 20 percent of the fiscal 1975 deferrals and 30 percent of those in FY 1976 resulted in the introduction of resolutions to disapprove, and Congress disapproved 38 deferrals amounting to almost $10 billion over the period.[39]

The congressional response to rescission proposals and deferrals was especially negative in the case of policy impoundments. When the President attempted to cut spending appropriated in excess of his budget requests, Congress generally enforced its initial spending decision.[40] But routine or statutorily authorized actions, which usually involved relatively small sums compared with the policy impoundments, did not represent a challenge to congressional budget priorities and were generally acceptable to Congress.

The Carter administration has also managed to raise a controversy over impoundment by attempting to end funding for certain water resources development projects. In his February 1977 revisions of the Ford administration budget for FY 1978, the President announced the elimination of water project funding amounting to almost $300 million in budget authority for FY 1978, with potential savings over future years amounting to over $5 billion. While no rescissions or deferrals were specifically proposed for fiscal 1977 spending, Congress was subsequently informed that over 300 additional projects would be reviewed by April 15 and that no future construction contracts would be awarded in cases where the administration decided to recommend that projects be deauthorized (or eliminated). Thus, contracting would end before Congress actually deauthorized a project. According to some members of Congress, this amounted to a policy impoundment, even though Carter spokesmen took great pains to distinguish the two. If there was any confusion about congressional sentiment, it was largely dispelled when the Senate, on March 10, approved by a vote of 65–24 an amendment to a public works employment bill that specifically disapproved any attempt to hold back spending for the water projects during the current fiscal year and stated in advance Congress' intention to oppose any rescission proposal or deferral during FY 1978. The floor debates on the amendment were reminiscent of some of the angrier confrontations of the Nixon years, with various Senators expressing their outrage over presidential attempts to frustrate established policy decisions.[41] When the administration announced the results of its review in April, however, attention shifted to the fiscal 1978 budget recommendations for the challenged projects, and the controversy was somewhat muted since most major projects were recommended for continuation or slight modification.

The fact that some impoundment proposals have resulted in serious conflict between Congress and the President should not obscure the more important point—that impoundment is no longer an executive weapon that can be used unilaterally to eliminate spending that the President opposes. While there have been problems with the massive number of reports now required by law—many of which are probably unnecessary since they are simply routine financial transactions—and occasionally with the reporting deadlines, the new impoundment procedures do allow the executive to monitor programs subsequent to appropriation and Congress to review presidential recommendations for delays or terminations in program expenditures. This provides a mechanism for managing the budget and responding to reduced spending needs without vesting sole discretion in the executive branch, and it also gives Congress a significant control over budget execution.

Reprogramming and Transfers

Impoundments have occurred when the President has sought to eliminate or reduce spending for programs and projects that have been supported by Congress. A different challenge to congressional spending decisions occurs, however, when the President attempts to use appropriated funds for purposes other than those which Congress had originally intended. In some cases, this means increasing spending for a program or project that has been approved by shifting funds from other programs or projects. In other cases, it can mean using funds to support activities that Congress has not approved or has even rejected. Reprogramming and transfers are discretionary spending tools that allow executive officials to alter congressional budget preferences and priorities, and they therefore represent an important aspect of budget execution.

In order to discuss reprogramming and transfers, it is necessary first to examine the content of an appropriations statute. Each appropriations statute consists of a number of appropriations accounts. These accounts include various program elements, which are broken down into separate projects. For example, the appropriations statute for the Department of Defense contains an appropriations account for research, development, test, and evaluation (RDT&E) for the Navy. This account is a broad category covering "expenses necessary for basic and applied scientific research, development, test and evaluation, including maintenance, rehabilitation, lease, and operation of facilities as authorized by law."[42] The Navy RDT&E account is then divided into program elements such as aircraft and related equipment; missiles and related equipment; and ships, small craft, and related equipment. These program elements then are divided into separate projects. The missiles and related equipment program element, for example, includes projects such as the Trident missile and the submarine-launched cruise missile.

While the actual appropriations statute does not usually specify in great detail how funds within an appropriation account are to be spent (in effect, the statute looks like a broad or lump-sum appropriation), there is a considerable amount of supporting material that does provide this specificity. Original budget estimates prepared by executive agencies, for example, are very detailed, providing justifications for spending on discrete projects. The congressional response to these estimates, as reflected in committee reports and floor action, provides additional information on how Congress wishes funds to be spent. Thus by the time action on an appropriations statute has been completed, the statute and supporting materials taken together provide a high degree of line itemization or specificity.[43]

Reprogramming. This is a procedure that allows "executive officials some latitude in shifting funds *within* an appropriation account, moving them from one program to another."[44] In the example noted above, this could take the form of shifting funds from one program element to another within the RDT&E/Navy account or of shifting funds between projects within a given program element. Thus, funds would still be spent in support of the same broad activity but for different programs or projects. As the executive branch's use of reprogramming increased during the 1950s and 1960s, Congress gradually moved to tighten its supervision of these actions. This response reflected the congressional view that reprogramming had been used in some instances to frustrate the intent of Congress by shifting funds for projects that had been approved to projects that had not been approved or had even been rejected.

Reprogramming has been utilized most heavily in the defense budget. In some years, particularly during the 1960s, there have been as many as 100 reprogramming actions amounting to several billion dollars.[45] Recently both the dollar amounts and number of reprogramming actions have declined, however, and congressional control in the form of prior approval of reprogramming requests has increased.

In general, congressional supervision over reprogramming requests rests with the Appropriations Committees and authorizing committees for a given agency. A formal procedure has gradually been developed to deal specifically with reprogramming by the Department of Defense. Starting in the mid-1950s, the Appropriations Committees required the Department to supply more information about major reprogramming actions and to submit periodic tabulations of reprogramming actions that exceeded specified dollar amounts. When this proved an insufficient means of control, the Appropriations Committees insisted that their prior approval be obtained for certain types of reprogramming actions. In 1961 the Armed Services Committees were also included in the procedures for prior approval.[46]

The system for dealing with reprogramming actions or requests now includes "prompt notification" of congressional committees by the Department of Defense where reprogramming actions within an appropriation account exceed specified dollar thresholds. Where one or more of the committees object, the Secretary of Defense will reconsider the action.[47] A more stringent check, prior approval, is required when the Defense Department wishes to shift funds to items that Congress has deleted from original budget requests or programs that Congress has specifically reduced from original agency requests. In the case of appropriations accounts for procurement, prior approval in these and other specified cases is required by the Appropriations and Armed Services Committees. In other cases, approval by the Appropriations Committees is generally sufficient. It is important to note, moreover, that approval must be in the form of explicit, written concurrence.[48]

On the nonmilitary side, reprogramming procedures have not been clearly established. Proposals have been introduced in Congress to have the GAO compile, analyze, and screen reprogramming actions and provide congressional committees with more adequate information about agencies within their jurisdiction. Thresholds and guidelines paralleling those used for Defense Department reprogrammings could thus be extended to domestic agencies.

One of the persistent criticisms of even the formal reprogramming procedures, however, has been that they allow a relatively small number of committee members to substitute their judgment for that of the entire Congress. In response to this, the Appropriations and

Armed Services Committees have in recent years been less willing to entertain major reprogramming proposals and have insisted that full congressional authorization and appropriation action be required instead.[49] Moreover, since open hearings are now held on reprogramming requests and transcripts of these hearings are printed, other members of Congress have access to more adequate information concerning reprogramming requests and committee actions.[50]

Transfers.   A related discretionary spending device is transfer authority. Unlike reprogramming, transfers involve the shifting of funds *between* appropriations accounts and are based on a statutory delegation of authority. Executive officials acting under statutory authorization are thereby allowed to use appropriated funds for a different purpose. Just how different this purpose can be has been a persistent issue. As noted previously, transfer authority is frequently used to finance intelligence activities. For example, under the Central Intelligence Act of 1949, the CIA is permitted to transfer funds to and from other agencies in order to perform functions or activities authorized by the National Security Act of 1947.[51] But there has been considerable controversy over the specific functions or activities that the 1947 law actually authorizes the CIA to perform, making the limits of permissible transfer authority difficult to define.

A much clearer pattern of abuse developed with the Nixon administration's use of transfer authority to finance the 1970 intervention in Cambodia and, subsequently, three years of air operations over Cambodia. Foreign assistance and Department of Defense transfer accounts were used in this fashion, and despite administration agreements to submit such transfers for prior approval by Congress, funds were effectively committed well in advance of requests being sent to Congress. Rather than being resorted to as even a short-term emergency measure, transfer authority was actually employed in order to circumvent the normal budgetary process and to effect a long-term financial commitment that Congress could not easily avoid.[52]

The Nixon experience illustrates an inherent problem with transfer authority. It is difficult for Congress to specify in advance those purposes for which transfers are to be used. Indeed, if Congress were able to foresee all contingencies, emergencies, and unexpected events, one of the major justifications for most discretionary spending would be eliminated. Yet in seeking to provide executive officials with some flexibility in responding to changing circumstances and events, particularly in the areas of defense and foreign affairs, Congress is necessarily dependent on the reasonable judgment and good faith of those officials. Thus, all that Congress can do in many instances is specify those purposes for which transfer authority cannot be used, a tactic that it finally resorted to in the case of Cambodia. Since 1974, Congress has also prohibited the use of transfer authority by the Department of Defense to fund items or programs that have previously been rejected by Congress.[53]

Congress has not yet developed an effective set of procedures for defining and supervising the use of transfer authority. Indeed, there is little information about the extent to which such authority is used by domestic agencies and the effects of this utilization. It would be possible to employ notification and prior approval requirements similar to those used for defense reprogramming and to provide for joint oversight by the Appropriations Committees and the authorization committees having jurisdiction over a particular agency, but transfer authority has thus far proved to be a difficult spending tool for Congress to control.

Summary

The final stage of the budgetary process includes budget execution—the actual obligation and expenditure of funds—and procedures for review, audit, and evaluation designed to ensure that funds have been spent in accordance with law, that spending has been economical and efficient, and that programs are effective. Budget execution is carried out by executive agencies, and there has been considerable controversy in recent years over the relative degree of presidential versus congressional control of budget execution. In particular, administrations have sometimes utilized discretionary spending tools such as impoundments, reprogrammings, and transfers to alter the spending and policy decisions contained in authorization and appropriations legislation. As a result, Congress has moved to strengthen its control of budget execution by imposing statutory restrictions on executive impoundments and by developing procedures to ensure congressional committee participation in reprogramming and transfer decisions. At the same time, the visibility of budget execution decisions has been broadened by imposing more stringent reporting requirements on executive agencies and by providing members of Congress with more information about executive agency and congressional committee actions.

Much of the review, audit, and evaluation process is conducted within the executive branch, involving the individual agencies and the OMB. This includes reviews of financial management and operations as well as assessments of program performance and effectiveness. In addition, Congress is responsible for conducting legislative oversight through its standing committees and through the review and audit functions of the GAO. Here, too, Congress has attempted to strengthen its power of the purse by encouraging its committees to provide more systematic and aggressive oversight and by expanding the authority and jurisdiction of the GAO to monitor executive agency performance and to assist in committee oversight.

There has been a growing recognition that the impact of congressional spending decisions depends on effective congressional supervision of budget implementation. While a degree of administrative judgment of executive discretion is necessary during budget execution, it is important that Congress be able to control those discretionary acts that have significant policy effects. Similarly, more effective congressional supervision of ongoing programs is required in order to assess the utility and desirability of current or proposed spending. An expanded congressional role with respect to budget implementation, then, is now viewed as essential to the strengthening of Congress' power of the purse.

Notes

1. *Congressional Quarterly Weekly Report*, 34, no. 48 (November 27, 1976), 3232–3233. See also *Economic Report of the President, Transmitted to the Congress January 1977* (Washington, D.C.: Government Printing Office, 1978), pp. 69–74. A different scenario unfolded in 1977. The new Carter administration proposed an economic stimulus package in January, with a portion of this package designed to increase outlays and reduce taxes during FY 1977. Congress reacted favorably to much of this program, indicating that budget execution need not involve executive-congressional conflict. The focus of the discussion in this chapter, however, is on discretionary spending actions that can intensify the conflict over budget control.

2. See Louis Fisher, *Presidential Spending Power* (Princeton, N.J.: Princeton University Press, 1975), pp. 257–266.

3. *United States Statutes at Large, Vol. 84,* 91st Congress, 2nd Session (Washington, D.C.: Government Printing Office, 1971), p. 1156.

4. President Wilson vetoed the Budget and Accounting Act because this appointment and removal procedure removed the Comptroller General from presidential control. However, Wilson's successor accepted an altered arrangement, which changed the removal procedure from a concurrent resolution that did not require a presidential signature to a joint resolution that did. See Arthur Smithies, *The Budgetary Process in the United States* (New York: McGraw-Hill, 1955), pp. 75–76; Joseph P. Harris, *Congressional Control of Administration* (Washington, D.C.: Brookings Institution, 1964), p. 61.

5. Statement of Elmer B. Staats, Comptroller General of the United States. House Select Committee on Committees, *Working Papers on House Committee Organization and Operation, General Accounting Office Support of Committee Oversight,* 93rd Congress, 1st Session (Washington, D.C.: Government Printing Office, 1973), p. 2.

6. Ibid., p. 3.

7. *Comptroller General of the United States, Annual Report 1975* (Washington, D.C.: Government Printing Office, 1976), p. 1.

8. Ibid., pp. 10, 38–49.

9. Comptroller General of the United States, *Report to the Congress, Summary of Open GAO Recommendations for Legislative Action as of December 31, 1976* (Washington, D.C.: Government Printing Office, February 16, 1977), p. 2.

10. Fisher, *Presidential Spending Power,* p. 273.

11. See James A. Thurber, "Legislative-Administrative Relations," *Policy Studies Journal, 5,* no. 1 (Autumn 1976), 57-58.

12. Ibid., p. 62. See also Randall B. Ripley and Grace A. Franklin, *Congress, the Bureaucracy and Public Policy* (Homewood, Ill.: Dorsey Press, 1976), pp. 5–7.

13. Fisher, *Presidential Spending Power,* p. 66. On the rationale for this, see also Smithies, *Budgetary Process,* pp. 175–197.

14. Fisher, *Presidential Spending Power,* pp. 202–228.

15. Ibid., p. 207.

16. Ibid., p. 214.

17. Early in 1977, the Carter administration announced that it would not oppose releasing a figure for the total amount of U.S. intelligence spending, but it did oppose the release of additional information relating to the composition and structure of the intelligence budget. *Congressional Quarterly Weekly Report, 35,* no. 18 (April 30, 1977), 800.

18. Fisher, *Presidential Spending Power,* p. 213.

19. Quoted in "Controversy in Congress over the Presidential Impoundment of Appropriated Funds," *Congressional Digest, 52,* no. 4 (April 1973), 100.

20. Senate Committee on the Judiciary, *Comptroller General's Opinion of the Legality of Executive Impoundment of Appropriated Funds,* 93rd Congress, 2nd Session (Washington, D.C.: Government Printing Office, 1974), p. 3.

21. See *Congressional Quarterly Almanac, Vol. V, 1949* (Washington, D.C.: Congressional Quarterly News Features, 1950), p. 225.

22. "Controversy in Congress," p. 128.

23. Fisher, *Presidential Spending Power,* pp. 177–192.

24. Louis Fisher, "Congress, the Executive and the Budget," *Annals of the American Academy of Political and Social Science, 411* (January 1974), 102–113.

25. Quoted in Fisher, *Presidential Spending Power,* pp. 191–192.

26. This section is based on the categorization and analysis provided in Fisher, *Presidential Spending Power,* pp. 147–174. This work presents an extremely valuable examination of the effect of various executive discretionary tools on budget execution.

27. Quoted in ibid., p. 149.

28. Ibid., p. 152.

29. Ibid., pp. 157–158.

30. *United States Statutes at Large, Vol. 64,* 81st Congress, 2nd Session (Washington, D.C.: Government Printing Office, 1952), pp. 765–766.

31. Senate Committee on the Judiciary, *Legality of Executive Impoundment,* p. 19.

32. See Fisher, *Presidential Spending Power,* p. 156.

33. David A. Martin, "Protecting the Fisc: Executive Impoundment and Congressional Power," *Yale Law Journal, 82* (1973), 1656.

34. William Rehnquist, "Memorandum Regarding Presidential Authority to Impound Funds Appropriated for Assistance to Federally Impacted Schools," in *Hearings, Impoundment of Appropriated Funds by the President,* Senate Committees on Government Operations and on the Judiciary, 93rd Congress, 1st Session (Washington, D.C.: Government Printing Office, 1973), p. 395.

35. Ibid.

36. House Committee on the Budget, *The Congressional Budget and Impoundment Control Act of 1974, A General Explanation,* 94th Congress, 1st Session (Washington, D.C.: Government Printing Office, 1975), p. 18.

37. Fisher, *Presidential Spending Power,* p. 201.

38. The numbers of rescissions and deferrals actually considered by Congress are somewhat confusing, since some rescissions and deferrals were reclassified by the Comptroller General, who also notified Congress of two rescission actions that had not been reported by the President. Allen Schick, *The First Years of the Congressional Budget Process* (Washington, D.C.: Congressional Research Service, June 30, 1976), pp. 31–35.

39. Ibid., pp. 36–38.

40. Ibid., pp. 31–38.

41. See "Carter vs. Congress: At War over Water," *Congressional Quarterly Weekly Report, 35,* no. 12 (March 19, 1977), 481–484.

42. House Committee on Appropriations, Subcommittee on the Department of Defense, *Hearings, Department of Defense Appropriations for 1976, Part 4, Research, Development, Test and Evaluation* (Washington, D.C.: Government Printing Office, 1975), p. 118.

43. Fisher, *Presidential Spending Power,* pp. 75–76.

44. Ibid., p. 75.

45. Ibid., pp. 86–87.

46. Ibid., p. 85.

47. Ibid., p. 86. According to Fisher, this "usually means that the action will be placed on hold until the committees approve."

48. Ibid.

49. Statement of Louis Fisher, House Select Committee on Committees, *Working Papers on House Committee Organization and Operation, Congressional Control of Budget Execution*, 93rd Congress, 1st Session (Washington, D.C.: Government Printing Office, 1973), pp. 3–4.

50. Ibid.

51. Fisher, *Presidential Spending Power*, pp. 214–215.

52. Ibid., pp. 107–117.

53. Ibid., p. 121.

Five

Budget Decisions and Policy Issues

Because the federal budget has significant implications for the economy, emphasis is naturally placed on budget totals or aggregates —what the level of spending is, how large a share of the nation's economy it represents, and what the relationship is between outlays and revenues. Assessments of the current state of the economy and the impact of a budget deficit (or surplus) at a given level are therefore major considerations in analyzing budget decisions. Since Congress has now instituted a process that allows it to deal explicitly with fiscal policy issues, at least one aspect of the annual budgetary debate will be easier to follow.

It must be recognized, however, that the fiscal policy choices embodied in the budget are not the only important decisions. Within the budget totals, decisions are made about the funding of specific programs, which reflect the relative importance that political leaders assign to various government activities. Of course, specific spending decisions are made within certain constraints—available revenues and other resources, the competing claims of other programs, and political feasibility. Each year the vast majority of funding decisions are simply marginal changes from the previous year and, as a consequence, receive little attention.[1] But significant policy issues do sometimes emerge during the budgetary process. In this chapter, the relationship between budget decisions and policy issues will be examined by focusing on two of the largest current spending programs—defense and income programs—and one potentially large program now being considered—national health insurance. These are not what might be termed "representative" types of budget decisions, since they are extremely controversial and do receive sustained attention. But they are useful in illustrating the various factors that political leaders take into account when making budget choices. Moreover, the short-term budget decisions for these programs will have a substantial impact on the size and composition of federal spending in the future. Defense outlays and benefit payments to individuals—of which income security programs are the largest component—now account for approximately three-fourths of the total budget. Because of this budgetary impact, there has been considerable competition between defense spending and the various benefit programs for budget shares.

Defense Spending

Among the most persistent and important budgetary debates are those concerning defense spending. Theoretically, determinations of defense budgets should be relatively straightforward, but as a 1976 Congressional Research Service study stated, this is rarely if ever the case:

> Ideally, national security interests are the bases for objectives and commitments which, within policy guidelines, shape strategy. Strategic concepts conditioned by threats generate military force requirements. Budgetary assets then are allocated to satisfy needs.
>
> That Utopian sequence rarely occurs in real life. National defense competes with other sectors. There never is enough money to go around. The trick is to walk a tightrope between excessive defense expenditures that emasculate political, economic, social, scientific, and ecological programs on one hand, and deficient defense expenditures that actively endanger national security on the other. Equally important, overallocations in any given military sector can undercut essential capabilities elsewhere.[2]

As discussed in Chapter One, the portion of the budget allocated to defense has changed markedly over the past two decades. In the mid-1950s, for example, national defense outlays represented approximately 58 percent of total federal outlays.[3] By the mid-1960s, despite the Vietnam war, outlays for defense had declined to considerably less than one-half of total outlays (43 percent in FY 1966); by 1976 defense spending accounted for only about one-fourth of the federal budget.[4]

There have been, however, two more serious trends than this proportional decline in spending. First, from 1968 through 1976 there was an actual reduction in real defense spending (that is, spending corrected for inflation to show actual purchasing power). In FY 1975, real defense spending was decreased by some $7 billion because of unanticipated price increases.[5] During this period, moreover, the proportion of the defense budget allocated to manpower costs rose sharply, meaning that spending for supplies and military equipment was even more sharply curtailed.

Second, while U.S. defense spending was declining, the military capability of the Soviet Union was rapidly improving. Since many consider the military balance between the United States and the Soviet Union to be the best available yardstick for measuring the sufficiency of U.S. defense forces,[6] this trend has been especially disturbing. Quantitative comparisons of U.S. and Soviet capabilities, for example, have shown substantial shifts in favor of the Soviet Union.[7]

Against this background, the Ford administration in its fiscal 1976, 1977, and 1978 budgets proposed real increases in defense spending, especially for procurement of military hardware. In his 1977 budget message, Ford stated his assessment of priorities with a focus on defense:

> Clearly, one of the highest priorities for our Government is always to secure the defense of our country. . . . If we in the Federal Government fail in this responsibility, our other objectives are meaningless.
>
> Accordingly, I am recommending a significant increase in defense spending for 1977. . . . The amounts I seek will provide the national defense it now appears we need. We dare not do less. And if our efforts to secure international arms limitations falter, we will need to do more.[8]

As was the case four years earlier, defense spending was a campaign issue in 1976, and the partisan lines were similar if less sharply drawn. In 1972 the Democratic presidential nominee, Senator George Mc-Govern, repeatedly called for cuts in defense spending, suggesting that savings of up to $30 billion were possible without significant reductions in defense capability. The Democratic party's 1976 candidate, Jimmy Carter, emphasized his commitment to a strong defense but implied that some $5 to $7 billion could be saved by eliminating "waste."[9] The Republican candidates, on the other hand, stated their commitment to current or increased spending. Ford's 1977 defense budget, for example, called for $7 billion in real growth.[10] Clear divisions have also existed in Congress. For many years, liberal Democrats have attempted to cut defense spending, while conservatives in both parties have opposed such reductions.

Whatever the partisan or ideological breakdowns, assessments of "how much is enough" are extraordinarily complex, involving considerations of U.S. national security interests and objectives, U.S. commitments, the manpower and resources available, and the threats posed by current and future rivals.[11] Since reliable information on the actions or intentions of rival governments is difficult to obtain, calculations of sufficiency or readiness are even more uncertain. In this section we will not attempt to answer the question of how much is enough but rather will examine the components of defense spending and the conflicts that have arisen over defense spending.

Components of Defense Spending

The broad budget categories used in the defense budget are shown in Table 5.1, along with the Ford and Carter recommendations for outlays and budget authority in the fiscal 1978 budget. As indicated, a major portion of defense spending goes toward manpower costs (current and retired personnel); this part of the budget is difficult to reduce appreciably without corresponding reductions in personnel levels.[12] Recent budgets have attempted to moderate future increases through legislative changes affecting military pay and retirement benefits. Other major categories include operation and maintenance, and procurement. It is the latter that reflects important differences between the Carter and Ford budgets. Budget authority for procurement in the Carter budget was almost $3 billion below the Ford recommendation, re-

Table 5.1

The Defense Budget, Fiscal Year 1978 Recommendations (in millions of dollars)

	Outlays		Budget authority	
	Ford budget	Carter revision	Ford budget	Carter revision
Department of Defense, Military				
Military personnel	26,005	25,959	26,193	26,140
Retired military personnel	9,035	9,035	9,036	9,036
Operation and maintenance	33,539	33,686	34,168	34,358
Procurement	23,786	23,510	35,143	32,209
Research, development, test and evaluation	11,350	11,181	11,980	11,717
Military construction	2,046	2,058	1,376	1,677
Family housing	1,518	1,518	1,329	1,339
Revolving funds and other	− 71	− 71	95	95
Allowances				
Civilian and military pay raises				
Existing law	2,417	2,417	2,493	2,493
Proposed legislation	− 160	− 160	− 167	− 167
Other legislation	58	33	58	33
Military assistance	577	576	−1,218	−1,220
Atomic energy defense activities	2,162	2,162	2,380	2,380
Defense-related activities	3	45	7	49
Deductions for offsetting receipts	− 3	− 3	− 3	− 3
Total, national defense	112,262	111,947	122,871	120,136

Source: Office of Management and Budget, *Fiscal Year 1978 Budget Revisions* (Washington, D.C.: Government Printing Office, February 1977), pp. 29–30.

flecting cancellations of some weapons systems and a slowing down of the rate of procurement for others. However, both budgets represented real spending increases over previous years. In FY 1976, for example, actual outlays for procurement were slightly under $16 billion, while outlays for FY 1978 were projected at over $23 billion. At the same time, the budget authority recommended for procurement increased from less than $21 billion in FY 1976 to the $32 to $35 billion levels proposed by Carter and Ford. Another area in which real spending increases were recommended is research, development, testing, and evaluation (RDT&E). Here the Ford and Carter recommendations are quite similar.

Another way to examine defense spending is to allocate the costs according to the combat mission of major military programs. This breakdown is presented in Table 5.2, and a discussion of some of the principal elements shown is helpful in understanding what defense budget issues actually involve.

Strategic Forces.   Included under strategic forces are several offensive and defensive weapons systems. The offensive forces are composed of land-based missiles as well as strategic bombers and submarines. Active defensive forces now include air defense forces and warning and control communications systems. The principal consideration in assessing strategic force requirements is, of course, the Soviet Union's capabilities and intentions.

During the past several years, the United States and the Soviet Union have reached agreement on certain strategic arms limitations, although major uncertainties remain as to the interpretation, im-

Table 5.2

Department of Defense Major Military Programs (in billions of dollars)

	Total obligational authority		
	Actual fiscal 1976	Estimated fiscal 1977	Estimated fiscal 1978
Strategic forces	7.3	9.8	11.0
General purpose forces	33.0	38.2	44.3
Intelligence and communications	6.7	7.5	8.2
Airlift and sealift	1.4	1.5	1.7
Guard and reserve	5.4	6.0	7.2
Research and development	8.7	10.1	11.1
Central supply and maintenance	9.8	11.1	11.8
Training, medical, and other general personnel activities	21.6	22.7	24.3
Administration and associated activities	2.1	2.1	2.3
Support of other nations	1.6	1.3	1.3
Total	97.5	110.2	123.1

Source: *The Budget of the United States Government, Fiscal Year 1978* (Washington, D.C.: Government Printing Office, 1977), p. 78.

plementation, and extension of these agreements. Under the 1974 agreement, for example, each side agreed to a 10-year limit of 2400 strategic delivery systems (land, air, and submarine), with up to 1320 of these missiles to be equipped with multiple independently targetable reentry vehicles. Another 1974 agreement limited indefinitely the number of antiballistic missile systems and the number of interceptor missiles. These limitations and subsequent SALT agreements will obviously be key elements in U.S. strategic planning.

Budget issues relating to strategic nuclear forces have recently involved several major new weapons systems. Although President Carter originally reduced President Ford's budget for strategic forces by only $400 million in budget authority, his decisions on specific weapons systems have been dramatically different. On June 30, 1977, for example, President Carter announced that production of the B-1 would be discontinued. The B-1 was a new strategic bomber that was designed to replace the B-52. President Ford had pushed development and production of the B-1, and his budget called for continuation of the program. Carter had attacked the B-1 as too expensive and exotic during his presidential campaign, but there was still considerable surprise over his decision. The President argued, however, that there were alternative weapons systems that were more cost-effective, particularly deployment of the newly developed cruise missiles using modernized B-52s. Cruise missiles, which can also be launched from submarines, thus became a central component of President Carter's defense program, and his budget proposals have called for accelerated development and production of the 1500-mile air-launched version (ALCM B), which could be launched outside the reach of Soviet defense forces. Carter has also slowed development of another weapons system that his predecessor had supported—the M-X intercontinental ballistic missile, a successor to the Minuteman ICBM. Another major strategic system is the Trident program, which calls for deploying a new strategic submarine armed with Trident missiles. The Ford administration had strongly supported this program, and while Carter has not yet announced any significant changes, there will be important funding decisions on extending the program once the original program authorization expires in 1980.

In addition to these weapons systems, there has been some attention to new defensive technologies, but the key issues now and in the future are likely to involve the "Triad" (land, air, submarine) of U.S.

strategic offensive forces—whether the Triad should be continued, what type of modernization should be planned, and what type of "mix" among the various elements should be adopted. The Carter administration has maintained the triad concept, but it has emphasized the necessity for careful and critical review of current and planned weapons systems.

Spending for strategic offensive and defensive forces has declined considerably as a share of the defense budget since the early 1960s. Even with indirect costs added, strategic forces now account for less than one-fifth of defense spending, as compared with approximately one-third in 1963.[13] The budgetary impact of strategic forces spending, then, has decreased markedly. Sharp reductions in the strategic forces share are unlikely, and at current levels they would not significantly reduce total defense spending.[14] Cost considerations can be critical for certain weapons systems, as in the case of the B-1, but the primary consideration regarding strategic forces will be U.S. strategic doctrine.

General Purpose Forces.   The single largest component of the defense program is general purpose forces. The major elements of these forces include ground forces (Army and Marine), naval forces with the exception of ballistic missile submarines, and the tactical air forces (Air Force, Navy, and Marine Corps). The responsibilities are global, although the major potential threats that they are designed to meet come from the Soviet Union and the Warsaw Pact nations in Europe and the People's Republic of China and North Korea in Asia.[15]

Here, too, the budget debate has centered on modernization and expansion. The Ford administration supported the establishment of new combat units, major new weapons systems (such as tanks and attack helicopters) to support ground forces, and accelerated procurement of air combat fighters and naval vessels, including guided missile frigates and a nuclear-powered strike cruiser. There has been, however, considerable congressional opposition both to the overall expansion and to specific weapons procurement decisions. President Carter has proposed that the rate of modernization be slowed. His fiscal 1978 budget, for example, reduced Ford's request by $2.3 billion in budget authority. Carter has, however, recommended that funding be increased for NATO forces to improve combat readiness and capability. Thus, the size of general purpose forces, the degree and pace of modernization of the several components, and the addition of new or planned weapons systems will likely continue as major defense issues in the future.

Research and Development. Expenditure for research and development of new weapons systems is another area of the defense budget that is sensitive to the activities of potential enemies. The United States has generally placed a premium on technological supremacy, although significant Soviet advances in recent years mean that such superiority cannot simply be assumed any longer. As a result there has been pressure to increase support for research and development. Increases in real spending occurred in FY 1977, and subsequent increases are probable. The programs currently being considered, which necessarily extend well into the future, cover a wide range, from strategic missile improvements, to new tanks and aircraft, to more exotic weapons such as high-energy lasers. As might be expected, disagreements here usually focus on the specific weapons system or development program, but given the size of this budget—less than 10 percent of total outlays—the effects of increases or decreases on total defense spending are minimal.[16]

Airlift and Sealift Forces. The United States has been especially dependent on effective airlift and sealift forces to support American forces abroad and also to assist allies. This capability was extremely important during the 1973 Middle East war, when the United States found it necessary to send large amounts of weapons and supplies to Israel.

The major components of these mobility forces are strategic (long-range) and tactical (short-range) airlift squadrons, both active and reserve. At the present time there is a general program to improve strategic airlift capabilities, particularly to deploy troops and equipment to Europe. This includes improvements in existing aircraft, such as extending the lifetime of the giant C-5A transport by strengthening the wings and providing the C-141 transport with in-flight refueling equipment to reduce the reliance on overseas bases in the event of another war in the Middle East. A long-range program is also under way to replace the aging tactical airlift fleet.

As these programs are considered, a central factor is conflict over deployment requirements in Europe. Congress has been reluctant to accept the rationale that this capability must be improved, while the Department of Defense has argued that a shorter deployment time is necessary to stabilize the balance of conventional forces in Europe during the early stages of a conflict. So here, again, assessments of Soviet capabilities and intentions play a major role in decisions about program requirements.[17]

Other Programs.   It is possible to allocate some of the remaining program costs in Table 5.2, along with research and development costs, to measure total spending for what are termed *baseline forces* (see Table 5.3). Since the 1980 projections are based on Ford administration recommendations with respect to weapons procurement, force levels, manpower, and so forth, these figures serve as a yardstick to measure the budgetary impact of alternative policies. It is likely that real defense spending will continue to increase for the next several years unless there are dramatic and unforeseen changes in international politics. At issue, however, will be the extent of this increase, which will depend on congressional reactions to presidential defense policies.

Congressional-Presidential Conflicts

During the early 1970s, Congress consistently reduced the defense budget. In FY 1976, for example, it cut the administration's request by over $7 billion, bringing the total cuts over a four-year period to some $23 billion.[18] Debate on the fiscal 1977 budget, however, differed considerably in tone and substance from that of previous years, with Congress much more receptive to requests for increased defense spending.

Table 5.3

Defense Budget for Baseline Forces (in billions of dollars)

	Total obligational authority[a]	
	Estimated fiscal 1976	Projected fiscal 1980
Strategic nuclear forces	18.0	29.8
General purpose forces	72.3	101.0
Mobility forces	3.8	6.2
Total	94.1	137.0

Note: Figures include direct and indirect costs.

[a]Based on Ford administration defense policies.

Source: Adapted from Barry M. Blechman, Edward M. Gramlich, and Robert W. Hartman, *Setting National Priorities, The 1976 Budget* (Washington, D.C.: Brookings Institution, 1975), p. 91. Copyright © 1975 by The Brookings Institution, Washington, D.C.

While the administration's request was reduced by several billion dollars, Congress agreed to increase appropriations by more than $13 billion over the original fiscal 1976 appropriations. Its reductions in subsequent budgets have been similarly moderate.

Without exaggerating the extent of change in Congress regarding defense spending, it does appear that 1976 represented a turning point. While such factors as the lingering unpopularity of the war in Vietnam, loss of confidence in the military, and detente had played an important role in fueling previous attacks on defense spending, the major consideration in 1976 was the military balance between the United States and the Soviet Union. By examining some of the information and interpretations regarding this balance as well as the public's response, it is possible to explain at least in part this turnabout and to identify some of the factors that affect defense budget decision making.

The "Dollar Gap." In February 1976, the CIA released a report comparing U.S. and Soviet defense activities for the period 1965–1975.[19] Acknowledging that it was extremely difficult to compare the U.S. and Soviet military establishments (because of major differences in missions, structure, and characteristics), the report utilized what it termed dollar cost comparisons—"how much it would cost in dollars to reproduce individual Soviet military programs in the U.S. and then to compare these estimates with expenditure data of the Department of Defense."[20]

According to the report, Soviet and U.S. defense spending over the entire decade was roughly similar, but from 1970 on, Soviet spending had consistently exceeded U.S. spending. For 1975, for example, Soviet defense spending was estimated to be about 40 percent higher than U.S. spending (see Figure 5.1). Moreover, the disparity was especially pronounced for strategic offense and defensive forces—in 1975 the estimate of Soviet strategic defense spending was nine times U.S. spending.[21] While the United States had consistently spent more on military weapons research during the 1960s, the Soviets were investing consistently more in RDT&E during the early 1970s. According to the director of Defense Research, Malcolm R. Currie, this threatened to give the Soviet Union "dominance" in military technology by the 1980s.[22]

Although similar data and interpretations had obviously been avail-

U.S. Expenditures and Estimated Dollar Costs of Soviet Defense Programs [a]

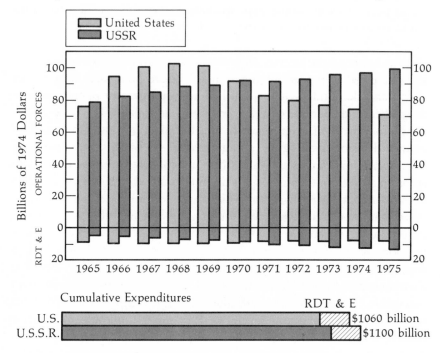

Cumulative Expenditures

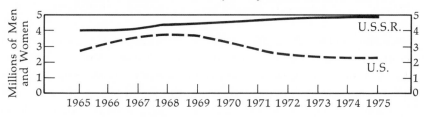

U.S. and Estimated Soviet Active Military Manpower [b]

Figure 5.1

United States and Soviet defense spending from 1965 through 1975 [[a]The dollar figures for the U.S.S.R. are estimates of what the Soviet forces and programs would cost if developed, purchased, and operated in the United States. For operational forces the figures are obtained by costing directly individual Soviet forces and programs. The estimated dollar costs of Soviet RDT&E are derived in the aggregate using a less certain methodology and should be viewed only as rough measures. For this reason they are shown separate from the dollar costs of operational forces. The U.S. defense expenditure series is based on Total able in past years, Congress was much more receptive to the potential threat posed by the "dollar gap" in 1976. Part of this reaction could no doubt be attributed to supporting evidence from other quarters.

Military Balance.   In January 1976 the Senate Armed Services Committee published a report on the military balance between the Soviet Union and the United States that had been prepared by the Congressional Research Service of the Library of Congress.[23] This was an attempt to provide Congress with an analysis that could be used in budget decision making by going beyond statistical comparisons of U.S. and Soviet forces to show "how much defense" was needed to accomplish various U.S. aims. As the report noted, "bolstering budgets is the *last*, not the *first*, resort."[24]

Certain aspects of the balance were clear. In quantitative terms—especially in regard to strategic nuclear weapons, tactical nuclear weapons, ground forces, and naval forces—the Soviets had achieved superiority by the mid-1970s. More important, however, when the asymmetries between U.S. and Soviet forces were assessed in terms of seriousness (taking into account quality, U.S. aims and objectives, and so forth), the report found several key U.S. shortcomings—in strategic forces, mobility forces, naval forces, and NATO.[25] While no solutions were proffered, it was stated that "U.S. budgetary projections paint a bleak picture when related to pressing U.S. problems, even though absolute outlays are very large."[26]

Public Perceptions.   Accompanying this growing congressional concern about the adequacy of U.S. defense spending was a shift in public attitudes. One element of this was the American public's growing pessimism concerning American power in the world (see Table 5.4). Gallup surveys in 1976 showed 63 percent of the public (the highest level in 16 years) believing that Soviet power would increase during the

Obligational Authority (TOA) data from *The Five-Year Defense Program*, January 1976 (Department of Defense). The U.S. data are in fiscal year terms and the estimated dollar costs of Soviet programs are in calendar year terms. [b]The manpower series for the U.S.S.R. includes border guards, internal security troops, and construction troops, for which the U.S. Armed Forces have no counterpart.] [Source: Central Intelligence Agency, *A Dollar Comparison of Soviet and U.S. Defense Activities, 1965–1975* (February 1976), p. 2.]

Table 5.4

U.S. Public's Perceptions of United States and Soviet Power

	Power position in world[a]					
	Power will increase		Power will decline		Don't know	
	U.S.	Soviet	U.S.	Soviet	U.S.	Soviet
1976	42%	63%	44%	18%	14%	19%
1974	29	55	50	14	21	31
1969	62	58	21	19	17	23
1968	63	56	22	22	15	22
1967	66	49	20	26	14	25
1965	64	38	19	33	17	29
1960	72	53	10	23	18	24

[a]At the beginning of each year, a national sample was asked if, during that year, "the United States will increase her power in the world, . . . or U.S. power will decline." The same question was then asked about the Soviet Union.
Source: Gallup Opinion Index, Report No. 126 (January 1976), pp. 24–25.

year, while a slight plurality—44 to 42 percent—expected U.S. power to decline. Attitudes on U.S. power were substantially more positive during the 1960s, even during the years of the Vietnam war.

Also in 1976, public opinion on defense spending became more supportive. As Table 5.5 shows, there was a decline between 1974 and 1976 in the percentage who thought that "too much" was being spent on defense and a commensurate increase in the percentage thinking that "too little" was being spent. Thus by 1976, for the first time in the period shown, a majority favored current or increased spending and, at least by implication, opposed cuts in defense spending. It should be noted that few persons had any idea of what defense spending actually was. Some 70 percent admitted that they did not know what percentage of the federal budget was spent on defense and only about 8 percent had a reasonably accurate idea.[27] However, knowledge about defense spending was, curiously enough, unrelated to attitudes about its adequacy.[28]

"How Much Is Enough?"   The changed congressional reaction to defense spending was no doubt conditioned by a variety of factors—the growing disparities in spending and forces, disillusionment because detente had led not to a decrease but rather a wholesale expansion of Soviet forces,[29] growing public apprehension concerning Soviet inten-

Table 5.5

Public Response to Defense Spending, 1969–1976

	U.S. defense spending[a]			
	"Too much"	"Too little"	"About right"	No opinion
1976	36%	22%	32%	10%
1974	44	12	32	12
1973 (September)	46	30	13	11
1973 (February)	42	8	40	10
1971	49	11	31	9
1969	52	8	31	9

[a]Those interviewed were asked the following question: "There is much discussion as to the amount of money the government in Washington should spend for national defense and military purposes. How do you feel about this: Do you think we are spending too little, too much, or about the right amount?"

Source: Gallup Opinion Index, Report No. 129 (April 1976), p. 20.

tions and U.S. strength, and so forth. This broad range of considerations illustrates the complexity of defense budget decision making. Neither the President nor Congress can deal with the defense budget as if "how much is enough" is equally clear to everyone. Intangible factors such as public moods and unpredictable factors such as enemy intentions to help shape calculations of readiness and sufficiency. Because the stakes are so high, this is one policy area where controversy is likely to continue.

Income Programs

A number of federal programs have been established to provide income security and income assistance to groups such as the poor, the disabled, and the aged. Through cash payments or other forms of assistance, the government transfers resources to individuals and households in order to alleviate poverty, facilitate access to important services, and prevent severe losses in economic well-being resulting from largely involuntary disruptions in earnings.[30] While the defense share of the budget has declined dramatically, the proportion of federal spending used to support these programs has increased sharply. As shown in Figure 5.2, benefit payments to individuals now account for approximately 45 percent of total federal outlays, compared with some

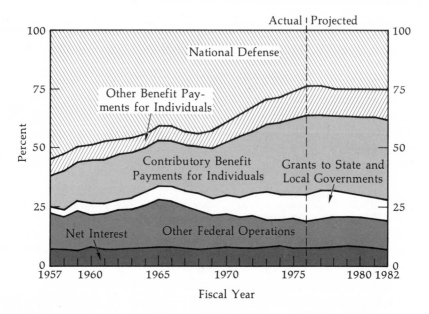

Figure 5.2

Composition of federal spending as a percentage of federal outlays. [Source: Congressional Budget Office, *Budget Options for Fiscal Year 1978: A Report to the Senate and House Committees on the Budget* (Washington, D.C.: Government Printing Office, February 1977), p. 11.]

20 percent in 1957. The contributory benefit programs, such as social security, currently account for about one-third of the federal budget. Noncontributory programs, such as Aid to Families with Dependent Children (AFDC) and food stamps, are roughly 12 percent of total outlays. Under current policy the combined share is projected to increase slightly through the early 1980s.

The substantial cost increases in income programs reflect several factors. Major new programs, such as Medicaid and food stamps, have been established. Benefits have been repeatedly increased for virtually all programs. Legislative changes and demographic trends have increased the eligible population for many programs. Finally, inflation has increased program costs appreciably. Benefits for certain income programs are now raised automatically as the cost of living increases. Whether by design or not, however, the growth in income program costs has been so large and has occurred so rapidly that major budgetary and other policy issues have developed. By examing social security and certain income assistance programs, it is possible to analyze these issues and some of the existing budget options.

Social Security

This is by far the largest single income security program, covering over 90 percent of private civilian employment and accounting for approximately one-fifth of federal outlays (almost $84 billion in FY 1977). Social security benefits are drawn from a trust fund that is financed by the payroll taxes of currently employed workers. Over 33 million persons are currently receiving benefits, which are paid to those who qualify because of old age or as survivors (widows, widowers, and orphans) under the original program established in 1935, to the permanently disabled under 1956 program amendments, and for medical treatment under the Medicare program, established in 1965.

Over the past decade, outlays for social security have risen sharply, as the number of beneficiaries has grown and average benefits have been increased. Fiscal 1976 outlays, for example, were $50 billion greater than fiscal 1966 outlays. Between 1967 and 1972, average monthly benefits were increased by 67 percent (discounting inflation, a real annual increase of about 6 percent). Over the past decade, social security taxes have also increased rapidly. Both the maximum salary base (the amount of wages on which social security taxes are paid) and the tax rate (the percentage tax on wages within the maximum salary base) have been periodically increased. The base was $6600 in 1966. This increased to $16,500 in 1977, and current law provides for automatic annual increases. The tax rate is currently 11.7 percent, compared with 8.4 percent in 1966 (with one-half of the tax paid by the employer and one-half by the employee).[31] The result is that the maximum tax more than tripled in one decade—from $555 in 1966 to $1790 in 1976; projected future increases are substantial.

Despite this increase in taxes, which have made social security taxes second only to individual income taxes as a source of federal revenues, the social security system has serious short-term and long-term financial problems. The short-term difficulties have developed since the early 1970s, when outlays began to grow at a faster rate than revenues. The 1974 recession, moreover, decreased revenues sharply as unemployment increased and people left the work force; as a result, outlays actually exceeded revenues. In FY 1976, for example, the deficit was over $4 billion, and continuing deficits are now being projected through the early 1980s. Accumulated reserves have been falling steadily, and current estimates are that reserves will be depleted by the early 1980s.[32] Current policy, then, is inadequate to meet the demands of the social security system over the next five to ten years, leading to proposals for increasing revenues by raising social security taxes or using general revenues to offset program deficits, limiting future benefit increases, and shifting certain social security outlays, such as Medicare, to funding through general tax revenues. However, each of these proposed solutions raises political or economic objections, and Congress has therefore been reluctant to adopt major revisions.

President Carter has proposed, for example, that "countercyclical" transfers of general revenues be used to offset lowered revenues during economic slowdowns. When the unemployment rate reaches a specified level, the transfer would be triggered automatically, and the trust fund would not encounter the severe drain on reserves that occurred as a result of the 1974–1975 recession. The use of general revenues, however, has been opposed by some as a threat to the contributory nature of the program. Moreover, there is concern that the use of general revenues would loosen the restraints on raising benefits, since payroll taxes would not have to be increased proportionately. Conservatives in particular object to moves that would further weaken the link between contributions and benefits. Tax increases of the magnitude necessary to eliminate projected deficits have also run into heavy opposition. Raising the tax rate above current levels, for example, is attacked as worsening the regressive feature of the existing tax system and thus placing an even heavier burden on low-income workers and their families. Increasing revenues by raising the tax base well above the projected automatic increases, on the other hand, could aggravate long-term deficit problems by requiring higher future payments. And substantial tax increases of either type retard economic recovery and increase inflation (because of increased labor costs). Moreover, since social security taxes are currently quite high, any major increase could obviously have a negative political impact.

Congress therefore has limited enthusiasm for increasing social security taxes. But it has even less enthusiasm for limiting benefit increases. As a result, Congress has moved very slowly in considering program revisions. The same is true of the long-term financing situation. Some of the factors influencing future costs are not susceptible to control. Future fertility rates, for example, will substantially affect the social security system. It is now expected that the number of workers per beneficiary will slowly decline—from 3.2 workers per beneficiary in 1975 to only about 2 workers per beneficiary by 2050.[33] Higher life expectancy and lower birth rates will therefore require adjustments between taxes and benefits. Inflation and the rate of real wage growth will also have a substantial impact. Under current benefit formulas, an annual inflation rate of 10 percent, real wage growth of 2 percent, and current fertility rates would necessitate a payroll tax rate of over 40 percent by the middle of the next century. If the inflation rate is 4 percent and the other conditions remain the same, a payroll tax rate of over 20 percent would be required.[34]

The impact of inflation is increased by a technical flaw in the 1972 legislation, which provides the formula for calculating future benefits. The law allows increases in wage levels and prices to affect the benefit levels for future retirees. This overcompensates for inflation and therefore raises future benefits substantially. It is estimated that "decoupling" benefits from both prices and wages could reduce the projected long-term deficit in the social security system by one-half.[35] There is, however, sharp disagreement over how future benefits should be calculated. One point at issue is whether all workers should be guaranteed the same percentage of their final earnings. Another involves the appropriate level(s) of the replacement rate—that is, the ratio of benefits to earnings in the year before retirement. High replacement rates that are equal for all workers would cost significantly more than rates that decrease as income increases. Those who advocate a decreasing rate argue that workers with high lifetime earnings will be relatively less dependent on social security than workers with lower earnings, since they will be more likely to have other resources, such as pensions or savings, to draw upon.[36] Some form of decoupling, however, is essential to control long-term costs.

The social security program, then, has become a budgetary issue, because of immediate and long-term imbalances between revenues and outlays. Decisions must be made about appropriate benefit levels, acceptable tax rates, and the extent to which future generations should depend on social security for postretirement support. The social security program has now reached such a high level—on both the revenue and outlay sides—that these decisions will have serious political and economic consequences.

Income Assistance Programs

There are a number of major federal income assistance and income supplement programs. For many of these, the spending increases of recent years have not been paralleled by positive perceptions about their value. Indeed, programs such as Aid to Families with Dependent Children (with approximately 11.4 million recipients during FY 1977) have been attacked for fraud and waste, inequities in coverage and benefits, and deleterious effects on work incentives and family stability. As shown in Table 5.6 for selected programs, estimated future cost increases under current law are substantial. These totals, moreover, do not reflect state and local benefit payment outlays (which are expected to reach $16 billion in FY 1978).[37]

Most of the noncontributory income assistance programs are entitlements, which means that any individual meeting the legal requirements is entitled to benefits. Thus program costs depend on the size of the eligible population and the rate of participation. Legislative changes

Table 5.6

Income Assistance and Income Supplement Program Outlays
(in billions of dollars)

	Actual fiscal 1976	Estimated fiscal 1979
Aid to Families with Dependent Children (cash assistance)	$ 5.8	$ 6.7
Supplemental Security Income (cash assistance to needy aged, blind, and disabled)	5.1	6.0
Food Stamps (coupons redeemable for food for needy households)	5.6	5.8
Medicaid (government payment for medical services for income assistance recipients)	8.6	13.6
Housing Assistance (public housing, rent and mortgage subsidies for low-income households)	2.5	4.6
Child nutrition programs (school lunch and other food assistance)	2.3	3.3
Veterans pensions (cash assistance to disabled and aged low-income war veterans)	2.8	3.1
Total	$32.7	$43.1

Source: The Budget of the United States Government, Fiscal Year 1978 (Washington, D.C.: Government Printing Office, 1977).

can affect both these factors. For example, the food stamp program revisions that President Carter sponsored in 1977 revised the eligibility criteria so as to eliminate the highest-income households from the program. The cash purchase requirement for the actual food stamps, however, was dropped in order to encourage participation by the very poor. The projected impact of these and related changes would increase overall participation by some 2 million persons.

Program costs are also affected by benefit levels. Here again, policy and therefore costs can be changed by legislation. The amount of cash assistance provided to persons within a specific income and need category will obviously affect total costs. Moreover, by what amounts benefits will be reduced if recipient earnings rise (how much income will be disregarded) raises questions about not only costs but also about work incentives for recipients and equity for the working poor not receiving benefits. One of the most complex problems affecting guaranteed income proposals, for example, has been how to mesh equitably benefits with earned income.[38] Of course, income assistance program costs are significantly affected by inflation. For cash benefits, there is pressure to increase payments as inflation reduces purchasing power. For in-kind forms of assistance, the rising cost to government automatically increases expenditures.

Finally, costs depend on actual participation, and this is affected by administration. Since state and local governments participate financially and actually administer certain income assistance programs, their actions can influence actual coverage. The effectiveness of administration in not only limiting fraud and waste but also encouraging participation by those who are eligible is therefore another factor affecting costs.

The major issue with regard to income assistance programs is whether the current program-by-program approach should be continued, or whether there should be a major revision along the lines of a guaranteed income system in which comprehensive cash benefits would be substituted for most of the existing programs. One of the principal constraints on any major revision, however, is cost. The Congressional Budget Office has estimated that, under current policy, federal outlays for the programs listed in Table 5.6 will increase from $38.5 billion in 1977 to $57.8 billion in 1981. What it terms a *low-budget option*—reducing costs by reducing benefits to those who are less poor—could limit this increase to approximately $5 billion by revising the eligibility and benefits for individual programs. The high option—a comprehensive cash program with standard eligibility determined by income and discontinuation of in-kind programs—was projected as adding over $26 billion to the amount that would be required to fund current policy in 1981.[39]

Current income assistance programs, then, have serious problems in terms of structure and costs. Incremental changes, while more attractive in relation to the short-term controllability of costs, are unlikely to solve the inequities and inadequacies in coverage and benefits that now exist. Major revisions, on the other hand, are likely to be very costly —an even more serious drawback given the intensifying pressures on the budget from other programs.

There are differences in many of the specific problems affecting contributory and noncontributory income programs, but one overriding concern affecting both is cost. Previous increases have been significant, and future cost projections indicate that, under current policy, cost pressures will become more severe. The budgetary shift that has occurred over the past decade—when the budget share for these programs almost doubled—has effectively run its course. The difficulty now is how these programs can be adapted to the new constraints and at the same time achieve their objectives.

National Health Insurance

While cost problems have obviously affected defense and income programs, their impact on federal health programs has been little short of overwhelming. In 1974, for example, the Ford administration sent to Congress a proposal for a national health insurance system. When the 94th Congress convened in 1975, the Democratic Speaker of the House, Carl Albert, announced that a national health bill would be one of the first major pieces of legislation to be reported. Shortly thereafter the administration announced that it would veto any new spending legislation and withdrew its support for a national health insurance program. Although the House Democrats promised that a health bill would be reported by summer, committee jurisdictional squabbles broke out and nothing was produced. Of the two dozen national health insurance proposals introduced during the 94th Congress, none made substantial progress toward passage in both chambers. On April 16, 1976, Jimmy Carter called for decisive action on a "universal and mandatory" national health insurance program. Although such a program was endorsed in the Democratic platform, Carter later spoke of the need for a careful "phasing in" as money was made available in the budget. Once in office, Carter moved first to limit health cost increases, arguing that national health insurance could not be implemented until such costs were contained.

National health insurance provides a good example of how budget constraints can effectively limit program innovations, even when support for them appears to be widespread. Moreover, the government's experience with existing health care programs provides additional evidence about the budgetary impact of entitlement programs. Prior to the mid-1960s, federal health expenditures were limited largely to support of biomedical research and to public health services, along with related health services for veterans and for military personnel and their families. In 1966 total federal health expenditures were approximately $6 billion. By 1976 federal expenditures had climbed to over $33 billion, with more than $26 billion of this accounted for by two programs established in the mid-1960s, Medicare and Medicaid. Current estimates are that non-defense-related federal health expenditures will increase to $58 billion by 1981, with Medicare and Medicaid costs totaling almost $49 billion.[40] Since tax expenditures in the health area are large (estimated at $6.6 billion in 1976 and $11.3 billion in 1981), the budgetary impact of federal health programs is now quite substantial.[41]

In addition to Medicare, Medicaid, and the veterans and national defense-related health services programs, the federal government also supports health research, training and education of health personnel, public health programs, and health planning and construction. The major budget items, however, are Medicare and Medicaid, and their budgetary impact continues to increase. Of the projected increase in federal non-defense-related health expenditures from 1976 to 1981, 90 percent of the increase is accounted for by Medicare and Medicaid. Most of this increase (about 80 percent), in turn, is due to higher medical costs rather than to more beneficiaries or higher utilization.[42]

Medicaid and Medicare

The Medicaid and Medicare programs were established to help finance health services for certain groups not well served by the private health insurance system, primarily the aged, welfare recipients, the medically indigent, and, most recently, the permanently disabled. Medicaid is a federal-state program covering the poor, and there is considerable variation in eligibility and coverage from state to state. Of the estimated $17 billion in program costs during FY 1977, the federal share came to slightly over $10 billion, with the remainder supplied by state and local governments. Almost 25 million persons were receiving benefits under the program during FY 1977.[43] Medicare is a federal program that finances health services for the aged and disabled. Fiscal 1977 outlays were approximately $22 billion. Approximately 26 million persons are covered by Medicare, and about 5 million of the aged also receive Medicaid benefits to supplement Medicare.[44]

There are serious problems affecting both programs. It is estimated, for example, that 28 percent of the poor are not covered by Medicaid and that less than 40 percent of the working poor have even limited health insurance. Moreover, nearly one-half of the population does not have major medical coverage.[45] Under Medicare, while most of the aged receive benefits, less than 40 percent of their total health costs are paid for by the current program.[46] The utilization of Medicare benefits is uneven because of deductibility and coinsurance requirements under the law. Under the current system of governmental programs and private insurance arrangements, coverage is incomplete and protection against extremely high medical bills is quite limited for many who are covered. Moreover, some states have responded to the increased costs of Medicaid by restricting eligibility and benefits.

A different type of problem involves access to and utilization of health care services, regardless of financial barriers. Many of the rural poor and low-income minority groups do not have adequate access to health facilities or health personnel. Moreover, many of these individuals are unaware of or inexperienced in obtaining available services.[47] The removal or at least modification of the nonfinancial barriers to health care represents a continuing and perplexing problem for policy makers.

Perhaps the most serious difficulty in financing health care, however, has been the enormous increase in costs. As Figure 5.3 indicates, health service prices have increased at a higher rate than prices generally (as measured by the overall consumer price index) in recent years. The only period during the past decade in which health service cost increases did not far outstrip the consumer price index was fiscal years 1971 through 1974, when for 32 months controls were imposed on health service costs as part of the Economic Stabilization Program.

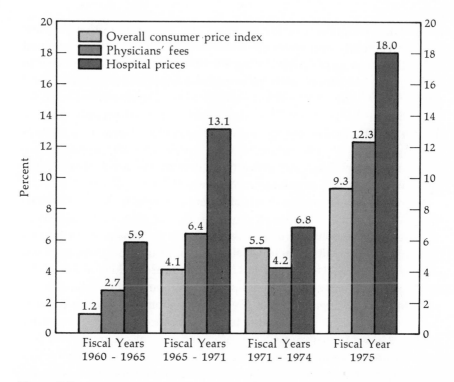

Figure 5.3

Average annual increase in the consumer price index for all items, physicians' fees, and semiprivate hospital rooms for selected fiscal year periods from 1960 through 1975. [Source: Congressional Budget Office, *Budget Options for Fiscal Year 1977: A Report to the Senate and House Committees on the Budget* (Washington, D.C.: Government Printing Office, March 15, 1976), p. 154.]

Much of the annual increase in Medicare and Medicaid outlays, therefore, has been a result of increased costs rather than expanded coverage or utilization. While such cost problems affect all levels of government, they have been especially acute at the state and county level. In Idaho, for example, the cost of Medicaid has tripled since 1972, although the eligible population has remained constant. In Westchester County, New York, total medical expenditures have been estimated at $400 million, with over one-fourth of this amount financing the care of 60,000 eligible persons under Medicaid and the remainder taking care of the other 800,000 individuals in the county.[48]

The gaps in coverage and utilization under current programs are thus exacerbated by the high costs of health care. What the future federal role in this policy area should be is therefore not confined to issues concerning the scope, financing, and administration of health programs but also involves efforts to control or limit costs. It is on these questions that the major health bills now being considered differ.

Health Policy Options

There are numerous options relating to health policy. One approach is to revise the current system program by program. This could include, for example, a federalized Medicaid program with uniform eligibility criteria and benefit standards. Coverage and costs would depend, of course, on these criteria and standards. Based on the most liberal state plans, benefits would be made available to an estimated 35 million persons, health care spending would be increased by $17 billion in FY 1978, and additional federal costs would be over $7 billion in 1978.[49] Other proposals would extend Medicare benefits and protection and, in particular, provide increased federal assistance for the long-term care of the aged and disabled.

Cost control proposals have also been recommended to limit future increases under existing programs. These proposals, including the Carter administration plan that was sent to Congress in 1977, focus primarily on hospital costs, since these have increased much faster than other medical service costs or prices generally and are now the largest component (40 percent) of total health care spending and also of total federal Medicare and Medicaid costs (58 percent).[50] The Carter plan, for example, calls for limiting hospital cost increases to 9 percent in FY 1978 with smaller increases in subsequent years. Alternative plans would control hospital costs by limiting reimbursement rate increases under Medicare and Medicaid. Requirements that recipients pay a larger share of their bills for short-term care—cost-sharing or coinsurance approaches—have also been recommended as a means of cutting utilization and costs, but Congress has been very resistant to this last approach.

Other approaches include targeted plans, mixed insurance plans, and public insurance plans. The objectives, costs, and federal role under these plans differ significantly. Within each of these categories, there are distinctions between proposals in terms of coverage, benefits, financing, costs, and administration. The plans examined below are representative of the various health program options that have been introduced in Congress during recent years.

Targeted Plans.   A number of health program proposals would increase federal responsibility over health care but restrict coverage and services to specific groups. One of the more prominent plans, sponsored by Senators Long (D-La.) and Ribicoff (D-Conn.), would provide catastrophic illness protection for all persons covered by Social Security but would pay virtually all medical expenses only for the poor. It would also provide incentives to encourage private medical insurance for the nonpoor. Financing for the program would come from payroll taxes and general revenues, and the program would be federally administered. It is estimated that over 24 million individuals would meet the income eligibility requirements for low income, with another 20 million nonpoor eligible under a provision allowing medical outlays to be deducted from income. Benefits for the latter would be financed by state as well as federal revenues. While it is generally conceded that the Long-Ribicoff plan would represent an improvement over Medicaid, especially in terms of eligibility and uniformity of benefits, there are reservations concerning its effect on work incentives and costs. Moreover, there is considerable doubt that the program would encourage substantially expanded private insurance coverage for the nonpoor. With respect to costs, incremental federal expenditures under the plan have been estimated at $8.1 billion (using 1975 as the base year), while state expenditures would remain unchanged.[51]

Mixed Insurance Plans.   This alternative involves expansion of coverage but continuation of the present system of private insurance. The National Health Care Act endorsed by the Health Insurance Association of America, for example, would use tax incentives to encourage the purchase of approved private health insurance through employer-employee or individual plans and provide the states with grants to purchase insurance for the poor through state insurance pools. Coverage would be voluntary for all citizens. There would be deductibility and coinsurance requirements, benefits would initially cover major health care services and be gradually broadened, and administration would be primarily handled by the states. The American Medical Association has endorsed the Comprehensive Health Care Insurance Act. This would require employers to offer approved health insurance plans, with the federal government providing tax credits or subsidies to cover a portion of the costs. The government would also provide insurance for the poor, and Medicare benefits would be extended. The plan would provide for voluntary acceptance of coverage and implement a coinsurance requirement for all services, and administration would be the responsibility of an advisory board including federal officials, health professionals, and private citizens. Under the mixed insurance plans, financing would be drawn primarily from premiums, and federal involvement would be restricted to providing financial assistance in support of the private insurance plans (largely through tax incentives), purchasing or otherwise providing insurance for the poor or unemployed, and establishing general standards that would actually be implemented by the states and the private sector.

Public Insurance Plans.   The most far-reaching plan for changing the health care system is the comprehensive, tax-financed national health plan. The leading proposal of this type has been the Health Security Act, sponsored by Representative James Corman (D-Calif.) and Senator Edward Kennedy (D-Mass.), and endorsed by the AFL-CIO and several consumer organizations. The Health Security Act would cover the entire population, benefits would extend to a very broad range of health care and services, there would be no deductibility or coinsurance requirements, and costs would be controlled through a complex budgeting system that would allocate funds to regions and health service areas. It is estimated that 90 percent of personal health care expenditures would be federally financed under this proposal, with general revenues and payroll taxes providing the funding. While the Health Security Act generally receives high marks for removing financial and nonfinancial barriers to health care, there are questions about its long-term impact on utilization and costs and the efficacy of its regulatory mechanism. Under a comprehensive tax-based plan, federal expenditures would necessarily increase, while private and state government expenditures would decrease. Total national spending —public and private—on health services would probably increase slightly during the first year under a comprehensive plan. It has been estimated, for example, that total spending of $161 to $163 billion would occur during the first year compared to $151 billion for the current system (using 1977 as the base year). The short-term increases for any plan, however, would be limited by the current availability of services. By 1981, total spending for a tax-financed comprehensive plan could be in the range of $229 to $289 billion compared with $252 billion under current policy, with the actual amount depending on the effectiveness of cost controls.[52]

The cost factor, then, is critical for the comprehensive plan, as it is for any revision. Unless effective means are adopted to control health costs, federal health outlays will continue to grow with little or no corresponding improvement in health care. There is, for example, a greater potential for controlling costs under a national plan covering the entire population than there is under the current system, since the difficulty of controlling costs increases with multiple sources of funding. At the same time, if this potential is not fully realized, a national plan would probably be much more inflationary than the existing system.[53] There are, as might be expected, very sharp differences of opinion about the federal government's likely performance under a national plan and, hence, the eventual costs.

Summary

The policy areas examined here have had and will continue to have an enormous impact on budgetary politics. Defense, income programs, and health programs account for the major portion of federal spending. Almost three-fourths of the annual budget is allocated to contributory and noncontributory benefit payments to individuals and to defense. Within this combined budget share, however, there have been important shifts that have substantially altered the composition of federal spending. Between the late 1960s and middle 1970s, expenditures for social welfare programs, such as income security, income assistance, and health, increased at a rapid rate, while defense spending was curtailed. The result was that defense spending declined to approximately one-fourth of annual outlays, while contributory and noncontributory benefit payments became the largest component of the budget. In terms of priority setting, the budget reflected a clear movement away from defense and toward social welfare.

Beginning with the fiscal 1976 budget, however, the executive branch mounted a major effort to increase real defense spending, an effort that has continued despite the subsequent change in administrations. While Congress has still cut executive defense budget requests, its cuts have been extremely moderate compared with those of the early 1970s. This has not occurred, however, without a considerable struggle. Efforts to control total spending combined with defense spending increases inevitably impose constraints on social welfare spending that were not present during the "welfare shift" in the budget. This has resulted in sharp ideological and partisan divisions in Congress. Liberal Democrats have sought large annual budget increases, using these additional funds to expand existing social welfare programs and establish new ones. Conservatives in both parties have attempted to limit the size of the increments but also increase real defense spending. The balance that Congress has managed to impose thus far in response to these divergent pressures suggests that priorities have been altered slightly—there will be an emphasis on controlling the size of the annual increment, and annual increments will be apportioned so that the relative budget shares for defense and social welfare will be kept at or near existing levels. With severe competition for budgetary resources, however, the possibility of establishing major new spending programs is obviously quite limited.

There has also been a change in emphasis regarding the factors that affect budgetary decisions in these policy areas. Defense spending is now being assessed in a much more traditional fashion than was the case for much of the past decade. That is, budget decisions are being considered more in the context of U.S. policy objectives, strategic requirements, enemy capabilities and intentions, and the like and less in terms of the social desirability of defense spending versus social welfare spending. Judgments based on social desirability are not absent, particularly in Congress, but they have become much less prevalent as expert opinion and public opinion about defense spending have changed.

Social desirability has also become less dominant as a decision-making factor with respect to social welfare spending. This type of spending is now much more susceptible to judgments about acceptable total costs—that is, to limits on overall spending—and to considerations of acceptable cost increases for specific programs. This does not mean that the "welfare shift" will be reversed, which is highly unlikely. It does mean that the portion of the budget devoted to social welfare is now so large that any attempt to increase it further will be sharply contested. Moreover, the share of future annual budget increases that goes to social welfare will be limited by the competing demands from other program areas, including defense. Spending for one social welfare program is now much more likely to be assessed in relation to spending for another social welfare program—in other words, to either/or judgments—than in the past. Social desirability is still a powerful factor, but it is subjected more explicitly to the practical constraint of available resources. This also affects program innovations, such as national health insurance, where the effects on current spending may not be dramatic because of limited availability of services, but where long-term spending will be substantial and could be highly inflationary without strict cost controls on hospital prices and other medical services. Costs are therefore a major determinant of the acceptable rate of increase in existing programs and an even more crucial factor in decisions about new spending programs.

Members of Congress and the President, then, are finding their choices increasingly restricted as they attempt to incorporate their spending preferences into the budget. These restrictions will likely become more severe, at least for the next five to ten years, and portend increasing conflict over budget aggregates and budget priorities within Congress and also between Congress and the President.

Notes

1. See Aaron Wildavsky, *The Politics of the Budgetary Process*, 2nd ed. (Boston: Little, Brown, 1974), chap. 2.

2. Senate Committee on Armed Services, *United States/Soviet Military Balance, A Frame of Reference for Congress, A Study by the Library of Congress Congressional Research Service*, 94th Congress, 2nd Session (Washington, D.C.: Government Printing Office, 1976), p. 53.

3. In FY 1956, Department of Defense outlays were $35.8 billion, with an additional $4.8 billion for military assistance, atomic energy defense activities, and defense-related activities. This represented 58 percent of total federal outlays during that year. Congressional Budget Office, *Budget Options for Fiscal Year 1977: A Report to the Senate and House Committees on the Budget* (Washington, D.C.: Government Printing Office, March 15, 1976), p. 74.

4. Ibid.

5. Barry M. Blechman, Edward M. Gramlich, and Robert W. Hartman, *Setting National Priorities, The 1976 Budget* (Washington, D.C.: Brookings Institution, 1975), p. 85.

6. Senate Committee on Armed Services, *United States/Soviet Military Balance*, p. 1.

7. Ibid., pp. 3–9.

8. *The Budget of the United States Government, Fiscal Year 1977* (Washington, D.C.: Government Printing Office, 1976), pp. M4–M5.

9. In their second televised debate, Ford charged that Carter had called for $15 billion in cuts the previous year, a charge whose accuracy Carter denied.

10. Congressional Budget Office, *Budget Options for Fiscal Year 1977*, p. 36.

11. See Senate Committee on Armed Services, *United States/Soviet Military Balance*, pp. 47–54.

12. "Personnel-related outlays" including military pay, civilian pay, military retirement pay, as well as personnel support actually account for more than one-half of the Department of Defense budget. See *The Budget of the United States Government, Fiscal Year 1978* (Washington, D.C.: Government Printing Office, 1977), pp. 82–84.

13. See Barry M. Blechman, "Towards a New Consensus in U.S. Defense Policy," in *Setting National Priorities: The Next Ten Years*, ed. Henry Owen and Charles L. Schultze (Washington, D.C.: Brookings Institution, 1976), p. 82.

14. Congressional Budget Office, *Budget Options for Fiscal Year 1977*, p. 91.

15. Ibid., p. 78.

16. The research and development figure shown in the budget understates actual spending, since it excludes research and development spending in other program areas where systems have been approved for production.

17. Blechman et al., *Setting National Priorities*, pp. 118–121.

18. *National Journal, 8*, no. 13 (March 27, 1976), 414; *Congressional Quarterly Almanac, Vol. XXI, 1975* (Washington, D.C.: Congressional Quarterly Service, 1976), pp. 873–874.

19. Central Intelligence Agency, *A Dollar Comparison of Soviet and U.S. Defense Activities, 1965-1975* (February 1976).

20. Ibid., p. 1. The limitations of this type of comparison are discussed on pp. 1–2.

21. Ibid., p. 5.

22. *National Journal*, p. 414.

23. *United States/Soviet Military Balance*.

24. Ibid., p. vii.

25. Ibid., p. 27.

26. Ibid., p. 32.

27. *Gallup Opinion Index*, Report No. 129 (April 1976), pp. 19–20.

28. Ibid.

29. For an "early warning" on this, see Senate Committee on Armed Services, Subcommittee on Arms Control, *Detente: An Evaluation*, 93rd Congress, 2nd Session (Washington, D.C.: Government Printing Office, 1974).

30. John L. Palmer and Joseph J. Minarik, "Income Security Policy," *Setting National Priorities: The Next Ten Years*, ed. Henry Owen and Charles L. Schultze (Washington, D.C.: Brookings Institution, 1976), p. 505.

31. There is general agreement, however, that the employer's share of the tax is largely, if not totally, passed on to the employee in the form of lower wages. Ibid., p. 539.

32. Ibid., p. 540.

33. Blechman et al., *Setting National Priorities,* p. 178.

34. Ibid., p. 180.

35. Congressional Budget Office, *Budget Options for Fiscal Year 1977,* p. 131.

36. Congressional Budget Office, *Budget Options for Fiscal Year 1978: A Report to the Senate and House Committees on the Budget* (Washington, D.C.: Government Printing Office, 1977), pp. 168–172.

37. Ibid., p. 181.

38. See Daniel P. Moynihan, *The Politics of a Guaranteed Income: The Nixon Administration and the Family Assistance Plan* (New York: Random House, 1973).

39. Congressional Budget Office, *Budget Options for Fiscal Year 1977,* pp. 136–143.

40. Ibid., p. 152.

41. These tax expenditures estimates include personal income tax deductions for health expenditures and contributions to health charities and institutions, as well as the tax-exempt status of employer contributions to employee health insurance plans. Ibid., pp. 151–152.

42. Ibid.

43. *Congressional Quarterly Weekly Report, 35,* no. 18 (April 30, 1977), 794.

44. Congressional Budget Office, *Budget Options for Fiscal Year 1978,* p. 143.

45. Karen Davis, *National Health Insurance: Benefits, Costs, and Consequences* (Washington, D.C.: Brookings Institution, 1975), p. 3.

46. Congressional Budget Office, *Budget Options for Fiscal Year 1977,* p. 153.

47. Ibid.

48. John K. Iglehart, "The Rising Costs of Health Care—Something Must Be Done—But What?" *National Journal, 8,* no. 42 (October 16, 1976), 1462–1463.

49. Congressional Budget Office, *Budget Options for Fiscal Year 1978,* p. 152.

50. Ibid., p. 147; *Congressional Quarterly Weekly Report, 35,* no. 18 (April 30, 1977), 787.

51. Davis, *National Health Insurance,* p. 134.

52. Congressional Budget Office, *Budget Options for Fiscal Year 1977,* pp. 162–164.

53. Congressional Budget Office, *Budget Options for Fiscal Year 1978,* p. 155.

Six

Budgets and Politics

The federal budget that is adopted each year provides authoritative answers concerning the size and scope of government activities. The policy decisions recorded in the budget are the subject of continuing competition between the President and Congress for dominant influence in deciding what the government does, who benefits from what it does, and ultimately, who pays for it. Even when this competition does not result in the acrimonious battles that have characterized some administrations, it has profound implications for institutional prerogatives and powers.

The assumption that influence over budget decisions is a basic component of legislative or executive power has been characteristic of national politics since the adoption of the Constitution. From the beginning, Congress has sought to guard its power of the purse against executive intrusions, an endeavor that has never been entirely successful. In a similar fashion, Presidents and other executive officials have attempted to extend their influence over budget decisions and budget implementation. At times, budget-related conflicts have been largely internal, with congressional committees vying among themselves or with other groups in Congress for control over taxing and spending decisions, or with Presidents seeking to limit the independence of executive agencies and officials. But at least in recent years, these internal conflicts have usually been subordinated to the broader issue of presidential versus congressional control.

Despite a continuity in the tensions between the Presidency and Congress, there have been substantial changes in the budgetary process and in the social and economic impact of budget decisions. Over the past half century, the President has assumed the major responsibility for budget initiation. In addition to its formal, statutory involvement in budget planning and formulation, the Presidency has also acquired staff and advisory groups to assist in budget preparation. Finally, contemporary Presidents cannot avoid the political consequences stemming from the economic and programmatic effects of the budget. The budget has been and will continue to be one of the major components of presidential leadership.

As the President's role in the budgetary process has grown, Congress has attempted to preserve its own powers and prerogatives. During the post–World War II period, it has tried to utilize legislative budgets, omnibus budgets, and spending ceilings in order to gain close control over government spending. When these proved ineffective, Congress finally moved in 1974 to revise drastically its procedures for handling the budget and to coordinate its consideration of taxing and spending measures. Under the new process, Congress can deal explicitly with the economic implications of the budget, a subject that previously was left largely to the executive branch, and it can also challenge the President directly over program priorities.

Both the President and Congress, however, face a common set of budgetary problems. Over the past two decades, government spending has increased dramatically, even when factors such as inflation and overall economic growth are taken into account. Federal government spending has grown faster than the economy. Federal outlays now are more than one-fifth of the gross national product (GNP), up from approximately 17 percent during the mid-1950s. Even adjusting for inflation, spending has more than doubled over the past twenty years. Accompanying this growth in spending have been frequent budget deficits—from 1956 to 1976, deficits occurred in all but four years, and the recent and current deficits have been unusually large. This means that serious attention must be paid to the overall relationship between federal taxing and spending policies and the economy, not only with respect to deficits but also with respect to the limits that a given level of economic activity might impose on government activities.

As these complex economic questions are debated, controversial policy issues must also be confronted. Much of the increase in federal spending has been the result of various social insurance and assistance programs designed to assist the elderly, the unemployed, the poor, and the sick or disabled. These and other benefit payments to individuals now constitute the single largest category of federal expenditures. At the same time, spending for national defense, when measured in constant dollars, has only recently increased above the level of the mid-1950s, and there is considerable concern that as a result U.S. defense capabilities have declined relative to the Soviet Union's. If spending for existing social insurance and social welfare programs increases, as is probable, and as pressure builds to increase defense spending by even moderate amounts, the likelihood of initiating major new spending programs, such as national health insurance, will be considerably reduced. The political, practical, and legal constraints in current budgets are formidable, reflected not only in the 70 to 80 percent of spending technically classified as uncontrollable but also is much of the remaining spending, which is difficult if not impossible to change significantly over the short term. This limits any major budgetary initiative, whether sponsored by the Congress or the executive branch, and it also tends to increase the controversy over even marginal changes in existing programs.

Budgetary issues in future years, then, will not be less complex or easier to resolve than they have been in the past. Participants in the budgetary process, whether executive or congressional, will continue to make decisions on the basis of admittedly inadequate information and imperfect knowledge. As in the past, there will be considerable disagreement over the effectiveness or desirability of past spending and over the economic and social implications of current and future spending. The scope of budget conflict between the President and Congress, however, has now been broadened to include fiscal policy and program priority issues. The institutional stakes are considerable, and this lends special significance to the new budget techniques that each side is now developing and to the general perspective that governs each side's approach to the annual budget debate.

Zero-Base Budgets and Sunset Legislation

The limited flexibility in current budgets has led the executive branch and Congress to consider new methods of spending control. *Zero-base budgeting* is an executive budgeting process that the Carter administration is implementing for the fiscal 1979 budget. Modeled on the system that he installed as governor of Georgia, zero-base budgeting would provide, according to Carter, cost reductions through more efficient and effective management techniques and planning.[1] *Sunset legislation* is a congressional device that would require the periodic review of all authorizations. While not tied directly to the annual budget process, this review would encompass most spending programs. According to some, zero-base budgeting and sunset legislation are potentially complementary and could increase joint presidential and congressional control over the budget. Others, however, argue that the changes likely to result would be limited at best, so that the additional time, energy, and other resources required would be largely wasted.[2] Despite the obvious enthusiasm for the zero-base and sunset concepts in the White House and among many members of Congress, there are questions about their potential impact on budget choices.

Zero-Base Budgeting

Budgeting in the United States has traditionally been incremental— that is, budget review has been primarily concerned with the funds requested above the current level of spending.[3] Under incremental budgeting, most agencies and programs have a base—that is, certain commonly accepted activities and expenditures—which is continued from year to year and is not ordinarily subject to detailed examination. There is, as a consequence, a high degree of stability and continuity from one year's budget to the next. Over time, the incremental changes that are made can have a dramatic cumulative effect, but the room for immediate maneuver is limited.

Zero-base budgeting, on the other hand, requires detailed examination of the entire budget, not just the increment. Its emphasis on comprehensiveness means that the same scrutiny must be applied to all programs and agencies, regardless of their longevity, legislative mandates, and past commitments. No prior assumptions are made about the justification for or inviolability of an agency's base. Indeed, each agency has a "zero base." In effect, zero-base budgeting simply requires that all items in the budget be reexamined each time a new budget is prepared.

To achieve this general objective, a zero-base system requires that certain kinds of information be collected and that specific analytical tasks be performed. For each discrete activity within an agency, descriptions and justifications, goals and objectives, and performance measurement standards must be provided. Then the effects of alternative courses of action must be assessed. This includes identifying and examining the different ways of performing an activity. It also involves analyzing the impact of different spending levels on that activity: What is the minimum funding level below which the activity cannot realistically be conducted? What is the funding level required to maintain the existing level of activity? What is the funding level required to improve or expand the existing level of activity? This information is utilized in "decision packages" for each activity, which are then ranked in order of priority.[4]

Decision packages are initially prepared and evaluated at a low organizational level—typically the minimum level that can formulate a budget. At successively higher levels within an organization, the priority rankings are consolidated. As this occurs, it is unlikely that all of the packages and alternatives developed at lower levels will be reviewed by top officials, since these can number in the hundreds or thousands.[5] However, these officials do have access to very detailed information about programs and activities, which can be useful in making management and budgetary decisions. With regard to the latter, zero-base budgeting is aimed at developing a final priority ranking for programs or activities. This ranking can then be utilized in allocating budgetary resources.

The appeal of this type of comprehensive budgetary examination is substantial, but there are limits on what zero-base budgeting can accomplish, particularly in terms of crucial, high-level budget decisions. Perhaps most important, zero-base budgeting is useful primarily as a management tool. By forcing the consideration of alternative methods and funding, it can promote economy and efficiency. It generates data and analyses that administrators can use in assessing what an agency is doing and how it is doing it. There is, then, the potential for better utilization of existing resources through reallocations of personnel and funds, as well as through revised operating methods.

There are, however, some significant limitations to the zero-base process. First, zero-base budgeting cannot provide much, if any, assistance in making choices between broad policy goals. Choices between increased defense spending, expanded income programs, or a new national health insurance program involve a complex mix of political and philosophical considerations. Defense spending cannot be realistically compared, for example, with national health insurance in terms of relative costs and benefits. Political decision makers in the executive branch and Congress must deal with allocations to a number of government functions that likewise cannot be comparatively assessed using any budgeting system. Second, it is difficult to affect significantly the content of the budget with the zero-base process. In part, this results from the budget itself. Outlays classified as "relatively uncontrollable under existing law" can perhaps be evaluated or challenged by zero-base budgeting. They cannot be changed, however, unless basic legislative revisions are made first, and this is not easy to accomplish. Since the remaining one-fourth of the budget—the controllable portion—is taken up largely by personnel and operating costs, it is equally difficult for zero-base budgeting to have an appreciable impact. These costs are not easily adjusted over the short term.[6] In addition, it does not appear feasible for budget review at higher executive levels to include comprehensive consideration of all or even most of the priority rankings and decision units generated at lower levels. In the state of Georgia, for example, zero-base budgeting now includes some 10,000 elements.[7] One cannot realistically expect a chief executive—governor or President—to examine all of these elements. Indeed, at this level budget review under zero base is likely to resemble budget review under conventional procedures. It will focus on a relatively small number of policy issues, essentially those issues that high officials consider to be most pressing and important.[8] Moreover, since these issues will no doubt be considered important by others—legislators, interest groups, or segments of the public—executive decisions must invariably take into account political realities.[9]

Congressional use of zero-base budget materials also poses difficulties. There is, for example, the problem of access to the alternatives and priorities that the agencies develop as opposed to those that the President finally chooses. In the past, Congress has been able to obtain original estimates from only a limited number of executive agencies. What estimates it usually receives are presidential recommendations, a restriction that serves the President's purposes. If this practice is continued, the implementation of zero-base budgeting will not give Congress information that is appreciably different from what it now receives. However, if Congress does receive detailed zero-base data and priority rankings from agencies, it will have significantly altered its role and the President's role in the budgetary process.

The kind of information that Congress appears to want from zero-base budgeting is illustrated by an experiment that a House Appropriations subcommittee conducted during the fiscal 1978 budget cycle. It required two agencies—the Consumer Product Safety Commission and the National Aeronautics and Space Administration (NASA)—to prepare zero-base budgets in addition to their conventional budgets. The legislators found that the massive information generated by a "from the bottom up" approach in NASA—with detailed descriptions, analyses, and justifications for all programs, work, and activities—could not be used effectively by Congress. The Consumer Commission was directed to provide priority rankings for all its activities and to prepare estimates of minimum, current, and improvement funding. It did not provide the rankings, which the House members recognized as the most politically difficult task to perform. Moreover, the Commission reported that one-third of its activities were already at their minimum level. The Commission's defensiveness appeared well warranted, since the committee members and staff had indicated that priority rankings for the various projects within an agency would be helpful in making funding decisions and in particular that low-priority projects would be prime candidates for cuts by Congress.[10]

What Congress apparently wants, then, is more material about agency views on programs and funding, as opposed to presidential recommendations only. This is information that Congress can use effectively in making program changes,[11] but it is also information that does not necessitate Congress' comprehensively examining all agencies, programs, and activities. In this manner, Congress could use zero-base budgets to get what Presidents have resisted providing in the past— agency views and estimates on programs and funding; it could then use this information to review a selective range of policy issues. In all probability, this review would also resemble the incremental budgeting approach, since in most cases the issue would doubtlessly be alternative funding levels rather than abolition.

It is also instructive that the congressional subcommittee that used zero base cautioned against applying it immediately to all federal programs. Immediate implementation was described as useless or even counterproductive; instead, emphasis was placed on the necessity for carefully evaluated experiments to develop appropriate procedures and guidelines for different programs.[12] The need for caution is related to the limits of the zero-base approach with regard to specific programs. Many programs are not in question, since they are proper and necessary government activities. Detailed justifications of national defense, for example, are wasted efforts.[13] Also, the effectiveness of many programs is difficult to measure. Objectives may not be clear or quantifiable, and even if they are, it may not be possible to examine the impact and effectiveness that a program has had over time. It is not always feasible, in other words, to ignore the history of a program, since that history may have the greatest impact on the current program. Crucial decisions on social security, for example, are not made and cannot be made "from the bottom up." It is difficult, if not impossible, to evaluate the effectiveness of the social security program, unless effectiveness is defined in terms of such measures as income amounts and numbers of recipients. It is not possible to determine what society would be like today without social security, since the program's existence has had an impact on such matters as workers' savings and private pension plans,[14] to say nothing of family living patterns or mandatory retirement programs. In sum, program evaluation is difficult. This does not argue against attempts to do it, but rather suggests that there are limits on knowledge and resources that must be recognized.

Zero-base budgeting, therefore, is not a panacea for budget control. It appears to have some benefits as far as management is concerned, and its emphasis on periodic examination of what the government is doing is a useful corrective to a purely incremental approach. But zero-base approaches cannot be substituted for political judgments. Decision makers do not operate in a historical or political vacuum. Their decisions are affected by experience and conditioned by political feasibility. Information that supplements these factors is useful, and this is where zero-base budgeting can be utilized. In addition, it is essential to examine the flexibility and workload associated with a zero-base system. Different approaches and techniques may need to be developed for different programs and activities, and some programs may not be amenable to a zero-base approach at all. The time intervals between periodic review may also need to be varied based on program requirements. Finally, a zero-base approach will increase the budgetary workload for agencies by significant amounts—more people will have to spend more time generating more information—and this will adversely affect current operational capabilities.

A flexible and deliberate attitude toward zero-base budgeting would not encourage unrealistic expectations about what it can deliver and would at the same time allow executive officials and Congress to concentrate on those specific areas of the budget where there are problems and where detailed review would be helpful. If it simply accomplishes the latter, zero-base budgeting will have made a significant contribution. To expect much more is to ignore the fact that members of Congress and executive officials have always had ample opportunity and authority to review everything "from scratch." That they have not done so indicates that the justifications for most governmental commitments have not been seriously challenged. Until they are, there is no need for detailed scrutiny.

Sunset Legislation

While there have been conflicts over specific guidelines and requirements, the general concept of sunset legislation has received widespread, bipartisan support in Congress. The primary objective of a sunset plan is to force reconsideration of spending commitments by mandating periodic, detailed evaluations. Sunset legislation sets an automatic termination date for a program's statutory authority. Unless this authority is reenacted, the program is terminated.[15] Consideration of reenactment (or reauthorization), however, is tied to systematic review and evaluation. Sunset legislation, therefore, establishes a fixed reauthorization schedule and a review and evaluation process for existing legislation.

For Congress, the sunset plan could complement the existing budgetary process by providing an in-depth review of the individual programs that make up the functional categories and the total budget. In effect, the required comprehensive approach to totals would be matched by mandatory comprehensive examinations of components. Sunset legislation could also complement the zero-base executive budgetary process. Since it reaches the basic legislation affecting spending, the sunset process provides the opportunity for making those changes that the zero-base budget process can only identify.[16]

Sunset plans do not create new authority for Congress, since nothing in the budget is exempt from any type of review Congress wishes to employ. Many programs have annual or limited-term authorizations already, so they presumably are reconsidered by authorizing committees. What the sunset concept actually represents is a technique designed to force Congress to do what it has been reluctant to do in the past. There are several important manifestations of this.

The sunset concept is aimed particularly at uncontrollable spending and therefore at the authorizing committees that have sponsored the bulk of this spending. Under a sunset plan, periodic reauthorization would be required for all spending programs, and this reauthorization would be linked to a detailed examination of past program performance and an analysis of available options. Sunset legislation would therefore institute systematic review of many programs that have not been closely studied. Moreover, since the sunset approach provides for simultaneous review of all programs within a functional or subfunctional category, it would allow Congress to make comparative assessments of similar programs and to consider policy options in a coordinated manner. Thus, the authorizing committees are required to provide more information about specific programs, to review in a comprehensive fashion programs with similar aims or objectives, and to mount an active defense of those agencies and programs within their jurisdiction. Reauthorization by program area also allows Congress to make more informed decisions about program duplication or to consider more carefully the effects that related programs have on each other than is possible when programs are reconsidered one by one. Since program areas cut across committee jurisdictions in many cases, the same opportunity for coordinated examination would be available to the authorizing committees.

The sunset approach, then, is aimed at forcing decisions through deadlines, but what distinguishes it from the traditional system is the kind of review that it attempts to establish. By imposing guidelines and requirements on how the authorizing committees review their programs, sunset legislation implicitly acknowledges that most, if not all, authorizing committees have not usually engaged in strenuous, systematic review and that they have instead directed their efforts toward supporting and expanding their individual spending programs. A related judgment would be that authorizing committees have not adequately considered the budgetary impact of the backdoor spending mechanisms they have employed to circumvent the appropriations process. However, if these charges are accurate, similar ones would be appropriate for Congress generally—Congress has not adequately reconsidered many of its spending programs and has allowed its authorizing committees to promote long-term spending commitments without sufficient scrutiny. Even Title IV of the 1974 Budget Act imposes only limited restrictions on backdoor spending—existing forms of backdoor spending as well as the major trust funds were exempted from review by the Appropriations Committees.[17] Congress has not decided to shift control of what are now substantial segments of the budget away from the authorizing committees and back to the Appropriations Committees, so the sunset requirements could provide a partial corrective to the fairly weak controls that now apply to many uncontrollable outlays. The requirements would force Congress to do what it has not done in the past, and that is to pay serious attention to all spending commitments, even popular ones, and to do so under circumstances that make it difficult to ignore congressional responsibility for those commitments. This is not something for which Congress has shown much enthusiasm in the past, and it could also prove the eventual undoing of a sunset plan. If the pressure to control spending were to abate substantially—which does not appear probable—there would be little reason to expect a sunset plan to work. As long as that pressure remains, however, sunset legislation could force Congress to strengthen spending discipline.

The most prominent sunset proposal during the 95th Congress was reported by the Senate Governmental Affairs Committee in June 1977. This was a revised version of a sunset bill that had been considered during the previous Congress. The Senate bill requires reauthorizations every six years. Federal programs are divided into three groups, and each group is to be considered over a two-year period. The initial cycle would begin in 1981–1982, with the first group of programs—military assistance, space, agriculture, labor, and elementary and secondary education—being reviewed for reauthorization. A second group of programs would be considered in 1983–1984, and the third group in 1985–1986. In 1987, the second review cycle would commence.

Within the two-year review period designated for a broad program area, the spending authority for individual programs would be automatically terminated unless Congress reenacted the statutory authorizations. (Exempted from the automatic termination are Social Security and other federal retirement programs, interest on the national debt, the federal judiciary, and civil rights enforcement activities.)[18] Authorizing committees would be required to develop review plans assigning priorities to the examination of different programs, specifying the criteria and standards to be used during review, and outlining the information and other assistance required from executive and congressional agencies. The amount of discretion accorded to committees in developing these review plans is a distinct contrast to earlier sunset proposals, which had mandated extremely detailed or zero-base reviews for program evaluations.[19] The Senate bill allows committees greater leeway in choosing which programs to evaluate in depth, and therefore recognizes the need for at least limited flexibility in program evaluation requirements.

As conceived in this plan, the sunset approach would emphasize decisions by broad program areas. This would, according to the Senate Committee, allow Congress to deal more effectively with the vast number and complexity of federal programs, with uncontrollable spending, and with programs that are permanently authorized and that therefore have escaped periodic congressional review. While sunset does establish a process that forces Congress to deal with spending in a different fashion—and perhaps to face up to matters it might otherwise neglect—it is not a magic solution to these problems. The Senate bill exempts from termination several important, permanently authorized programs, and this means that almost one-third of the budget will still be effectively outside the sunset sanction. Review is possible, of course, but review is also possible without sunset. Therefore, implementation of the Senate plan would affect many permanently authorized programs only marginally. With respect to uncontrollables, there is the potential for more effective control under the sunset approach. As indicated previously, Congress can discipline itself on spending without sunset requirements. Sunset simply makes it easier to impose that discipline. The number and complexity of federal programs are also perhaps easier to deal with if specific programs are not considered separately but rather within broad program areas.

What the sunset approach cannot solve, however, is the kind of problem that also affects zero-base budgeting—the difficulty of conducting program evaluations and making accurate estimates about program performance at different levels of funding. These evaluations and estimates are especially difficult for many programs that are now considered uncontrollable. It may well be that the sunset approach will simply overwhelm Congress with detailed information that it cannot effectively utilize and that does not provide answers to the kinds of questions that Congress is asking. If this occurs, then Congress may neglect those troublesome areas that are apparent but present the most difficult political as well as evaluative issues. It does not require any special insight to identify those areas of the budget that are serious problems in terms of current and future spending. Whether Congress is more likely to deal with these problems if it is also forced to reconsider everything else is the crucial question about the sunset approach.

Congressional interest in sunset legislation reflects concern over spending control, but sunset is a technique. It does not resolve the serious internal disagreements in Congress about spending for defense versus social welfare programs, fiscal policy, or the need for major program innovations. The President can determine his spending goals with relative ease and certainly with less publicized disarray than can Congress. When those goals differ from Congress'—as they often do—the conflict cannot be avoided through techniques. The techniques may represent an appealing strategy for appealing to the public—since they presumably reflect each institution's serious approach to spending control—but the sunset concept is not especially useful in terms of the annual budget debate. Neither zero-base budgeting nor sunset legislation is likely to change the budgetary perspective of the President or Congress.

Presidential Budget Perspectives

Despite the constraints on budget planning and formulation, the budget can still serve a number of presidential purposes. First, the budget can be used to improve administrative control and management of agencies and programs. The executive budgetary process provides opportunities for planning, supervising ongoing programs, and evaluating program implementation. The zero-base budgeting system is simply the latest attempt to capitalize on these opportunities. When coupled as it has been by President Carter with executive reorganization, the zero-base budget reflects a renewed presidential concern with planning and management. While there are limits on what the zero-base budget or any budgeting system can achieve, it is probable that the pressures on current and future budgetary resources will continue to direct presidential attention to administrative efficiency and economy and to the so-called routine management functions that most Chief Executives have tried to avoid.[20]

The budget serves a second purpose, relating to the President's responsibility for economic management and stabilization. The fiscal policy effects of the budget have serious political implications for any administration, and recent Presidents have as a result directed much of their participation in budget decision making toward consideration of budget totals and the balance between spending and revenues. Until the recent congressional reform, the task of relating spending to revenue was left largely to the executive branch, which meant that the presidential budget provided an overview and a policy focus that the Congress' budget decisions lacked. While this has been altered by congressional budget resolutions, the President will no doubt still emphasize the importance of budget totals in justifying his administration's budget recommendations, if for no other reason than to surround these recommendations with the cloak of rationality.[21] What has changed, of course, is that the President's totals no longer represent the only authoritative overview, since Congress develops its alternative totals. Moreover, discretionary spending tools that Presidents have used in the past in order to defend their totals are now subject to congressional control, as in the case of impoundment. Thus, while the fiscal policy effects (or, at least, intended effects) of presidential budgets will continue to command serious attention, they will no longer confer an unchallenged initiative on the President.

Third, budget decisions can affect a President's political support, image, and reputation. Presidents do have an advantage over Congress in publicizing their actions and initiatives. Their philosophies about government spending and responsibilities and their pronouncements concerning congressional spending policies are more likely to benefit from media coverage and find a reasonably attentive electorate than are similar judgments or pronouncements by members of Congress. Indeed, there is good reason to suspect that Presidents may be able to portray themselves as guardians of the federal purse strings much more effectively than Congress is able to do. If the public can be led to perceive a President as uniquely committed to fiscal restraint, economy, and efficiency, resisting on the one hand the limitless financial appetite of the bureaucracy and on the other the free spending habits of an amenable Congress, the President's leverage in dealing with both is increased considerably. If this type of symbolic leadership serves to enhance a President's image and support with the public, and at the same time to enhance his reputation with the political professionals in Congress and the bureaucracy, the President stands a much better chance of defending his budget decisions effectively.

Finally, the budget allows the President to determine in large part the debate about national priorities. Just as a President has a natural advantage over Congress in drawing public attention to the philosophical assumptions and beliefs embodied in his budget, he can also publicize with relative ease his specific policy preferences and innovations. The annual budget submission can therefore be used to structure debate about cutting, continuing, or expanding existing programs or about establishing new ones.

For the President, then, the budget continues to provide opportunities for achieving a variety of purposes—administrative, programmatic, and political. The relative emphasis that past administrations have placed on these has differed, although the administrative objective has generally lagged considerably behind the others. No President is likely to neglect the programmatic or political opportunities that the budget represents, but greater concentration on the administrative uses of the budget might become necessary and desirable, given the projected limits on available budgetary resources. Control of spending through better management was, of course, a major justification for the 1921 Budget and Accounting Act, which gave the President a formal, statutory responsibility for preparing an annual budget. Now that attention is once again on controlling federal spending, the President might find that administrative control and management have a renewed relevance for executive leadership.

Congressional Budget Perspectives

The 1974 Congressional Budget and Impoundment Control Act is potentially the most significant aspect of the broad reassertion of congressional authority and prerogatives that has taken place over the past several years, because it provides Congress with the means to compete with the President over the broad range of public policy. The budget reorganization was a response to internal problems and external challenges that had developed over time and that became more acute with the economic dislocations of the early 1970s. The central weakness of the prereform budgetary process was the growing decentralization of spending control in Congress and the corresponding lack of any mechanism to coordinate budget decisions. This made it difficult for Congress to determine fiscal policy, make priority choices, and exercise effective short-term control over the budget. Widespread concern over rising spending and deficits made Congress susceptible to presidential challenges over spending and to impoundments. Congress lacked the institutional resources—in terms of information, expertise, and procedures—necessary to counter presidential influence over budget decisions.

This inability was clearly evidenced with respect to determining fiscal policy. The lack of coordination and comprehensiveness in budget decision making made it impossible for Congress to plan alternative budget aggregates—total spending, total revenues, and the resulting deficit or surplus. Taxing and spending decisions were made piecemeal, unrelated to each other and to congressionally determined fiscal policy needs. While budgetary totals are far less precise than many imagine, the inability of Congress to fashion them led to charges of irrationality and irresponsibility, allowing Presidents to characterize themselves as guardians of the public purse and to justify accordingly the use of impoundments to control spending.[22] As the controversy over the Nixon proposal for a 1972 spending ceiling indicated, many members of Congress, if not a majority, were sufficiently worried about these charges that they were willing to cede to the President unprecedented control over spending. A key element in the budget reorganization, therefore, was the concurrent budget resolution. Each spring, Congress must establish expenditure and revenue targets and a planned deficit or surplus. This first resolution guides the subsequent consideration of spending and revenue legislation. The second resolution, passed in the fall, sets expenditure ceilings, a revenue floor, and a final deficit or surplus level. The concurrent resolutions therefore provide a mechanism through which Congress can state its preferences about fiscal stimulus or restraint and then act on specific budget decisions accordingly.

The concurrent resolution also provides the means for Congress to deal explicitly with budget priorities. Prior to 1974, spending decisions were not considered in relation to each other or in relation to any predetermined total. Congress could and did affect priorities, as it did with defense spending and social welfare programs, but its actions in terms of the relative support for competing spending programs were unclear until the last spending bill had passed. Since this was usually well into the fiscal year, it was difficult to determine what overall approach, if any, was guiding congressional spending decisions. Congressional spending priorities were, as a consequence, fairly well hidden. Moreover, the absence of any prior decision on totals also provided Congress with the luxury of not having to make clear choices between spending. As long as budget growth could accommodate competing spending pressures, then conflicts could be resolved without difficult either/or choices.[23] But the increasingly severe spending pressures that developed in the early 1970s, coupled with concern about rising totals and deficits, made it clear that hard choices would have to be made and that a procedure was required to aggregate budget decisions so that such choices could be made. The functional category targets and ceilings in the budget resolution, therefore, were established to allow Congress to make choices between spending programs. Since these functional categories are also used in the President's budget, there is a clear statement of the differences between congressional and presidential spending priorities.

A much more complex and intractable problem was also developing under the traditional budgetary process—the gradual erosion of short-term spending control resulting from uncontrollable outlays. By the mid-1970s, approximately three-fourths of the budget was "relatively uncontrollable under existing law." Congress could not alter these outlays without changing the authorizing statutes for the many uncontrollable programs. Congress was determining spending—in that it had approved the authorizing legislation in the first place—but it was doing so in a manner that limited the margin for change in any given year's budget. Since the bulk of uncontrollable spending is accounted for by direct benefit payments to individuals, Congress could not realistically be expected to lower benefits and thereby increase the available margin. The same distinction between potential control and real control applied to backdoor spending. By approving legislation creating expenditure obligations outside the normal appropriations process, Congress was shifting a portion of spending control to its authorizing committees and away from its Appropriations Committees.

This meant that by 1974 less than one-half of the budget was directly controlled by the Appropriations Committees on an annual basis.[24] Again, Congress could have reversed this trend by eliminating the backdoor routes and reestablishing control by the Appropriations Committees, but this would have made little sense, since the authorizing committees were obviously acting in accordance with congressional spending preferences.

The problem was not that Congress lacked spending control. It was that this control could not be effectively exercised under short-term conditions requiring that budget growth be curtailed. Inflation, high rates of unemployment, and reduced economic growth occurred simultaneously beginning in the early 1970s, and the budgetary effects were dramatic. Revenues were curtailed, while direct benefit payments increased substantially. These increases were not simply a result of the economic downturn; they also reflected the changes in eligibility and benefits that had been legislated earlier. Since these outlays could not be controlled on any short-term basis, budget deficits of unusual size were generated. This placed Congress in the uncomfortable position of defending large deficits in order to finance its past spending commitments.

Congress could do little to change the immediate effects of these past commitments. What it could do, however, was attempt to limit their growth and the future utilization of backdoor spending routes. The budget reform made at least some progress in this direction by giving the Appropriations Committees limited review of certain new or expanded backdoor spending and by providing estimates of the long-term spending implications of new legislation. It also focused attention on the current and future costs of existing uncontrollables by relating these costs to spending by function and total spending.

A third shortcoming that Congress attempted to resolve in 1974 was the lack of a staff organization, responsible to Congress, that could provide fiscal policy and program analyses to be used in budget decision making. This had led, as far as some members of Congress were concerned, to an unhealthy reliance on information and analyses supplied by the executive. A permanent staff was therefore established as the Congressional Budget Office to assist congressional committees, especially the new Budget Committees, during the budgetary process. In addition, Congress conferred additional responsibilities on the General Accounting Office to conduct program analyses and evaluations to be used in general oversight activities and in review of budget implementation.

Finally, the 1974 budget legislation included provisions to establish congressional control over executive impoundments. While impoundment is only one type of executive spending discretion, its use by the Nixon administration represented a direct challenge to Congress' constitutional authority. Through the elaborate reporting, review, and control procedures of Title X, Congress has insured that it can defend its budget decisions against similar presidential challenges in the future. There has also been some movement toward limiting other discretionary spending tools. Congressional review and control of reprogramming and transfers have been gradually increased, particularly in terms of committee involvement. To the extent that these changes result in sustained congressional attention to budget execution, they allow Congress to enforce its spending decisions much more effectively than it has in the past.[25]

The congressional budget perspective, then, has been widened considerably. The primary congressional emphasis remains on particular spending decisions, but consideration of these decisions now takes place as part of a process that also includes related decisions about taxation, fiscal policy, and spending priorities. Moreover, the impact of congressional spending decisions has been increased through restrictions on executive discretion during budget execution.

There are, of course, limits within even this broader perspective. Congress has not seen fit to eliminate backdoor spending entirely, and a considerable portion of uncontrollable spending is still not subject to any serious review. Procedures to control reprogramming and transfers have been directed primarily toward defense spending. For most domestic spending, the monitoring and supervision of budget execution is sporadic. It may be that the sunset concept will provide at least a partial solution to these limitations by forcing congressional reconsideration of past spending commitments. Indeed, sunset legislation could complement the 1974 budget legislation by requiring detailed examination of the individual programs that make up the functional categories and budget totals. This, in turn, could encourage greater congressional scrutiny to budget execution.

Congress has attempted, then, to protect its power of the purse by revising its procedures and organization and also extending its participation in budget decision making to stages of the budgetary process that had been left largely in the hands of the executive. It is now equipped to deal much more effectively with executive budget initiatives at each stage of the process—a truly major modification in executive-congressional relations. At the very least, Congress has indicated that it is willing to fight to protect its powers and prerogatives. It might well be that Congress has been able to establish and will be able to maintain a high degree of parity with the President over the broad range of government programs and activities.

The Future of Budget Politics

The federal budget has been and continues to be at the center of national politics. As the social and economic effects, and thus the political importance, of federal taxing and spending policies have become increasingly pronounced, both the executive branch and Congress have sought to strengthen their influence over budget decisions and to develop more effective mechanisms for handling the complexities of budget decision making. Within Congress this has resulted in the establishment of a significantly different budgetary process and a gradual tightening of controls over executive spending discretion. The new budget system and spending controls enable Congress to deal with the executive on a more equal basis in determining fiscal policy and budget priorities. For the President, this means that the political context of budgetary politics has been substantially altered. Since Congress can now produce alternative budgets in a coherent fashion, Presidents are now confronted with the necessity of debating and defending publicly not only their programmatic choices but also the economic assumptions and fiscal policy choices embodied in their budgets. Whether they will be able at the same time to convince the electorate that Congress should also share the responsibility for final budget decisions and their effects is less apparent.

Both Congress and the President, moreover, must confront a persistent and perplexing feature of budgetary politics—the contradictory public attitudes toward government spending. The public is typically upset about the size of government and about increases in taxes and spending, and it wants something to be done about these things. But the public also supports a wide range of governmental commitments —particularly with respect to social welfare programs—that inevitably require more government intervention, increased spending, and more taxes. This is not, of course, a recent phenomenon. Nor is it surprising that the President and Congress often respond differently to these public sentiments. The recent and current presidential emphasis, for example, has been on spending restraint, suggesting that Presidents now perceive real political benefits to be gained from acting as guardians of the Treasury, rather than as program innovators or spending advocates. Congress, on the other hand, has encountered considerable difficulty in trying to resolve these conflicting demands for spending and restraint, as reflected in the House of Representative's problems in developing budget resolutions. This indicates that Congress continues to feel significant pressures to increase spending for many specific programs, pressures that for certain blocs in Congress are more intense than the more generalized pressure for spending discipline.

Institutional differences over priorities and the importance of spending control obviously characterized relations between the Democratic-controlled Congress and the Nixon and Ford administrations. They have not disappeared with the election of a Democratic President. President Carter and Congress face severe constraints in effecting any sweeping changes in the budget. A major portion of future outlays has already been determined by past commitments. Economic growth rates will apparently not be substantial enough to relieve budgetary pressures within the next several years. President Carter's pledge to submit a balanced budget by the end of his first term further narrows the possibilities that major new programs can be initiated. A related Carter goal of reducing federal outlays to 20 percent of GNP represents another source of potential conflict with Congress. The large Democratic majorities have difficulty in accepting these goals, since they implicitly exclude significant expansions in social welfare programs. The President and many of his fellow Democrats in Congress see the road to reelection differently, and this makes the debate over budget policy even more serious. Thus, while few expect that the budgetary disagreements between the Carter administration and Congress will be as bitter or as protracted as those under Nixon, there is equally little reason to expect that no serious disagreements will arise as these difficult choices are faced.

The budgetary issues of the next several years, then, will not be substantially dissimilar from those of the recent past. But the manner in which they are debated and resolved will differ. There have been major changes in the budgetary process, particularly on the congressional side, that may have far-reaching effects on executive-congressional relations. Moreover, these issues will likely command greater public attention than they have in the past. If this results in a better understanding of the inherent complexities, imprecisions, and compromises of democratic government, the budget might provide a valuable educational service.

Notes

1. *The GAO Review,* 12 (Spring 1977), 80.
2. See Aaron Wildavsky, "Policy Analysis Is What Information Systems Are Not," in *Hearings, Zero-Base Budget Legislation,* House Committee on the Budget, 94th Congress, 2nd Session (Washington, D.C.: Government Printing Office, 1976), pp. 121–131.
3. The incremental approach is, according to Wildavsky, institutionalized in the rich, industrialized countries. See Aaron Wildavsky, *Budgeting: A Comparative Theory of Budgetary Processes* (Boston: Little, Brown, 1975). For a contrary view on the importance of incrementalism in recent U.S. budgets, see John R. Gist, " 'Increment' and 'Base' in the Congressional Appropriations Process," *American Journal of Political Science,* 21 (May 1977), 341–352.
4. See, for example, Joseph F. Delfico, "Proposed Sunset and Zero-Base Legislation," *The GAO Review,* 11 (Winter 1977), 34–40. Statement of Allen Schick, Congressional Research Service, in House Committee on the Budget, *Hearings, Zero-Base Budget Legislation,* pp. 51–55.
5. Schick, in House Committee on the Budget, *Hearings, Zero-Base Budget Legislation,* p. 52.
6. Ibid.
7. Wildavsky, "Policy Analysis," p. 130.
8. Schick, in House Committee on the Budget, *Hearings, Zero-Base Budget Legislation,* p. 52.
9. It has been argued that budget outcomes reached under zero-base procedures are not significantly different than those produced under the incremental approach. See Wildavsky, *Budgeting,* pp. 281–296.
10. *Congressional Quarterly Weekly Report,* 35, no. 11 (March 12, 1977), 441–443.
11. House Committee on the Budget, *Hearings, Zero-Base Budget Legislation,* p. 58.
12. *Congressional Quarterly Weekly Report,* 35, no. 11 (March 12, 1977), 443.
13. Statement of Alice B. Rivlin, Director, Congressional Budget Office, in House Committee on the Budget, *Hearings, Zero-Base Budget Legislation,* p. 148.

14. Ibid., p. 149.

15. At the federal level, sunset legislation would not eliminate all statutory authority for programs or agencies but rather would apply to the termination of funding. See Schick, in House Committee on the Budget, *Hearings, Zero-Base Budget Legislation*, p. 52.

16. Ibid., p. 54.

17. The jurisdiction of the Appropriations Committees extends to entitlements that provide budget authority in excess of the amount for that function in the latest budget resolution.

18. *Congressional Quarterly Weekly Report, 35,* no. 29 (July 16, 1977), 1463.

19. Zero-base review differs from zero-base budgeting. The zero-base review examines past program performance and different funding levels. It is not primarily concerned, as is the zero-base budget, with manpower levels and internal organizational effects. The zero-base review, then, is oriented toward legislative needs.

20. For an analysis that suggests that these functions should receive considerably more presidential attention than they have in the past, see Thomas E. Cronin, *The State of the Presidency* (Boston: Little, Brown, 1975), pp. 250–256.

21. See Aaron Wildavsky, *The Politics of the Budgetary Process*, 2nd ed. (Boston: Little, Brown, 1974), pp. 210–213.

22. Ibid.

23. John W. Ellwood and James A. Thurber, "The New Congressional Budget Process," in *Congress Reconsidered*, ed. Lawrence C. Dodd and Bruce I. Oppenheimer (New York: Praeger, 1977), pp. 166–167.

24. Ibid., p. 166.

25. Louis Fisher, *Presidential Spending Power* (Princeton, N.J.: Princeton University Press, 1975), pp. 257–266.

Index